D1188354

METALITERATE
LEARNING
FOR THE
POST-TRUTH
WORLD

ALA Neal-Schuman purchases fund advocacy, awareness,
and accreditation programs for library professionals worldwide.

METALITERATE LEARNING FOR THE POST-TRUTH WORLD

EDITED BY
THOMAS P. MACKEY
and
TRUDI E. JACOBSON

FOREWORD BY
TROY A. SWANSON

ALA
Neal-Schuman
CHICAGO   2019

© 2019 by the American Library Association

Extensive effort has gone into ensuring the reliability of the information in this book; however, the publisher makes no warranty, express or implied, with respect to the material contained herein.

ISBNs
978-0-8389-1776-3 (paper)
978-0-8389-1839-5 (PDF)
978-0-8389-1838-8 (ePub)
978-0-8389-1840-1 (Kindle)

Library of Congress Cataloging in Publication Control Number: 2018049837

Cover design by Kim Thornton. Cover image © AndreasG/Adobe Stock.

Text design in the Chaparral, Gotham, and Bell Gothic typefaces.

♾ This paper meets the requirements of ANSI/NISO Z39.48-1992 (Permanence of Paper).

Printed in the United States of America

23 22 21 20 19   5 4 3 2 1

The editors dedicate this book to all of those
who are working, in their disparate ways, to restore
meaning to the concept of truth. We would especially
like to acknowledge the critical work of professional
journalists, the Fourth Estate, who provide invaluable
information others would suppress.

It is only when the oppressed find the oppressor out and become involved in the organized struggle for their liberation that they begin to believe in themselves. This discovery cannot be purely intellectual but must involve action; nor can it be limited to mere activism, but must include serious reflection: only then will it be a praxis.

PAULO FREIRE
Pedagogy of the Oppressed
(1997, 47)

Contents

Figures and Tables

Tables

TROY A. SWANSON

Foreword

Nearly twenty years ago I started my career as a librarian focusing on information literacy and instruction. At that time the *Information Literacy Competency Standards for Higher Education* (Association of College & Research Libraries [ACRL] 2000) was fairly new and I had a feeling of exuberance around the potential that information literacy presented as an avenue for entering the curriculum and offering valuable skills to students.

But as a new librarian, some of my excitement fell away as I read James Marcum's 2002 article "Rethinking Information Literacy" in *Library Quarterly*. This article laid bare the problem that I had refused to recognize up to that point but could not ignore once Marcum defined it. Essentially, many instruction librarians made grand claims about the impact and value of information literacy to transform higher education but, in practice, many of us were mostly teaching students to search for books in the library catalog. As Marcum (2002) states:

> What conclusions can be drawn from this discussion? One implicit message is that information literacy reaches too far. As developed to date, IL sets too broad a target and must clarify realistic objectives. . . . On the other hand, information literacy as practiced is too limited, too grounded in text, and overly concerned with conveying basic skills to fully encompass the visual, the interactive, and the cultural domains required by the current situation. . . . (20)

As I read this in 2002, I knew that Marcum was right. Information literacy had the potential to be much more than it was, and as a profession, we needed a broader vision that went beyond simply searching with keywords.

Over the past two decades, librarians have stepped up to answer Marcum's challenge. We have created learning outcomes, lesson plans, and assessments focused on information literacy (Radcliff 2007). We have explored critical information literacy, considering power relationships and social justice issues within the information landscape (Accardi, Drabinski, and Kumbier 2010). We have identified core ideas connected to information literacy, as in the work of Townsend and colleagues (2016) who outlined information literacy threshold concepts through their Delphi study, providing fresh energy focused on helping learners make progress in learning.

Metaliteracy has been an important part of this conversation since Mackey and Jacobson's 2011 *College and Research Libraries* article "Reframing Information Literacy as a Metaliteracy" and both of their books, *Metaliteracy: Reinventing Information Literacy to Empower Learners* (Mackey and Jacobson 2014) and *Metaliteracy in Practice* (Jacobson and Mackey 2016). Metaliteracy, as a model, outlined a direction for revising the *Information Literacy Competency Standards for Higher Education* (ACRL 2000) and influenced the subsequent development of the *Framework for Information Literacy for Higher Education* (ACRL 2016), which transformed the conversation into a broader conceptualization of what information literacy could be. Specifically, metaliteracy helped move the conversation away from the skills and objectives orientation of the *Standards* and toward the more adaptable and reflective stance of the *Framework*.

This book that you hold in your hands or that you are reading online represents another meaningful step in this conversation about information literacy in general and metaliteracy in particular. This dialogue is crucial in our "post-truth" world where 9/11 Truthers, Andrew Wakefield anti-vaccers, and Trump's birthers have held sway. The 2016 US election and the firestorm of debates that followed emphasized the impact misinformation, disinformation, and accusations of "fake news" can have in undermining the credibility of institutions. The calls to address misinformation, disinformation, and political polarization have gone out through librarianship along with many other disciplines.

The chapters in this book are timely, as educators and librarians consider how to address our tumultuous information world. I am most excited by the metacognitive aspects of metaliteracy and how reflection can open up the affective domain. It is the affective domain that sets the traps that make misinformation and fake news effective. In our post-truth information environment, understanding the role of affect and the ways that information sources interact with emotion, identity, and worldview seems more urgent than ever. Metaliteracy presents a model whereby we can understand the complexities of affect in learning.

[handwritten margin notes: "claim on post-truth"; "conflating metaliteracy w/ affective awareness"]

It is my belief that much of our work around information literacy in higher education is built upon a misunderstanding of how we interact with information sources. The mental faculty of *reason* is mostly treated as a capability to help the individual process information better. But the work of Mercier and Sperber (2018), among others, argues that this is an inaccurate view of the purpose of reason. Most of the time, reason is put into practice in order to produce ideas that are used in arguments. These are arguments against others, with oneself, or in building new ideas with others. As educators, we think of reason as part of logic or at least as some kind of rules-based approach for decision making. *Reason should be used to discover capital-T Truth.* But Mercier and Sperber argue that reason did not evolve to find the *right* answer. Reason evolved as a cooperative mechanism to coordinate groups, and it does this fairly well. It makes *existing* arguments stronger. This is the source of the challenge.

Recent research from Kahan (2017) has noted that an individual's perception of his or her own identity is directly connected to ways that individuals interact with information. Our reasoning enables us to connect to groups that are important to some facet of our identity, such as political, religious, ethnic, class, or countless other aspects. Some are strong and well-defined. Others are not. We work to use reason to protect these identities. This *identity-protective cognition* is activated when information contradicts preexisting beliefs that align with group affiliations. The protection of identity is more central to how we interact with information than is seeking objective truth. This is why there are not heated debates about the theory of gravity but there are debates about the theory of evolution. As Kahan (2017) states:

> When individuals apprehend—largely unconsciously—that holding one or another position is critical to conveying *who they are* and *whose side they are on,* they engage information in a manner geared to generating identity-consistent rather than factually accurate beliefs. (6)

Identity-protective cognition explains a great deal of the debates that surround highly charged topics such as climate change, the social safety net, privacy rights, and immigration.

When we argue with others or interact with information that conflicts with our views, it is reasonable that we would give weight to our own arguments, especially when time and emotion have been given to creating them. Our tendency is to avoid falling prey to arguments presented by those who disagree with us. We are naturally skeptical. We don't want to be suckers, which makes sense. But in the current, highly polarized information environment where trust has been undermined and sources can be found to support almost any stance on any topic, our innate skepticism and our identity-protective motivations threaten to bring about an epistemological nihilism that allows no possibility of changing beliefs. Psychologists Taber and Lodge (2006) note:

> Skepticism is valuable and attitudes should have inertia. But skepticism becomes bias when it becomes unreasonably resistant to change and especially when it leads one to avoid information as with the confirmation bias. (768)

This brings us back to the value of metacognition in understanding affect. If our students are to actually learn—which means being open to utilizing new information to develop new beliefs—then they have to be open to reflecting on their own biases. They need to become aware of their affective and identity-driven connections to information. Most important, they have to recognize that their ideas may *feel* as if they are well-reasoned and built upon logic but that many other identity-driven factors may be hidden behind their ideas. How do we teach this? We need the applications presented in this book to help us develop approaches emphasizing the metacognitive.

As I read the chapters in this text, I celebrate. I celebrate the work of Mackey and Jacobson whose initial idea has taken root and borne fruit. This collection includes theoretical as well as on-the-ground applications of metaliteracy that connect to diverse disciplines and speak to one another in valuable ways. The contributors have answered Marcum's call to make information literacy something more than dressed-up bibliographic instruction, and as a profession, we should be proud about how many of the authors here are not librarians at all. Metaliteracy has its roots in information literacy, but the conversations have spread throughout higher education. In our post-truth world, this dialogue must expand and evolve if we are to meet the ever-changing needs of the students and communities that we serve.

REFERENCES

Accardi, Maria T., Emily Drabinski, and Alana Kumbier. 2010. *Critical Library Instruction: Theories and Methods*. Duluth, MN: Library Juice Press.

ACRL (Association of College & Research Libraries). 2000. *Information Literacy Competency Standards for Higher Education*. Chicago: American Library Association. www.ala.org/acrl/standards/informationliteracycompetency.

———. 2016. *Framework for Information Literacy for Higher Education*. Chicago: American Library Association. www.ala.org/acrl/standards/ilframework.

Jacobson, Trudi E., and Thomas P. Mackey. 2016. *Metaliteracy in Practice*. Chicago: ALA Neal-Schuman.

Kahan, Dan M. 2017. "Misconceptions, Misinformation, and the Logic of Identity-Protective Cognition." Cultural Cognition Project Working Paper Series No. 164; Yale Law School, Public Law Research Paper No. 605; Yale Law and Economics Research Paper No. 575. https://papers.ssrn.com/sol3/papers.cfm?abstract_id=2973067.

Mackey, Thomas P., and Trudi E. Jacobson. 2011. "Reframing Information Literacy as a Metaliteracy." *College and Research Libraries* 72 (1): 62–78.

———. 2014. *Metaliteracy: Reinventing Information Literacy to Empower Learners.* Chicago: ALA Neal-Schuman.

Marcum, James W. 2002. "Rethinking Information Literacy." *Library Quarterly* 72 (1): 1–27.

Mercier, Hugo, and Dan Sperber. 2018. *The Enigma of Reason: A New Theory of Human Understanding.* New York: Penguin.

Radcliff, Carolyn J. 2007. *A Practical Guide to Information Literacy Assessment for Academic Librarians.* Westport, CT: Libraries Unlimited.

Taber, Charles, and Milton Lodge. 2006. "Motivated Skepticism in the Evaluation of Political Beliefs." *American Journal of Political Science* 50 (3): 755–69.

Townsend, Lori, Hofer, Amy R., Lin Hanick, Silvia, and Brunetti, Korey. 2016. "Identifying Threshold Concepts for Information Literacy: A Delphi Study." *Communications in Information Literacy* 10 (1): 23–49.

Preface

This book examines metaliteracy as a pedagogical framework to develop metaliterate learners for the post-truth world. Although the term *post-truth* has been around for some time, it has become the definitive nomenclature for our connected yet partisan world, especially as a result of the 2016 presidential election. It is a descriptor for a set of interrelated issues about how we identify, define, and understand truth in the fractured era of divisive politics and disruptive social technologies. The idea of a post-truth world challenges us to consider how we are to believe or not the information that circulates in our online lives and real-world communities. This book argues that metaliteracy is an empowering pedagogical framework that prepares learners to be active and engaged participants in an oftentimes technology-mediated social information environment. Our goal is to positively contribute to the conversation about envisioning educational solutions to the post-truth world while supporting the fine work that continues to emerge in response to these profound challenges.

As a postmodern term with a now precise dictionary definition provided by Oxford Dictionaries (2018), post-truth effectively names and defines "circumstances in which objective facts are less influential in shaping public opinion than appeals to emotion and personal belief." The post-truth world is evident in the damaging nationalist rhetoric and divisive politics that wash across our television screens and mobile devices with unnerving frequency.

This situation challenges us to expand pedagogical theories and practices that teach learners to understand the issues while pursuing truth and reason through ongoing inquiry and discovery. The term *post-truth* also has limitations since it is difficult to fully describe how we consume, produce, and share information in a world seemingly *after* truth has been exhausted. Naming is a crucial step in defining and ultimately resolving, but these issues have been unfolding for decades and will not be easily fixed. One of the problems with post-truth terminology is that the continuous fading of truth may simply be accepted as the way things are now, and not persistently challenged or rebuked. Consequently, we have to be careful that simply identifying the issues does not normalize rhetoric and circumstances that would be considered unimaginable otherwise. We need to do much more than acknowledge the post-truth condition. This book addresses the challenges directly through learner-centered pedagogical strategies while thinking beyond a post-truth era to reinvent a connected world of knowledge, collaboration, and participation.

The specific application of metaliteracy to prepare metaliterate learners for the post-truth world is a logical extension of research that started with the first article in 2011, "Reframing Information Literacy as a Metaliteracy" (Mackey and Jacobson 2011). The introduction of a metaliteracy offered a unified approach to literacy while foregrounding the impact of social media and online communities on the consumption, production, and distribution of information in participatory environments. As the idea evolved in the book *Metaliteracy: Reinventing Information Literacy to Empower Learners* in 2014 (Mackey and Jacobson 2014), the metacognitive dimension of metaliteracy developed within four domains of metaliterate learning that also included the affective, behavioral, and cognitive areas. This expanded conceptualization of the model advanced in partnership with the Metaliteracy Learning Collaborative and led to specific metaliteracy goals and learning objectives (Jacobson et al. 2018). This work informed several grant-funded MOOC (massive open online course) projects and the design of a competency-based digital badging system. The edited volume *Metaliteracy in Practice* in 2016 featured educators who discussed the application of this model in a range of disciplinary settings and different pedagogical situations (Jacobson and Mackey 2016). Metaliteracy research and practice has strived toward better understanding the collaborative and constructive aspects of a connected world. This perspective is grounded in the idea that education is transformative and necessitates critical thinking, the active production of new knowledge, and thoughtful cooperation in the design and facilitation of communities of trust.

Applying metaliteracy to an emerging set of concerns related to the post-truth world moved quickly with the circumstances. Just one month after the 2016 presidential election, the *Conversation* published the article "How Can We Learn to Reject Fake News in the Digital World?" in which we applied metaliteracy to the destructive emergence of fake news during that deeply divisive time (Mackey and Jacobson 2016). This essay made the argument that we need to read online information with a critical eye, apply metacognitive thinking to the consumption of all information, and make purposeful and responsible contributions to the social media ecology as active participants. Unfortunately, fake news is still a pressing issue, especially since the term has been appropriated and redefined to discredit reputable news organizations that ask critical questions and report information that counters misleading or false narratives. In addition, an expansive and troubling set of issues about the post-truth era extends beyond fake news to include confirmation bias, personal privacy, online security, online trolling, and an overall lack of trust in the information we consume through the technologies we have become so dependent upon.

There is a particular urgency in publishing this book now, when truth itself has been questioned by partisan leaders for political purposes, professional journalism is under attack, science and climate change are doubted as factual, online hacking is prevalent, and personal privacy has been violated by commercial and political interests. During this post-truth era, education and health care have become more politicized than ever before, and the proliferation of false information through commercial social media networks has developed as a serious concern. It is profoundly clear that the competencies, knowledge, and attributes specific to metaliterate learning are critical to effectively traverse these challenges. Metaliteracy is an evolving concept that offers an empowering way to develop and support the metaliterate learner in a wide range of educational contexts, across multiple learning spaces, and through continuous lifelong learning experiences.

BOOK CHAPTERS AND ORGANIZATION

In this book, an exceptional team of authors examines several critical themes related to metaliterate learning in the post-truth world through multiple perspectives. The chapter authors build on and expand theoretical and applied approaches to metaliteracy through persuasive insights and strategies that are adaptable to multiple disciplinary settings. The first half of the book opens up primarily from a theoretical perspective and then we shift to mostly applied viewpoints, although theory and practice intersect throughout the volume.

In the first chapter, "Empowering Metaliterate Learners for the Post-Truth World," Thomas P. Mackey, PhD, Professor in the Department of Arts and Media at SUNY Empire State College and one of the editors of this book, examines metaliteracy as a pedagogical model for the post-truth world and beyond. This framing chapter includes a detailed analysis of the metaliterate learner characteristics and the revised metaliteracy goals and learning objectives developed with co-editor Trudi E. Jacobson and the Metaliteracy

Learning Collaborative. In this chapter, metaliteracy is envisioned as an empowering pedagogical model that supports reflective and self-regulated learning to advance the purposeful creation and distribution of new knowledge in participatory communities of trust.

The second chapter, "The Materiality of Metaliteracy: A Documentary Approach and Perspective for Information and Literacy Practices in the Post-Truth Era," is authored by Marc Kosciejew, MLIS, PhD, Faculty of Media and Knowledge Sciences in the Department of Library, Information, and Archive Sciences, University of Malta. According to Kosciejew, while there is implicit acknowledgment of documentation in the original metaliteracy framework, this key dimension must be developed further to support metaliterate learning. Kosciejew asserts an essential role for documentation in the metaliteracy model and argues that a stronger awareness and deeper understanding of the documents we consume, create, and share leads to ethical and responsible practices.

The next chapter, "Inoculation Theory and the Metaliterate Learner," is written by Josh Compton, PhD, from the Institute for Writing and Rhetoric at Dartmouth College. In this theoretical piece, Compton argues that inoculation theory is a valuable perspective for understanding metaliteracy in the post-truth world because of the focus on building resistance to influence. As Compton suggests, inoculation and metaliteracy are complementary theories that offer considerable promise for future research synergies in support of developing proactive learning strategies. Compton provides a detailed analysis of metaliteracy's four domains of learning and the metaliteracy goals and learning objectives through the lens of inoculation theory.

Allison B. Brungard, MLIS, from Slippery Rock University and Kristin M. Klucevsek, PhD, from Duquesne University co-authored "Constructing Scientific Literacy through Metaliteracy: Implications for Learning in a Post-Truth World." Brungard and Klucevsek argue that such factors as politics and emotion are now challenging evidence-based learning practices and scientific reasoning. The authors call for a holistic approach to scientific literacy that is enhanced through metaliteracy, including the four domains of metaliterate learning, and the associated emphasis on digital learning strategies. They offer a comprehensive methodology that reimagines scientific literacy for a wide range of disciplines within the STEM (science, technology, engineering, and mathematics) disciplines.

In the next chapter, "When Stories and Pictures Lie Together—and You Don't Even Know It," Thomas Palmer, MS, Digital Media Lecturer from the University at Albany, SUNY, and Editorial Design Director/News Editor at the *Times Union* newspaper, writes about the deceptive qualities of visual images. According to Palmer, the relationship between text and image is dynamic and complementary, while also leading to misrepresentations as well. Palmer analyzes the synergistic association of several visual-textual examples from photojournalism to illustrate how images are easily manipulated or misunderstood. He argues for an empowering pedagogical response to these concerns that develops detection and prevention strategies through the lens of metaliteracy.

The second half of the book shifts primarily to applied methodologies for advancing metaliterate learning. The collaborative chapter "Teaching and Learning with Metaliterate LIS Professionals" was co-written by Nicole A. Cooke, PhD, MEd, MLS, and Rachel Magee, PhD, MA, from the University of Illinois. The authors argue that information professionals in the field of library and information science (LIS) must be metaliterate as well to support and promote metaliteracy among learners. Cooke and Magee incorporate both metaliteracy and the ACRL (2016) *Framework for Information Literacy for Higher Education* into their work with communities, including peers and learners, to best serve students while transforming the curriculum.

Allison Hosier, MSIS, Information Literacy Librarian at the University at Albany, SUNY, wrote the next chapter, "First, Help Students Learn to Be Wrong," based on a freshman seminar she redesigned and taught at the University at Albany, SUNY. Hosier reimagined the course Empowering Yourself as a User and Creator of Information by applying concepts from both metaliteracy and the ACRL *Framework for Information Literacy for Higher Education*. The revised learning experience addressed such topical issues as fake news and misinformation in the post-truth world. Hosier argues that the development of a lesson on being wrong was a critical part of the course to empower learners about the responsibilities of creating information.

In the chapter "Fictional Affect and Metaliterate Learning through Genre," Jaclyn Partyka, PhD, in the English Department at Temple University, argues for developing metaliteracy through genre analysis and fictionality. The author focuses specifically on first-year writing instruction to develop students as analytical readers and writers capable of differentiating among the wide range of rhetorical strategies from a multitude of information sources. Partyka examines the application of the metaliteracy goals and learning objectives as well as the ACRL *Framework for Information Literacy for Higher Education* in her course Inventing Facts: Digital, Historical, Fictional for Temple University's First-Year Writing Program.

The book's closing chapter, "Poetic Ethnography and Metaliteracy: Empowering Voices in a Hybrid Theater Arts Course," was written by Kimmika L. H. Williams-Witherspoon, PhD, Associate Professor in the Department of Theater at Temple University. According to the author, Temple University's Department of Theater features a Theater Arts curriculum that demonstrates the application of the metacognitive domain of metaliteracy. Williams-Witherspoon examines THTR 2008 Poetic Ethnography from a metaliteracy perspective that inspires learners to create digital storytelling projects based on poetic narratives from neighborhoods in Philadelphia. The author argues that the development of metaliteracy and metacognitive learning strategies in the context of collaborative communities provides learners with a voice to challenge fake news and related concerns as critical consumers and creative producers of information.

BEYOND THE POST-TRUTH WORLD

As the authors of this book demonstrate, moving beyond the post-truth world requires pedagogical strategies that challenge learners to carefully analyze and reflect on all forms of information, as both consumers and producers. The chapter authors discuss theories and practices that encourage learners to critically adapt to new technologies, while investigating the social and political issues that influence perception, communication, and decision making in participatory environments. Each author explores metaliteracy as a pedagogical framework to advance metaliterate learning in the post-truth world. The authors innovate through metaliteracy while applying the metaliteracy goals and learning objectives and in some cases the ACRL *Framework for Information Literacy for Higher Education*. Collectively, they contribute to the continued development of metaliteracy as a comprehensive and unifying model in support of literacy and learning.

As the narratives unfold, it is important to remember that the believability of words and images will always be changeable through an evolving media ecosystem built on the virtual representation of ideas. The post-truth world has created a unique host of concerns, however, that exacerbate the virtualization of information and the inherent flaws of systems that were intended primarily to connect participants. As the current situation has demonstrated, uncertainty about truth itself reveals how people gravitate to their own communities and like-minded ways of thinking. The post-truth world has emerged as an unintended consequence of the first wave of social technologies that were idealistically developed to unite people in online communities. In designing the next wave of innovative social systems, developers, educators, and learners need to be wary of the proprietary and political interests that manipulate the openness of the social media ecology. Doing so will challenge the creation and distribution of false and unreliable information in these environments. In moving beyond a post-truth world, imagine a fully realized sense of community in which participants and producers take full responsibility for the systems to advance transparency, connectedness, and trust.

REFERENCES

ACRL (Association of College & Research Libraries). 2016. *Framework for Information Literacy for Higher Education*. Chicago: American Library Association. www.ala .org/acrl/standards/ilframework.

Jacobson, Trudi E., and Thomas P. Mackey. 2016. *Metaliteracy in Practice*. Chicago: ALA Neal-Schuman.

Jacobson, Trudi, Tom Mackey, Kelsey O'Brien, Michele Forte, and Emer O'Keeffe. 2018. "Goals and Learning Objectives: Draft Revision (April 11, 2018)." Metaliteracy.org. https://metaliteracy.org/learning-objectives.

Mackey, Thomas P., and Trudi E. Jacobson. 2011. "Reframing Information Literacy as a Metaliteracy." *College and Research Libraries* 72 (1): 62–78.

———. 2014. *Metaliteracy: Reinventing Information Literacy to Empower Learners*. Chicago: ALA Neal-Schuman.

———. 2016. "How Can We Learn to Reject Fake News in the Digital World?" *The Conversation*, December 5. https://theconversation.com/how-can-we-learn-to-reject-fake-news-in-the-digital-world-69706.

Oxford Dictionaries. 2018. "post-truth." Accessed August 16. https://en.oxforddictionaries.com/definition/post-truth.

Acknowledgments

The editors of this book gratefully acknowledge the exceptional contributions by all of our chapter authors. Thank you for taking this journey of discovery with us through your groundbreaking research and writing about metaliteracy and metaliterate learning. Your innovative theory and praxis advances the continued development of metaliteracy as a collaborative venture that is applied in a multitude of disciplinary settings and pedagogical situations, and now, through this book, thoughtfully addresses the significant challenges of the post-truth world.

Special thanks to Troy Swanson, Department Chair, Library/Teaching and Learning Librarian/Public Services at Moraine Valley Community College, for writing such an exceptional foreword. Troy, a key member of the Association of College & Research Libraries (ACRL) task force that developed the *Framework for Information Literacy for Higher Education*, has long supported metaliteracy. We appreciated his invitation to give the keynote address on metaliteracy several years ago at the Information Literacy Summit at Moraine Valley Community College.

Thanks to Rachel Chance, Acquisitions Editor at ALA Neal-Schuman and ALA Editions, who enthusiastically supported this project. We appreciate the creative and professional work of our copy editor, Amy L. Knauer, who brings so much energy and style to the manuscript review process. Thanks as well to Rob Christopher, Marketing Coordinator, for creative marketing ideas and support; to Kim Thornton, for the exceptional cover design; and to Angela Gwizdala, Director of Editing, Design, and Production.

We would also like to thank our colleagues from the Metaliteracy Learning Collaborative: Kelsey O'Brien, Senior Assistant Librarian in the Information Literacy Department at the University at Albany Libraries, and Michele Forte, Associate Professor at SUNY Empire State College and Open SUNY Project Manager Student Supports/Success at SUNY System Administration. Thank you for your collaborative efforts with our MOOC projects, digital badging system, and related research and writing that emerged from that work.

Lisa Stephens, Senior Strategist for Academic Innovation, Academic Technology & Instructional Services at the Office of the SUNY Provost, has helped to propel our work through her continued enthusiasm for our project ideas. We appreciate the support from Lisa and the SUNY Provost's office for our most recent SUNY Innovative Instruction Technology Grant (IITG) "Advancing Metaliteracy in a Post-Truth World through the Design of a Global MOOC," which will allow us to develop a new MOOC project based on the overarching theme of this book. Thanks as well to Christine Paige, Director of Instructional Design at SUNY Empire State College, for embarking with us on that project, along with Nicola Allain, David Dickinson, Christine Fena, Allison Hosier, Tom Palmer, and Lisa Stephens.

Special thanks to James R. Kellerhouse for encouraging a bolder statement related to metaliteracy in the post-truth era. And thanks to John R. Vallely, whose scope of reading and knowledge about current events provided valuable context for this work.

THOMAS P. MACKEY

1

Empowering Metaliterate Learners for the Post-Truth World

The emergence of the post-truth world reinforces the need to advance met-aliteracy in higher education and as a practice of lifelong learning. This book explores the metaliterate learner as an active and empowered partici-pant in information environments that are both connected and divided. This framing chapter examines the advent of a post-truth world in which metalit-eracy must play a vital role by supporting reflective learning and the informed production of new knowledge. The metaliterate learner is a critical consumer of information, continuously developing effective questions, verifying sources of information including authorship, and always challenging his or her own biases through metacognitive thinking. Metaliterate learners understand the social, political, and economic dimensions of information that often move instantly through mobile and social systems. Becoming metaliterate is an ongoing practice that requires learners to understand changing technologies and challenge assumptions about authority in these spaces, including the power we often give to the technology itself. This process is especially crucial during a time when truth is seen as mutable, requiring an unwavering com-mitment to the responsible and ethical participation in social networks and the critical reflection on how information is produced, shared, and consumed.

Metaliteracy prepares individuals to be thoughtful and collaborative producers of information in all forms including text, image, sound, and multimedia. It also supports learners in navigating and contributing to the networked environments of social media and online communities. Through this integrated consumer-producer dynamic, with a particular emphasis on metacognitive thinking, the metaliterate learner is a reflective and responsible digital citizen who understands that how we participate in social spaces has an ethical dimension that is reliant on effective contributions. Striving toward learner empowerment through metaliteracy is especially vital in a post-truth world when the distinction between truth and deception has been intentionally blurred and distorted.

The optimism that once surrounded social media as a participatory technology that connected us all in online communities has shifted to a more critical stance that exposes the fissures in the network that mislead and divide us. While these complex issues present many obstacles for educators and lifelong learners, the ability to overcome this post-truth reality is accomplished through meditative teaching and learning, in which teaching is a shared activity among the empowered, connected learners themselves.

THE POST-TRUTH WORLD

The term *post-truth* designates a significant cultural shift in the definition of truth as a result of the 2016 US presidential election and the Brexit movement in the United Kingdom. Oxford Dictionaries (2018c) identified both events as contributing factors when it named post-truth the 2016 word of the year. According to Oxford Dictionaries (2018b), post-truth, an adjective, is defined as follows:

> Relating to or denoting circumstances in which objective facts are less influential in shaping public opinion than appeals to emotion and personal belief.
>
> > 'in this era of post-truth politics, it's easy to cherry-pick data and come to whatever conclusion you desire'
> > 'some commentators have observed that we are living in a post-truth age'

As part of this description, a clear distinction is made between "objective facts" and "personal belief" and the related term "post-truth politics," which allows individuals to simply create their own reality based on their own belief system and not on objective and verified factual information. It is within this post-truth milieu that facts are contested as relevant and truth is determined by individual political or personal beliefs and feelings.

In his essay "Post-Truth and Its Consequences: What a 25-Year-Old Essay Tells Us about the Current Moment," Richard Kreitner (2016) traces the term back to Steve Tesich's article from 1992 and argues, "As Oxford Dictionaries has confirmed, that was a pioneering observation for its time. But now tens of millions of American voters have affirmed it." Kreitner emphasizes the emergence of this post-truth circumstance as a shared responsibility within a society that allowed a post-truth leadership to ascend.

Steve Tesich's 1992 essay for the *Nation*, "The Watergate Syndrome: A Government of Lies," argues, "In a very fundamental way we, as a free people, have freely decided that we want to live in some post-truth world" (13). According to Tesich, this new reality was the result of the Vietnam War, the Watergate scandal, and the pardon of Richard M. Nixon because at the time "we looked to our government to protect us from the truth" (12). Rather than acknowledge or celebrate that truths were ultimately revealed through each of these traumatic historical events, and that we emerged stronger than before, Tesich argues that "we came to equate truth with bad news and we didn't want bad news anymore, no matter how true or vital to our health as a nation" (12). Tesich's essay also examines the Iran/Contra scandal and the War in the Persian Gulf as two additional examples that led to a post-truth world, through our acceptance of a compromised understanding of truth itself. According to Tesich:

> We are rapidly becoming prototypes of a people that totalitarian monsters could only drool about in their dreams. All the dictators up to now have had to work hard at suppressing the truth. We, by our actions, are saying that this is no longer necessary, that we have acquired a spiritual mechanism that can denude truth of any significance. (13)

Tesich's essay is a sharp commentary directed at the leaders responsible for each of these circumstances, but he also focuses on the collective societal accountability for the post-truth world. As part of his argument, Tesich challenges the notion that the education system has failed and says that we need to "educate by example" (13). This is especially relevant today when education, as another pillar of society, has too been challenged in a post-truth context. In an opinion piece for *Time* magazine titled "AFT President: Betsy DeVos and Donald Trump Are Dismantling Public Education," Randi Weingarten (2017) argues, "It's dangerous in education when the facts don't matter to people." Tesich could not have envisioned the future, but he did suggest that we all must learn from the lessons of history, including the social, racial, and economic inequalities, and ultimately challenge the false assertions and assumptions of a post-truth world.

In 2004, Ralph Keyes, acknowledging the work of Steve Tesich, addressed the changing social and cultural understanding of truth in his book the *Post-Truth Era: Dishonesty and Deception in Contemporary Life*. According to Keyes, "We live in a post-truth era" in which "post-truthfulness exists in an ethical twilight zone" (13). Similar to Tesich's earlier argument that emphasized the flawed leadership that led to social and political upheavals from the 1970s to the 1990s, Keyes situates the post-truth era in the aftermath of the political scandals and controversies that followed, including those of the "Reagan-Clinton-Bush era" (12). Keyes writes, "Dishonesty has come to feel less like the exception and more like the norm. Along with our acceptance of lying as commonplace we've developed ingenious ways to let ourselves off ethical hooks" (12). He notes, for example, several terms that have become commonplace as substitutes for the word *lie*—as, he suggests, a softer way of making the same assertion—including *misspeak, exaggerate, exercise poor judgment,* and *spin* (13). According to Keyes, "When our behavior conflicts with our values, what we're most likely to do is reconceive our values" (13). He discusses the importance of language in defining what is true and what is not while describing the social and political factors that influence interpretations of truth.

In many ways, Keyes foreshadowed today's post-truth era by recognizing the important role public figures play in modeling and upholding the truth. Over decades, political leaders and individuals in the public eye have diminished the meaning of truth in society by lying and through political and personal scandals that demonstrate bad decision making. Today, the spread of false and misleading information accelerates through social media, cable television, and talk radio, while websites such as FactCheck.org publish research to counter the falsehoods. Glenn Kessler, Salvador Rizzo, and Meg Kelly (2018) from the *Washington Post*, for instance, have been tracking the precise number of false or misleading claims since President Trump has been in office. Similarly, David Leonhardt and Stuart A. Thompson (2017) from the *New York Times* have been cataloging all of the false or misleading statements to date and express concern that the public may simply get used to or even acquire a numbness to untruthful information. The ongoing tracking of falsehoods, and even the blatant use of the term *lie* in this context, illustrates the seriousness of the concerns. At the same time, the ongoing reporting about false and misleading information by elected officials also requires the public to take responsibility and to carefully reflect on and determine if this is an acceptable state of affairs. Ultimately, we are all responsible for accepting the deterioration of truth by leaders and institutions and through technologies such as social media. We are also accountable for the language and terms we use, as well as the normalization of behaviors and communications once considered inconceivable.

POST-TRUTH AND POSTMODERNISM

Keyes (2004) suggests that postmodernism explains how our definition of truth has changed. He writes, "To devout postmodernists, there is no such thing as literal truth, only what society labels *truth*. That is why they call concepts of truth *social constructs*, ones that vary from society to society, group to group, and individual to individual" (Keyes 2004, 139). According to this definition of postmodernism, there is no longer an objective truth because any individual or group is capable of defining its own reality based on particular social circumstances and explanations. Andrew Kirkpatrick (2017) looks at post-truth through a postmodern lens as well and states:

> We are "post-truth" not because truth is passé and we have moved beyond it as a concept. We are post-truth because we already have and possess our truths. This has only been amplified by the postmodern condition, whose little narratives serve as impenetrable bastions of certainty. (331)

In this context, then, postmodernism describes disparate communities with defined opinions and beliefs. Everyone is confident in the truths they consider as their own. Kirkpatrick suggests that what we are really lacking is the ability to try to understand others, and as he states, "Most alarming in post-truth discourse is the lack of empathy for and movement between these little narratives" (331). While the postmodern world opened up the opportunity for multiple perspectives by challenging linear historical narratives and traditional hierarchies, disparate groups are now talking past one another without the compassion needed for mutual understanding. At the same time, this fragmentation of communities and groups has been taken advantage of by those interested in fostering division and intensifying mistrust through false narratives.

In an opinion piece for the *New York Times*, Thomas B. Edsall (2018) explores postmodern theory in relation to the post-truth era and notes, "Scholars of contemporary philosophy argue that postmodernism does not dispute the existence of truth, per se, but rather seeks to interrogate the sources and interests of those making assertions of truth." This reading of postmodernism in a post-truth world supports the need for critical thinking that informs the ongoing questioning of statements presented as truth. Rather than assume that any assertion is inherently true, we must continuously investigate, challenge, and support assertions with evidence, no matter what the source of information may be, whether the individual is an anonymous blogger or a famous world leader.

In his essay "America's First Postmodern President," Jeet Heer (2017) writes, "Postmodernism brings with it the erasure of older distinctions not just between reality and fiction, but between elite and popular culture." Heer suggests a significant blurring of traditional boundaries between what is real and virtual as well as between truth and untruth. He argues that there is more to the ascension of Trump than "a fluke election or a racist and sexist backlash, but the culmination of late capitalism," and that postmodernism is key to understanding the connection to these "cultural changes with deeper economic transformations." Postmodernism provides a way to recognize the social, political, and economic factors at play that have led to such a contested and partisan post-truth environment. Heer asserts:

> In a world where commerce and media (including social media) reward performance above truth telling, it's not surprising that a figure like Trump rises to the top. Any moralistic condemnation of Trump is incomplete without acknowledging the institutions (notably the media) that both created him and allowed him to thrive.

As Heer suggests, we need to examine the role social media has played in the emergence of the post-truth condition. Social media was once seen as a way to level the playing field, as a democratic technology that provided wide access to transformative communications, interactivity, connectivity, and participation. In the post-truth world, however, the same technology is also understood as an immense social network that has created an editorial vacuum with confusing notions of expertise. This connected system functions through algorithms that simply present us with the kind of subjective information we want, while continuously selling products in the virtual marketplace. The vast amounts of information in these spaces can be truth or lies, and how this information is presented and shared, without editorial filters or collective agreements about what is reality or expertise, will impact how it is received and interpreted.

CONFIRMATION BIAS

As just described, the post-truth world has been advancing for some time and may be better understood through the lens of postmodern theory. Research into how we think and respond to data and information sources provides another explanation. In her book *The Influential Mind: What the Brain Reveals about Our Power to Change Others*, Tali Sharot (2017) argues that confirmation bias and prior beliefs play a significant role in how we interpret and understand information, whether factual or not. She defines confirmation bias as "seeking out and interpreting data in a way that strengthens our preestablished opinions" (22). In other words, we find and analyze information that supports what we already believe to be true. According to Sharot, "data has only a limited capacity to alter the strong opinions of others" (15), which means that the presentation of verified and objective facts will not necessarily convince anyone of anything. She notes, "Established beliefs can be extremely resistant to change, even when scientific evidence is provided to undermine those beliefs" (15). This suggests that a fact-based argument is not sufficient to impact opinions that people hold dear and the presentation of scientific proof is not enough to sway them. According to Sharot, "When you provide someone with new data, they quickly accept evidence that confirms their preconceived notions (what are known as *prior* beliefs)" (17). She argues that this response leads to only further "polarization" among people with differing perspectives and that every new argument will generate even stronger counterarguments (18). As a result, presenting individuals with information that contradicts their existing beliefs to persuade them or change their opinion is not entirely effective, even though it is grounded in the idea of a reasonable argument (Sharot 2017, 18).

Sharot's (2017) research presents educators with a considerable challenge since our intellectual frame is based on the development of rational, logical, and scientific arguments. Her assertion that "there is no single truth we all agree on" describes the current state of the post-truth world very well (18). In this environment, the meaning of truth itself is contested, as is the idea of one commonly understood truth. If everyone pursues and supports what each already believes to be true, the presentation of new ideas and counterarguments will not result in a shared understanding of truth. Sharot examines these issues through her research to identify the *motivations* that lead to change (34). Sharot's research provides awareness about how we think, and the biases we all have and continuously support through how we receive data and information. This is a valuable perspective in developing pedagogical strategies that address the post-truth world while moving beyond some of our own preconceived notions about how to do so.

PERSONAL PRIVACY

Concerns about personal privacy have been prevalent since the emergence of networked environments, and in a post-truth world, these issues relate to how individuals trust the platforms they engage with online. Personal data is not secure through social networks, as was evident in the vast security breach of over 87 million Facebook users before the 2016 presidential election. This issue raises serious concerns about personal privacy in a post-truth era since individuals freely post and share information about themselves with a false sense of security about the social systems. Both the New York Times and the *Observer* of London investigated Cambridge Analytica, a data analytics firm that "harvested private information from the Facebook profiles of more than 50 million users without their permission" (Rosenberg, Confessore, and Cadwalladr 2018). Facebook later increased the number of users impacted by this breach of trust to more than 87 million (Schroepfer 2018). This significant violation of consumer data revealed the failure of Facebook, the most popular social media platform in the world (Statistica 2018), to protect the personal privacy of millions of unsuspecting users.

According to Rosenberg, Confessore, and Cadwalladr (2018), Cambridge Analytica was able "to exploit the private social media activity of a huge swath of the American electorate, developing techniques that underpinned its work on President Trump's campaign in 2016." In addition, Cadwalladr and Graham-Harrison (2018) reported that Cambridge Analytica worked with both the Trump campaign and the Brexit campaign. They also stated that Facebook knew about this as early as 2015 but "failed to alert users and took only limited steps to recover and secure the private information of more than 50 million individuals." As evident in this massive security breach, personal data was simply a commodity that was appropriated and manipulated for a specific political purpose without the awareness of the users. This situation in particular demonstrates the need for continuous proactive strategies for protecting one's personal data, as well as knowledge about the security policies and practices of social media platforms. The revelations about Cambridge Analytica are a significant enough turning point to demonstrate the necessity for participant empowerment online to guard against current and future incidents.

FAKE NEWS

The term *fake news* is one of the most contested phrases in a post-truth world, but it exemplifies and magnifies the interrelated concerns of this era. Initially, fake news described the false and misleading information that circulated through social media, but then it was appropriated and its definition was intentionally altered to describe any news story or news organization that countered the prevailing narrative of the Trump administration. This tension was obvious when the Sinclair Broadcast Group required nearly 100 local news anchors throughout the United States to recite a script that claimed to argue against "the sharing of biased and false news" (Burke 2018) but did so in an orchestrated and nonnegotiable way that supported President Trump's position. This unprecedented attack on objective and professional journalism through a scripted performance that was delivered by local news anchors was edited together in a video that went viral through social media (Deadspin on Twitter, 2018). The video showed all of the anchors reading from the same exact script, as mandated by the Sinclair Broadcast Group. The visual mash-up of the incident reinforced the critique that followed by illustrating the concerns about objectivity in news reporting when the message is politicized by a media conglomerate that owns local television stations.

Claire Wardle and Hossein Derakhshan (2017) argue that the term *fake news* fails to adequately describe what they define as the proliferation of "information pollution" through global social technologies. They also avoid the fake news language because "it's becoming a mechanism by which the powerful can clamp down upon, restrict, undermine and circumvent the free press" (5). An essay in *Science* titled "The Science of Fake News," however, argues that while the terminology for fake news is being appropriated for political purposes, it is important to keep the original phrase and intent at the forefront "because of its value as a scientific construct, and because its political salience draws attention to an important subject" (Lazer et al. 2018, 1094). This group of authors defines fake news as "fabricated information that mimics news media content in form but not in organizational process or intent" (Lazer et al. 2018, 1094). In this environment, the generators of fake news "lack the news media's editorial norms and processes for ensuring the accuracy and credibility of information," further emphasizing the kinds of journalistic controls or mechanisms that have been lost through the proliferation of social technologies (Lazer et al. 2018, 1094). While these changes have resulted in phenomena such as fake news, this does not mean that individuals or a community of users cannot assert and monitor the veracity of information that circulates in open and social spaces. This issue reinforces the need for communities to define specific policies and practices that provide new kinds of filters and assurances for collaborative online settings.

Lazer and colleagues (2018) identify two ways to address fake news, including "those aimed at empowering individuals to evaluate the fake news they encounter," which is consistent with the critical thinking competencies associated with metaliteracy, and "structural changes aimed at preventing exposure of individuals to fake news in the first instance," which focus primarily on the technology platforms (1095). Since each method has limitations, the authors argue for a collaborative and interdisciplinary research strategy that brings together academics and industry from around the world to "redesign our information ecosystem in the 21st century" (1096). The challenges ahead are significant since the authors found that fact-checking websites, perceived as one possible fix to the problem, are actually mixed in effectiveness as a response to fake news. According to Lazer and colleagues, "Prior partisan and ideological beliefs might prevent acceptance of fact checking of a given fake news story" (1095). In addition, fact-checking could even work against the intended goal to correct false information since people may remember the falsity because it was repeated to them, even if done for clarification (Lazer et al. 2018, 1095). Guess, Nyhan, and Reifler (2018) arrived at a similar conclusion as part of an analysis of fake news data from the 2016 presidential election, arguing that "fact-checking failed to effectively counter fake news" (11). The authors also found "that fake news website production and consumption was overwhelmingly pro-Trump in its orientation" and that "Facebook played an important role in directing people to fake news websites—heavy Facebook users were differentially likely to consume fake news" (10–11). As Facebook gained in popularity, it became a vehicle for the creation and distribution of false information that generated profit for the company and failed to protect the consumer with appropriate checks and balances or detection resources.

Based on these initial findings related to fake news, it is clear that additional inquiry is needed across disciplines to fully understand this troubling aspect of the post-truth world. In many ways, the preliminary discoveries about fact-checking websites in particular support the need for a metaliteracy that goes beyond information verification to include a broader understanding of the whole person and how individuals interact, collaborate, create, and reflect in technology-mediated social environments.

REJECTING THE POST-TRUTH WORLD

As concerns about the post-truth world have grown, so has the response from scholars and educators. Kathleen Higgins (2016) examines post-truth from a philosophical perspective and notes, "Much of the public hears what it wants to hear, because many people get their news exclusively from sources whose bias they agree with." At the same time, she argues that unscrupulous politicians ironically "rely on truth" by taking advantage of the trust the public bestows upon them. As a response to these concerns, Higgins asserts that philosophers and scientists must be vocal when scientific reasoning is ignored and that scientists "should publicly affirm the intellectual virtues that they so effectively model: critical thinking, sustained inquiry and revision of beliefs on the basis of evidence." While individuals may pursue and selectively interpret information that simply supports their own beliefs, educators have a responsibility to make this bias known and to affirm the values of critical thinking and scientific reasoning in a connected world.

The science community has addressed the attacks on scientific evidence and the scientific method as well. In a guest editorial for *Current Science*, scholars from the International Organization for Chemical Sciences in Development argue, "Opinions in an open society can be plentiful and diverse, but need to be related to all the sound evidence available" (Krief et al. 2017). In this collaborative essay, these science scholars assert, "The time has come for all who support and respect the validity of the scientific method to step forward and take action to defend and promote it as a core value of society" (Krief et al. 2017). As part of this argument, the authors ask the scientific community to look internally as well to prevent the publication of false, misleading, or plagiarized information that damages the credibility of scientific research and practice. Ultimately, this team concludes that we need to "support the use of scientific evidence and logic in public discourse and decision-making at all levels" while promoting science education and science literacy (Krief et al. 2017). They call on the science community to reject false or misleading scientific information in any form, from their own peer-reviewed journals to social media (Krief et al. 2017).

In the field of library and information science (LIS), Ben Johnson (2017) discusses the critical role of libraries in a post-truth era because "libraries were established under the assumption that information is a tool of social good." If this core supposition has changed, however, what are the expectations for libraries and the role this institution plays in supporting information literacy in this new reality? According to Johnson, "Libraries, which offer curated and authoritative information, are champions of a dead assumption." He argues that if facts no longer matter, the very principles that support libraries, such as access to accurate and reliable information, raise questions about relevance as well. Johnson points out, however, that "insisting on facts is not a bias" and that libraries have an essential role to play in communities and are trusted to support diverse perspectives, objective facts, and accurate information. He concludes:

> Strong libraries build strong communities. We must insist that we provide quality information, even if our communities choose not to use it. And if false information wins the day, we can take comfort in knowing that we kept the option of truth available.

odd comfort

Johnson makes a convincing case to support one of the vital institutions that opens the opportunity for all to pursue accurate information, knowledge, and literacy. At the same time, in the article "Why Librarians Can't Fight Fake News," M. Connor Sullivan (2018) argues, "Rather than reaffirming core library values in the face of fake news, perhaps it is time to revisit and reassess those values" (4). From Sullivan's perspective, we need to gain a better understanding of the issues related to fake news by closely examining the research in disciplines outside of LIS. Sullivan challenges many of the assumptions found in the field, including the role of the library (3–4) and evaluative approaches to information literacy in particular (6–7). He also recognizes "an urgent need for LIS professionals to engage with and contribute to technological solutions that can assist in identifying unverified or outright false information" (9). In this context, new technology would provide verification resources to assist participants in identifying false information, although learners would still need to understand how to effectively consume and create information within these spaces.

In a post-truth world, it is important to build on the trust and reliability already garnered by the library and to stand by the core values and mission that ultimately drive action in a truly democratic society. Concomitantly, we need to challenge some of our own disciplinary and institutional assumptions about the ways to resolve fake news and related indicators of the post-truth milieu. Ultimately, our pedagogical strategies must be open and interdisciplinary to promote a transparent and honest dialogue across a wide range of digital learning spaces and for the larger societal benefit.

The emergence of the post-truth world has been caused by many factors, including historical circumstances that created mistrust of established institutions and beliefs. The post-truth era is now typified by an elected leadership that continues to perpetuate uncertainty, intentional fabrications, and division. This ongoing blurring of ethical boundaries and changing definitions of truth is a collective responsibility we all must fully understand and work against. Postmodernism described the emergence of multiple perspectives and communities with distinct narratives while the advance of social technologies offered the promise of purposeful collaboration and connected learning. But groups also coalesce around set ideas that fail to consider other perspectives as everyone seeks to confirm their own beliefs. In addition, personal information that was freely shared by active participants through social media platforms has been compromised due to failed security and a breach of trust by proprietary interests within these digital spaces. At the same time, while we have seen a large-scale manipulation of networked information environments and the intentional division of disparate communities, these developments do not negate the promise and potential of bringing people together to seek truth, effectively communicate, creatively collaborate, and make new knowledge in a pluralistic society.

Considering how both truth and reason have been challenged in today's political atmosphere and social media settings, we need to expand education and dialogue and reaffirm the values, theories, and praxis we embody as teachers and learners. We must repudiate lies with truth. Education is central to this process. In his essay "From Post-Truth to Post-Lies: Using Behavioral Science to Fight 'Alternative Facts,'" Gleb Tsipursky (2017) argues that "our survival depends on moving from the post-truth, alternative-facts present into a post-lies future." As we work toward a more promising outlook, metaliteracy is an essential framework for achieving this goal, knowing that the production of untruths and misinformation is not going away and will most likely compound, but that our strategies for critical, collaborative, and reflective learning must continue to advance.

METALITERACY IN THE POST-TRUTH WORLD

Metaliteracy is a reframing and reinvention of information literacy, grounded in critical thinking and the pursuit of lifelong learning (Mackey and Jacobson 2011, 2014; Jacobson and Mackey 2013). The original conception of metaliteracy challenged the traditional definition of information literacy by envisioning a comprehensive framework that pushed the bounds of standard institutional descriptions (Mackey and Jacobson 2011, 2014; Jacobson and Mackey 2013). This model was responsive to revolutionary changes in emerging technologies such as social media and online communities and reflected the pedagogical practices that many faculty and librarians were engaging with in the real world.

The introduction of a metaliteracy to reframe information literacy explored characteristics of cognate literacies, such as visual, media, and digital literacy, that were especially relevant in dynamic new media environments.

The intent of this unified approach was to recognize applicable attributes that were complementary and connected in an emergent environment of multimedia and social media, yet often overlooked in the prevailing information literacy definition found in the Association of College and Research Libraries' *Information Literacy Competency Standards for Higher Education* (ACRL 2000). At the time, this previous model emphasized the information consumer and primarily the behavioral and cognitive abilities. Metaliteracy promoted the evaluation and creation of dynamic content while "asking vital questions of other participants, critically evaluating the materials presented, and carefully incorporating the information into their own learning" (Mackey and Jacobson 2011, 74). This collaborative dimension and active role for producers of information was a core part of metaliteracy from the start, especially within the context of rapidly changing and interactive information environments and the proliferation of new formats, such as blogs, microblogs, wikis, digital media, virtual environments, and a range of digital resources in libraries and academe.

As metaliteracy developed as a pedagogical model, it emphasized metacognition within four domains of learning that also included affective, behavioral, and cognitive dimensions in support of a comprehensive set of goals and learning objectives (Forte et al. 2014). Metaliteracy integrates metacognition in a way that "allows us to move beyond rudimentary skills development and prepares students to dig deeper and assess their own learning" (Mackey and Jacobson 2014, 13). Metacognition supports both reflective thinking and self-regulation and challenges the skills-based approach of traditional information literacy definitions and practices. As the ACRL redefined information literacy and moved from the set of *Standards* to the *Framework for Information Literacy for Higher Education* (ACRL 2016), metaliteracy and metacognition were mentioned as influences but ultimately downplayed in the final document (Fulkerson, Ariew, and Jacobson 2017). This diminution of both concepts in the ACRL *Framework* reinforces the need to advance the connection between metaliteracy and metacognition since "without reflection learners will neither change to see themselves as empowered learners with authoritative voices, nor will they be conscious of their own attitudes" (Fulkerson, Ariew, and Jacobson 2017, 36). Both ideas have become especially critical in today's information environment that enables connectivity while also resulting in division and mistrust.

While metacognition is often understood as thinking about one's own thinking, it has an integral relationship to self-regulation that is crucial to metaliteracy. According to Fulkerson, Ariew, and Jacobson (2017), "Self-regulating learners have an enhanced awareness of their own strengths and weaknesses, are more resilient in adapting new tactics for problem solving, and are more adept at overcoming obstacles" (25). This integrated approach to metacognition is built into metaliteracy to promote learner agency and empowerment. Flavell (1979) argues that learners are faced with a range of challenging situations that "provide many opportunities for thoughts and feelings about your own thinking to arise and, in many cases, call for the kind of quality control that metacognitive experiences can help supply" (908). He describes how this process of "cognitive monitoring" plays out in the real world and asserts, "In many real-life situations, the monitoring problem is not to determine how well you understand what a message means but to determine how much you ought to believe it or do what is says to do" (910). Based on this key insight, metacognitive learning is more than the comprehension of information because it also supports verifying accuracy and believability. According to Flavell, this analytical approach requires us to promote the "critical appraisal of message source, quality of appeal, and probable consequences needed to cope with these inputs sensibly" (910). As we continue to grapple with how to differentiate between what is real and what is not, the ability to analyze the source and quality of communications is especially vital.

not a strong argument

The metacognitive aspect of metaliteracy is both reflective and self-regulating. As part of this dynamic, metaliteracy shifts the emphasis from teacher to learner by envisioning the learner as both. Metacognition supports this expanded role for learners:

> Metaliterate students will be prepared to fill the gaps in learning and develop strategies for understanding more than we, as teachers, present or discuss. Through this process, the learner is also a teacher and each individual is a collaborative partner in the learning experience. If learners gain new insights about their knowledge in these areas, they will be better prepared to critically evaluate information and technology systems common today and in the future. (Mackey and Jacobson 2014, 13)

Imagining the learner as teacher recognizes the pedagogical role we all play in social spaces by sharing this commitment in an equal way that promotes empowered learning and active participation with others. Metacognition provides an opening for individuals to consider their own strengths and areas for improvement and to check those strongly held beliefs and biases that may prevent the objective evaluation of information in any setting. In collaborative social environments, individuals have a responsibility to participate ethically and to contribute in meaningful ways but are often swayed by their own predetermined mind-sets. Within a variety of actual and virtual spaces, "Metaliteracy is more than descriptive; it identifies how learners critically evaluate and understand their knowledge as individuals and participants in social learning environments" (Mackey and Jacobson 2014, 13–14). Through this metacognitive process, metaliteracy prepares learners to effectively participate by integrating critical thinking and evaluation, production and sharing of information, adaptation to new technologies, teaching and learning, and ultimately the acquisition of new knowledge.

META LITERACY

In the aftermath of the 2016 presidential election, metaliteracy was discussed as a pedagogical framework to prepare learners to identify and reject fake news (Mackey and Jacobson 2016). In unfiltered information environments that shape and distribute false and misleading content masked as news, metaliterate learners "distinguish between formal and informal sources of information that may have very different or nonexistent editorial checks and balances" (Mackey and Jacobson 2016). This deep evaluation of online content includes a close examination of how information is packaged "to recognize whether the seemingly professional design may be a façade for a bias or misinformation" (Mackey and Jacobson 2016). In addition to understanding the evaluative aspects of information creation and sharing, the metacognitive dimension of metaliteracy "asks that individuals understand on a mental and emotional level the potential impact of one's participation" (Mackey and Jacobson 2016). This reflective approach to learning requires individuals to differentiate between cognitive and affective responses to online information by foregrounding any biases that may predispose viewpoints. Metaliterate learning combines multiple critical thinking competencies that promote the evaluation, production, and sharing of information while carefully reflecting on individual thinking in these spaces.

In her essay "Posttruth, Truthiness, and Alternative Facts: Information Behavior and Critical Information Consumption for a New Age," Nicole A. Cooke (2017) argues for a metaliteracy approach to address fake news by developing "critical consumers of information." She asserts, "Metaliteracy provides a holistic lens through which to consider how critical consumers can interact with information; this approach focuses on the individual consumer and puts equal emphasis on the context that shapes information production and consumption" (219). Cooke points out that fake news is not a new problem and is rooted in other forms of propaganda as well as misinformation and disinformation. She supports an emphasis on how we develop pedagogical strategies as a response to the concerns because "metaliterate learners are critically engaged researchers who can contribute to discourse and who can also successfully navigate the information landscape that is riddled with fake news, alternative facts, biases, and counterknowledge" (219). This approach empowers learners to effectively contribute in these connected yet divided environments through active participation and discovery.

Gibson and Jacobson (2018) argue for "transformative learning experiences" that encourage dialogue and debate to overcome individual biases and set beliefs in a post-truth world (189). They describe a range of "high-impact practices" that build trust among and across diverse communities in support of critical thinking and research-based inquiry (191). Gibson and Jacobson (2018) support metaliteracy in relation to the ACRL *Framework*, which was influenced by this model, although not to the extent as originally envisioned (Fulkerson, Ariew, and Jacobson, 2017). Gibson and Jacobson (2018) argue that we need to develop pedagogical practices that are "well integrated into a course that is designed to foster a community of inquiry in order to accomplish the goals that characterize transformative learning ,and metaliteracy" (191). Through this integrated approach, educators invent or reinvent a host of pedagogical practices to address the challenges of the post-truth world.

Overall, the collaborative and participatory aspects of metaliteracy allow us to build connected communities that reinforce the *empathy* and *understanding* Kirkpatrick (2017) envisions when arguing that "such empathetic movements can provide the sorely needed antidote to our post-truth plague" (331). In addition, advancing metacognitive reflection in these environments provides us with the chance to check our own biases and those of other participants. Seeing other perspectives while challenging our own assumptions makes us more open to new ideas in a network of disparate communities. Similarly, as Gleb Tsipursky (2017) argues, "We need to work tirelessly to educate everyone about the benefits of orienting toward truth" while "focusing on the values and emotions of those we communicate with in order to change their hearts and minds." This empathetic approach to education is reliant on openness and communication and must be embedded into our pedagogical strategies. Metaliteracy promotes the kind of metacognitive reflection, purposeful collaboration, and engaged participation that encourages individuals to improve communication and dialogue through mutual respect and support.

Metaliterate learning reinforces Tali Sharot's (2017) point: "Considering the other person's existing outlook will help clarify how we can present arguments in a way most convincing to them, rather than a way most convincing to us" (34). Sharot suggests that offering evidence alone is not sufficient because that approach will simply lead to counterarguments based on set beliefs rather than productive dialogue and exchange. We need to do more than gain access to social technologies and increase proficiency. We must also become critical consumers of information in these environments through meaningful participation and the creation of new knowledge. This is a key aspect of metaliteracy that works against the "technology-induced confirmation bias" that exists in the systems (Sharot 2017, 21). An ongoing adaptation to new technologies as a critical consumer offers the potential to challenge the algorithms that simply show us what we want to see based on our online behavior, for instance. Rather than accept the assumptions and automations of the system design, we need to learn how things work and build this knowledge gained into our critical thinking perspective.

CHARACTERISTICS OF A METALITERATE LEARNER

To gain a deeper understanding of the primary dimensions that comprise metaliteracy in support of the metaliterate learner, this section examines figure 1.1, Metaliterate Learner Characteristics. These essential attributes reinforce the four domains of metaliteracy (behavioral, cognitive, affective,

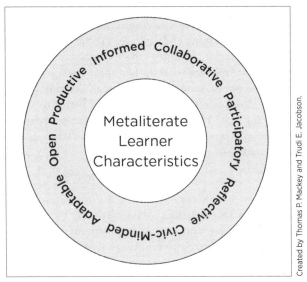

FIGURE 1.1
Metaliterate Learner Characteristics

metacognitive) and underpin the metaliteracy goals and learning objectives. This visual representation of the metaliterate learner provides an overview of the central metaliteracy concepts that we must further emphasize and develop in the post-truth world. The primary characteristics of the metaliterate learner include collaborative, participatory, reflective, civic-minded, adaptable, open, productive, and informed. Let us delve further into each of these interrelated attributes.

Collaborative

The metaliterate learner is open to creative collaboration that fosters responsible cooperation in social environments, including those mediated by technology. Through collaboration, the metaliterate learner is actively engaged in professional, personal, and collegial partnerships that include like-minded viewpoints but must also support diverse perspectives that expand and challenge individual preconceptions or beliefs. The collaborative characteristic supports dialogue among participants and reinforces the dual roles of learner and teacher. As Paulo Friere (1997) argues, "Through dialogue, the teacher-of-the-students and the students-of-the-teacher cease to exist and a new term emerges: teacher-student with students-teachers" (61). The idea of learner as teacher is core to metaliteracy because empowered learners actively contribute to the dialogue and teach others what they know or learn in social environments. Metaliterate learners are also open to learning from others in collaborative social spaces. Since evolving technologies such as social media have proven to be both unifying and divisive, a focus on constructive dialogue and productive collaboration reinforces the ways that diverse perspectives are capable of bringing people together rather than breaking them apart. This requires a conscious effort, however, to consider alternative viewpoints and to understand the downside of technologies that foster isolated groups that coalesce around the same ideas. It also means that teachers must consider learners in this social dynamic as co-creators of knowledge capable of teaching what they learn and know.

Participatory

Being participatory is an essential characteristic of the metaliterate learner because it promotes active and critical engagement with others in shared social environments. This attribute reinforces metaliterate learning through networked social media and emerging technologies and is beneficial in a variety of real-world settings as well. According to Henry Jenkins and colleagues (2006), a participatory culture is "a culture with relatively low barriers to artistic expression and civic engagement," one that encourages active participation that is both creative and community-driven (3). Individuals are free to express themselves online but must also consider the public responsibilities that accompany the production and sharing of creative works. Jenkins and colleagues also argue that in participatory cultures "members believe their contributions matter, and feel some degree of social connection with one another" (3). This idea suggests that individuals care about what they create and post online and are aware of the communities they are a part of and that surround them. In today's post-truth world, everyone must take responsibility for the digital information they produce and share and know that both original and repurposed information have meaning and consequences. In developing the metaliterate learner, we need to reinforce the creative possibilities of knowledge construction through connectedness and collaboration. Doing so requires supporting the participatory characteristic to build communities of trust that are accountable for the information that originates and circulates online.

Reflective

The reflective characteristic is core to metaliteracy because it emphasizes the metacognitive domain that fosters thinking about one's own thinking and the self-regulation of one's own literacy and learning. As described in *Metaliteracy: Reinventing Information Literacy to Empower Learners*, "To be metaliterate requires individuals to understand their existing literacy strengths and areas for improvement and make decisions about their learning" (Mackey and Jacobson 2014, 2). In the post-truth world, this reflective process takes on additional significance because awareness is required to check one's own biases. The reflective attribute reinforces meditative thinking, deeper understanding, and openness to other viewpoints and alternate perspectives. According to Tali Sharot (2017), "when people perceive their own agency is being removed, they resist. Yet if they perceive their agency as being expanded they embrace the experience and find it rewarding" (84–85). This suggests that a careful balance is needed between self-regulation and influence. Sharot argues, "Understanding why we are the way we are, and being conscious of our deeply rooted drive to make decisions, may help us hand over the wheel once in a while" (103). In other words, while people want control, they may be able to give it up at times and open up to other ideas and influences if it is understood as an expansion of their own agency (Sharot 2017, 84–85). In this context, reflection is necessary for the self-regulation of one's thinking and actions. According to O'Brien and colleagues (2017), metaliteracy is a pedagogical framework that supports "autonomous and self-regulated learners, as learners who do not reflect on their thinking and learning are incapable of self-regulation" (272). Combined with the other related metaliteracy learning characteristics, being reflective reinforces a holistic pedagogy that promotes learner empowerment through expanded awareness and control of one's behaviors in a range of social settings.

Civic-Minded

Being civic-minded emphasizes and supports the role of the metaliterate learner in collaborative social communities. Oxford Dictionaries (2018a) defines the term *civic-minded*, an adjective, as "concerned with or active in civic affairs; concerned with the welfare of the community as a whole, public-spirited." This definition suggests an expanded role of the individual in public and community settings that requires civic responsibility and a focus on the public interest. In today's post-truth world, being civic-minded must extend to social media environments and online communities that depend upon community-based accountability as well. The collaborative and participatory nature of the commons, which we find in many forms through online communities, social media platforms, and open learning initiatives, for instance, relies on the norms and expectations of the community, especially since many traditional editorial filters and processes have either changed significantly or disappeared as a result of networked social technologies.

Wikipedia was once seen as a Wild West of unverified information posted by anonymous users. While the communal standards and community-based editorial processes at *Wikipedia* address the concerns about anonymity and the reliability of information, the site still has a long way to go in terms of being fully open and transparent. Noam Cohen (2018) describes a plan by YouTube to use *Wikipedia* entries to counter false information that appeared on the video-sharing site, arguing that "in the past 15 years, Wikipedia has built a system of collaboration and governance that, although hardly perfect, has been robust enough to endure these polarized times." At the same time, *Wikipedia* has not gone far enough because a considerable gender gap has been identified in the authoring and editing of content (Kennedy 2017; Shane-Simpson and Gillespie-Lynch 2017; Ford and Wajcman 2017), suggesting that the online encyclopedia has not realized a vision for equitable participation. As shown in this example, pioneering approaches to developing and sharing content require innovative practices and processes for maintaining the integrity of that information. A critical perspective is also needed to make certain that the interface is designed in a way that is fully transparent and inclusive. Metaliterate learners are civic-minded contributors to collaborative spaces such as *Wikipedia* who understand how to effectively create and consume meaningful content in participatory environments, while demanding that the spaces be truly open and democratic.

Open

The open characteristic of metaliteracy defines personal and professional qualities needed to expand the learning process and to effectively engage with others in collaborative communities. Being open to new ideas, insights, and perspectives allows individuals to think beyond their own biases that might limit their learning experiences. Openness intentionally invokes open learning and open education as well, challenging educators to collaborate on teaching philosophies and practices while sharing learning objectives and learning resources. In his essay *Connectivism: A Learning Theory for the Digital Age*, George Siemens (2004) asserts, "Learning and knowledge rests in diversity of opinions," but in a post-truth world, we have seen multiple communities that connect internally but not across the divide. According to Siemens, "Connectivism presents a model of learning that acknowledges the tectonic shifts in society where learning is no longer an internal, individualistic activity." In many ways, connectivism reflects the optimism of the networked world, to bring people together to share ideas, learning, and knowledge through social communities. Similarly, metaliteracy promotes active and engaged learning in collaborative, participatory environments that rely on multiple perspectives and insights. In today's post-truth world, we also need an expanded and conscious emphasis on open-mindedness in these spaces. As Kirkpatrick (2017) argues, *understanding* "can only be appreciated in an active sense, requiring a movement that seeks to overcome a distance" (330–31). This empathetic approach requires an innovative sense of openness that seems unachievable in today's partisan world, but nevertheless it is an essential characteristic within a holistic metaliterate construct.

Adaptable

Being adaptable is especially relevant as emerging technologies change and evolve so quickly, requiring learners to continually familiarize themselves with new media platforms and information systems. This characteristic is intended to prepare learners to be responsive and flexible to new ways of learning and knowing, including approaches mediated by technology. Learner empowerment is gained as individuals become proficient with new media and effectively communicate and produce original and repurposed content in these spaces. In a post-truth world, however, we have also seen the negative consequences of posting and sharing personal information in commercial interfaces such as Facebook that have been caught sharing user data without permission. Keeping this in mind, then, we need a critical adaptability that takes into account the protection of personal privacy and information security while remaining open to new technologies and information environments. Metaliterate learners must be curious about changing technologies and be fearless in trying new devices and experiencing new environments while asking probing questions about the information architecture and policy implications of every system. The extent to which content is influenced by technologies and interpreted within information environments is a related understanding as well. This iterative process requires a specific understanding of the distinctions between open and commercial interfaces and the impact these different models have on how information is ultimately produced, secured, and shared.

Productive

The productive characteristic reinforces being a creative producer of original and repurposed content, both individually and in collaboration with others. Through this participatory and dynamic process, "Metaliteracy promotes active involvement with open, online, and mobile resources to advance self-reflection and critical thinking" (Mackey and Jacobson 2014, 52). From a metaliteracy perspective, the open space of *Wikipedia* and even the commercial setting of Facebook both have the potential to become environments for meaningful contributions among a productive and responsible community of learners (Mackey and Jacobson 2014, 52). In her discussion of digital literacy, Renee Hobbs (2017) argues, "Too many people graduate from college without having had experience composing memos, building a web site, writing a blog post, or creating a compelling photo" (8). She points out that learners "stumble when asked to create an infographic, deliver a speech, create a podcast, share a compelling story, or create a YouTube video" because "they have not had sufficient experience creating to learn" (8). Metaliteracy addresses similar concerns through the dynamic production of original and repurposed information and reflection on this work and one's own thinking during this process. While learners may have access to a range of technological devices, they may not see themselves as producers of content, and if they do, they may not have the chance to be creative originators of media in both educational and real-world settings. Metaliterate learners are productive creators of information and learn from these experiences through the trial and error of exploring new technologies while making meaning through content creation. But they also need to ask critical questions about the interface itself and insist upon an open and transparent environment that supports the ethical production and sharing of information.

As Hobbs asserts, the production of original materials is valuable and carries with it a clear sense of accountability. She argues:

> Today the burden of responsibility is on the consumer to sort out and evaluate the quality of human creativity in all its many forms. But if everyone tries hard to create and share what is true, what is beautiful, and what has value to others, and if we all avoided creating content that harms people, the world really would be a better place. Human creative expression has the potential to transform the world, by enabling people to construct and share work that has meaning and value. (Hobbs 2017, 26)

This emphasis on the positive and transformative dimension of producing and sharing creative works is integral to metaliteracy as well, and the emphasis on the integrity of this process resonates as a purposeful response to the post-truth world. In a holistic metaliteracy model, the productive characteristic supports the entire person who contributes both creatively and consciously to diverse communities of learning.

Informed

Being an informed consumer of information is essential to the consumer-producer dynamic of metaliteracy. This foundation concept traces back to the core information literacy principles that effectively differentiated between technology skills and broader information proficiencies. In today's technology-centric world, being informed is especially relevant in distinguishing between fact and fiction, real and virtual, truth and untruth. According to a study conducted by the Stanford History Education Group, the ability to use a range of technological devices is widespread since "Our 'digital natives' may be able to flit between Facebook and Twitter while simultaneously uploading a selfie to Instagram and texting a friend" (Wineburg et al. 2016, 4). At the same time, however, "when it comes to evaluating information that flows through social media channels, they are easily duped" (Wineburg et al. 2016, 4). As we have seen in today's connected world, being fooled by the proliferation of false information extends beyond the digital natives to a broader population. As the Stanford History Education Group observed, this concern has serious implications for society since "we worry that democracy is threatened by the ease at which disinformation about civic issues is allowed to spread and flourish" (Wineburg et al. 2016, 5). The informed characteristic underpins all of the other attributes in metaliteracy and reinforces the centrality of research in both academic and lifelong learning settings to consume and produce accurate and verifiable information. Being informed is crucial to understanding the implications of content production and distribution through all media and in comprehending how to effectively participate in democratic communities and societies.

❈ ❈ ❈ ❈ ❈

The characteristics outlined in this model support the development of the metaliterate learner in multiple contexts and are indispensable for preparing individuals for the post-truth world and beyond. These critical attributes are interrelated in a comprehensive metaliteracy framework that considers the four domains of learning: affective, behavioral, cognitive, and metacognitive. Further, the metaliterate learner characteristics inform the revised and expanded metaliteracy learning goals and objectives outlined in the next section.

PURSUING TRUTH THROUGH INQUIRY

As a pedagogical framework for literacy and learning, metaliteracy is enacted through a developing set of goals and learning objectives (Jacobson et al., 2018). The metaliteracy model has evolved from an original set of seven learning objectives (Mackey and Jacobson 2011, 70–76), followed by the comprehensive design of the metaliteracy goals and learning objectives, as defined by the Metaliteracy Learning Collaborative (Forte et al. 2014; Mackey and Jacobson 2014, 84–92). The expanded goals and learning objectives took into account the four domains of learning: affective, behavioral, cognitive, and metacognitive (Forte et al. 2014; Mackey and Jacobson 2014, 85–86). This comprehensive approach envisions the whole person with the ability to understand and develop emotions and attitudes (affective), skills and competencies (behavioral), comprehension and evaluation (cognitive), as well as reflection and self-regulation (metacognitive) (Forte et al. 2014; Mackey and Jacobson 2014, 85–86). The four domains of learning work together in a unified metaliteracy framework, informing the goals and learning objectives in support of the metaliterate learner characteristics.

In a post-truth world, the metaliterate learner pursues truth through ongoing inquiry, ethical participation, and informed knowledge production. This ongoing process requires a further refinement of the goals and learning objectives to address the current challenges. This renewed approach continues to be informed by the four domains of learning and supports the characteristics of the metaliterate learner (Jacobson et al. 2018; goals and objectives presented in the following sections are drawn from this source).

GOAL 1

Actively Evaluate Content While Also Evaluating One's Own Biases

This first goal promotes the critical evaluation of dynamic content in all forms while pairing this competency with the need for identifying individual biases. Doing so encourages individuals to be aware that the predispositions they bring to any information situation have an impact on how they understand and interpret the content therein. One of the affective and cognitive learning objectives related to this goal includes the ability to "verify expertise but acknowledge that experts do exist." This objective recognizes that sources of information must be genuine and confirmed while acknowledging that even in decentered environments, expertise is relevant, necessary, and verifiable. The ability to think critically in this context is supported by the cognitive objective to "acknowledge that content is not always produced for legitimate reasons, and that biases exist, both subtle and overt." This learning objective strengthens the ability to critically assess content while closely examining the preconceptions that may exist in any form of information.

Metaliterate learners are also expected to look internally and reflect on individual biases, as asserted in the affective and metacognitive objective to "reflect on how you feel about information or an information environment to consider multiple perspectives." This goal is further supported by another affective and metacognitive objective to "examine how you feel about the information presented and how this impacts your response." Building these two objectives into the evaluation process promotes the metacognitive reflection necessary to gain a deeper understanding of one's own predispositions and influences, heightening awareness to inform the critical analysis of both perception and interpretation. The importance of diverse perspectives that extend beyond one's own world is emphasized in the behavioral objective to "consciously seek information from a spectrum of viewpoints and sources." Overall this first goal contains associated objectives that promote the critical evaluation of content in all forms while taking into account the biases that may be embedded in information and related environments, while reflecting on individual preconceptions that influence our own understandings.

GOAL 2
Engage with All Intellectual Property Ethically and Responsibly

The second goal of metaliteracy emphasizes the ethical dimension of dealing with all forms of intellectual property as both a content creator and an informed consumer. This goal addresses the accountability associated with producing and sharing information through a range of technology-mediated environments. Metaliterate learners are encouraged to achieve the cognitive objective to "differentiate between producing original information and remixing openly licensed content" so that they grasp the differences in the origins of content and the distinctions among format types. In addition, they address the behavioral objective to "responsibly produce and share original information and ethically remix and repurpose openly licensed content" in an effort to understand the answerability of content creators. In today's complex information environment, individuals must be able to achieve the cognitive objective to "distinguish between public and personal information and make ethical and informed decisions about appropriately sharing information online." Social media environments in particular require an ongoing process of critical thinking that emphasizes the ability to draw the line between one's personal privacy and the public distribution and consumption of information.

The metaliterate learner has many options for creating and publishing information in open and proprietary environments and needs to "differentiate between copyright, Creative Commons, and open licenses in both the creation and licensing of original and repurposed content." This behavioral and cognitive objective reinforces the capacity to distinguish among a range of licensing methods, including those that promote open content and others that are proprietary or through some blend of the two. As part of this goal, metaliterate learners are also inspired to achieve the behavioral and cognitive objective to "identify and follow the specific intellectual property attribution expectations in the setting in which you are working." This learning objective reinforces the ability to understand and apply the appropriate acknowledgment of specific sources in various formats and in all settings. Overall, this goal emphasizes the ethical considerations of the consumer-producer dynamic and the attendant responsibilities of creating and sharing content.

GOAL 3
Produce and Share Information in Collaborative and Participatory Environments

This third goal addresses one of the key aspects of metaliteracy, which is focused on the metaliterate learner as an individual and collaborative producer of information in participating communities. Central to this goal is the affective and metacognitive objective for a learner to "see oneself as a producer as well as consumer of information." This learning objective reinforces the ability to first envision this dual role with the aim of enacting it in a variety of collaborative settings. As part of this process, metaliterate learners work toward the behavioral objectives to "participate conscientiously and ethically in collaborative environments" and to "share knowledge accurately and effectively through the production of content using appropriate and evolving formats and platforms." Both objectives address the ethical responsibilities associated with producing and sharing information. In addition, the behavioral and cognitive objective to "protect personal privacy and actively secure your online information" is especially relevant in a post-truth world in which proprietary interests have overlooked and betrayed the personal privacy of individual participants.

As metaliterate learners become insightful participants, they attain the behavioral and cognitive objective to "translate information presented in one manner to another in order to best meet the needs of a particular audience." This ability to translate information expands the understanding of information consumers to recognize varying forms of information and prepares content creators to adapt, apply, and repurpose mutable content in numerous formats. In doing so, metaliterate learners strive toward the behavioral and cognitive objectives to "critically evaluate and verify user-generated content and appropriately apply in new knowledge creation" while expanding the scope of their worldview to "recognize diverse cultural values and norms to create and share information for global audiences." As part of this developing process, the metaliterate learner is inspired to "recognize that learners are also teachers and teach what you know or learn in collaborative settings." This learning objective integrates the affective, behavioral, and cognitive domains because seeing oneself as a teacher involves an individual's attitude or emotion about this expanded role while taking into account how this ability is enacted and then understood or evaluated. Ultimately, this goal prepares metaliterate learners to be responsible knowledge producers and critical information consumers in situations that involve participation and support teaching and learning from community members.

GOAL 4

Develop Learning Strategies to Meet Lifelong Personal and Professional Goals

This fourth metaliteracy goal encourages metaliterate learners to reflect on their own education and to enact metaliteracy in personal and professional settings. Individuals seek to "recognize that learning is a process and that reflecting on errors or mistakes leads to new insights and discoveries." This metacognitive objective inspires learners to gain new perspectives from ongoing inquiry and discovery. In doing so, they work toward the cognitive and metacognitive objective to "assess learning to determine both the knowledge gained and the gaps in understanding." In an objective that combines all four domains of learning, individuals "recognize that critical thinking depends upon knowledge of a subject and actively pursue deeper understanding through inquiry and research." As part of this goal, metaliterate learners reach the metacognitive objective to "value persistence, adaptability, and flexibility in lifelong learning." This adaptability extends to the affective and behavioral objectives to "adapt to new learning situations while being flexible about the varied approaches to learning" and to "adapt to and understand new technologies and the impact they have on learning." Ultimately, this goal motivates individuals to reflect on and take control of their own learning strategies while working toward the metacognitive objective to "apply metaliterate learning as a lifelong value and practice" through situations that may be both constructive and demanding.

CONCLUSION

Metaliteracy prepares individuals for a post-truth world because it promotes metacognitive reflection and self-regulation at a time when the touch of a portable screen allows us to transmit and receive unfiltered information instantaneously. Reflecting on the information we search, post, or share provides time for us to pause and critically examine the documents in transit. Reflecting on one's own thinking in these spaces offers a chance to contemplate individual biases or beliefs through the analysis of evidence. Self-regulation places us in control of interpretation and response as well as individual literacy and learning. In addition, metaliterate thinking allows us to identify and analyze the preconceptions embedded in the multitude of sources we encounter. Metaliteracy advances the idea that energetic and meaningful participation is democratic and supports the egalitarian promise of a decentered and connected virtual space. This learner-centered pedagogical model is especially critical in a post-truth world where expertise is uncertain and often unchecked across a vast social network.

Metaliteracy recognizes that learners adapt to evolving technologies and understand the underlying architecture of the systems. It promotes the ability to actively contribute to social information environments as participants and designers of these spaces. Engaging with these ever-evolving communities is essential to a better understanding of the learning potential and possible perils of the devices and related virtual spaces we design and build. Metaliterate learners increase competence and gain confidence with technology while bringing a critical thinking perspective to how the associated environments are applied to consume and create information. In networked settings with an inherently social dimension, metaliterate learners engage with one another and collaborate both intuitively and consciously. They exchange roles as teachers and learners while translating multiple forms of information across platforms. Metaliterate learners engage in collaborative and productive dialogue to broaden conceptions of the world and to gain a deeper understanding of the beliefs and perspectives of others.

At this critical historical moment, metaliterate learners must be prepared to envision a newfound sense of community by taking responsibility for the social spaces we create, join, moderate, and share. Rather than harken back to the days of traditional narratives, with outdated checks and balances, we need to reaffirm our commitment to collaborative communities that are built on trust and compassion and that necessarily evolve and change in the face of unexpected challenges. This process involves both individual and collective accountability informed by innovative, transparent, and inclusive theories and practices. In a post-truth world, facts alone are not enough to cross the partisan divide or as a way to address the intentional misrepresentations and untruths that flood the social ecosystem. Metaliterate learners are optimistic that through reflective and empowered participation, and the strength of connected communities, we will purposefully reinvent a truthful world.

REFERENCES

ACRL (Association of College & Research Libraries). 2000. *Information Literacy Competency Standards for Higher Education*. Chicago: American Library Association. www.ala.org/acrl/standards/informationliteracycompetency.

———. 2016. *Framework for Information Literacy for Higher Education*. Chicago: American Library Association. www.ala.org/acrl/standards/ilframework.

Burke, Timothy. 2018. "How America's Largest Local TV Owner Turned Its News Anchors into Soldiers in Trump's War on the Media." *The Concourse*, March 31. https://theconcourse.deadspin.com/how-americas-local-tv-owner -turned-its-news-anc-1824233490.

Cadwalladr, Carole, and Emma Graham-Harrison. 2018. "Revealed: 50 Million Facebook Profiles Harvested for Cambridge Analytica in Major Data Breach." *The Guardian*, March 17. www.theguardian.com/news/2018/mar/17/cambridge -analytica-facebook-influence-us-election.

Cohen, Noam. 2018. "Conspiracy Videos? Fake News? Enter Wikipedia, the 'Good Cop' of the Internet." *The Washington Post*, "Outlook: Perspective," April 6. www.washingtonpost.com/outlook/conspiracy-videos-fake-news-enter -wikipedia-the-good-cop-of-the-internet/2018/04/06/ad1f018a-3835-11e8 -8fd2-49fe3c675a89_story.html?utm_term=.b47a28d9b98c.

Cooke, Nicole. A. 2017. "Posttruth, Truthiness, and Alternative Facts: Information Behavior and Critical Information Consumption for a New Age." *Library Quarterly* 87 (3): 211–21.

Deadspin on Twitter. 2018. "How America's Largest Local TV Owner Turned Its News Anchors into Soldiers in Trump's War on the Media." Posted March 31. https:// twitter.com/Deadspin/status/980175772206993409.

Edsall, Thomas B. 2018. "Is President Trump a Stealth Postmodernist or Just a Liar?" *New York Times*, "Opinion," January 25. www.nytimes.com/2018/01/25/ opinion/trump-postmodernism-lies.html.

Flavell, John H. 1979. "Metacognition and Cognitive Monitoring: A New Area of Cognitive-Developmental Inquiry." *American Psychologist* 34 (10): 906–11.

Ford, Heather, and Judy Wajcman. 2017. "'Anyone Can Edit,' Not Everyone Does: Wikipedia's Infrastructure and the Gender Gap." *Social Studies of Science* 47 (4): 511–27. doi:10.1177/0306312717692172.

Forte, Michele, Trudi Jacobson, Tom Mackey, Emer O'Keeffe, and Kathleen Stone. 2014. "Goals and Learning Objectives: 2014 Goals and Learning Objectives." Metaliteracy.org. https://metaliteracy.org/learning-objectives.

Freire, Paulo. 1997. *Pedagogy of the Oppressed*. New York: Continuum.

Fulkerson, Diane M., Susan Andriette Ariew, and Trudi E. Jacobson. 2017. "Revisiting Metacognition and Metaliteracy in the ACRL Framework." *Communications in Information Literacy* 11 (1): 21–41.

Gibson, Craig, and Trudi E. Jacobson. 2018. "Habits of Mind in an Uncertain Information World." *Reference and User Services Quarterly* 57 (3): 183–92. https://journals.ala.org/index.php/rusq/article/view/6603.

Guess, Andrew, Brendan Nyhan, and Jason Reifler. 2018. "Selective Exposure to Misinformation: Evidence from the Consumption of Fake News during the 2016 U.S. Presidential Campaign." Unpublished manuscript. www.dartmouth .edu/~nyhan/fake-news-2016.pdf.

Heer, Jeet. 2017. "America's First Postmodern President." *The New Republic*, July 8. https://newrepublic.com/article/143730/americas-first-postmodern-president.

Higgins, Kathleen. 2016. "Post-Truth: A Guide for the Perplexed." *Nature* 540 (December 1): 9.

Hobbs, Renee. 2017. *Create to Learn: Introduction to Digital Literacy*. Hoboken, NJ: John Wiley & Sons.

Jacobson, Trudi E., and Thomas P. Mackey. 2013. "Proposing a Metaliteracy Model to Redefine Information Literacy." *Communications in Information Literacy* 7 (2): 84–91.

Jacobson, Trudi, Tom Mackey, Kelsey O'Brien, Michele Forte, and Emer O'Keeffe. 2018. "Goals and Learning Objectives: Draft Revision (April 11, 2018)." Metaliteracy.org. https://metaliteracy.org/learning-objectives.

Jenkins, Henry, with Katie Clinton, Ravi Purushotma, Alice J. Robison, and Margaret Weigel. 2006. *Confronting the Challenges of Participatory Culture: Media Education for the 21st Century*. An Occasional Paper on Digital Media and Learning. Chicago: The John D. and Catherine T. MacArthur Foundation.

Johnson, Ben. 2017. "Information Literacy Is Dead: The Role of Libraries in a Post-Truth World." *Computers in Libraries* 37 (2): 12–15. www.infotoday.com/cilmag/mar17/Johnson--Information-Literacy-Is-Dead--The-Role-of-Libraries-in-a-Post-Truth-World.shtml.

Kennedy, Kara. 2017. "Why Women Should Be Editing Wikipedia." *Women's Studies Journal* 31 (1): 94–99. http://library.esc.edu/login?url=https://search.ebscohost.com/login.aspx?direct=true&db=a9h&AN=124612549&site=eds-live.

Kessler, Glen, Salvador Rizzo, and Meg Kelly. 2018. "President Trump Has Made More Than 5,000 False or Misleading Claims." *The Washington Post*, "Fact Checker: Analysis," September 13. www.washingtonpost.com/politics/2018/09/13/president-trump-has-made-more-than-false-or-misleading-claims/?utm_term=.a8736ab0b316.

Keyes, Ralph. 2004. *The Post-Truth Era: Dishonesty and Deception in Contemporary Life*. New York: St. Martin's Press.

Kirkpatrick, Andrew. 2017. "Understanding in a Post-Truth World: Comprehension and Co-Naissance as Emphatic Antidotes to Post-Truth Politics." *Cosmos and History: The Journal of Natural and Social Philosophy* 13 (3): 312–335.

Kreitner, Richard. 2016. "Post-Truth and Its Consequences: What a 25-Year-Old Essay Tells Us about the Current Moment." *The Nation*, November 30. www.thenation.com/article/post-truth-and-its-consequences-what-a-25-year-old-essay-tells-us-about-the-current-moment.

Krief, Alain, Henning Hopf, Goverdhan Mehta, and Stephen A. Matlin. 2017. "Science in the Post-Truth Era." *Current Science* 112 (June): 2173–74.

Lazer, David M., Matthew A. Baum, Yochai Benkler, Adam J. Berinsky, Kelly M. Greenhill, Filippo Menczer, Miriam J. Metzger, Brendan Nyhan, Gordon Pennycook, David Rothschild, et al. (2018). "The Science of Fake News" (cover story). *Science* 359 (6380): 1094–96.

Leonhardt, David, and Stuart A. Thompson. 2017. "Trump's Lies." *New York Times*, "Opinion," December 14. www.nytimes.com/interactive/2017/06/23/opinion/trumps-lies.html.

Mackey, Thomas P., and Trudi E. Jacobson. 2011. "Reframing Information Literacy as a Metaliteracy." *College and Research Libraries* 72 (1): 62–78.

———. 2014. *Metaliteracy: Reinventing Information Literacy to Empower Learners*. Chicago: ALA Neal-Schuman.

———. 2016. "How Can We Learn to Reject Fake News in the Digital World?" *The Conversation*, December 5. https://theconversation.com/how-can-we-learn-to-reject-fake-news-in-the-digital-world-69706.

O'Brien, Kelsey L., Michele Forte, Thomas P. Mackey, and Trudi E. Jacobson. 2017. "Metaliteracy as Pedagogical Framework for Learner-Centered Design in Three MOOC Platforms: Connectivist, Coursera and Canvas." *Open Praxis* 9 (3): 267–86. doi:http://dx.doi.org/10.5944/openpraxis.9.3.553.

Oxford Dictionaries. 2018a. "civic-minded." Accessed August 20. https://en.oxforddic tionaries.com/definition/us/civic-minded.

———. 2018b. "post-truth." Accessed August 20. https://en.oxforddictionaries.com/ definition/post-truth.

———. 2018c. "Word of the Year 2016 Is . . ." Accessed August 20. https://en.oxford dictionaries.com/word-of-the-year/word-of-the-year-2016.

Rosenberg, Matthew, Nicholas Confessore, and Carole Cadwalladr. 2018. "How Trump Consultants Exploited the Facebook Data of Million." *New York Times*, "Politics," March 17. https://nyti.ms/2GCv9EI.

Schroepfer, Mike. 2018. "An Update on Our Plans to Restrict Data Access on Facebook." Newsroom. Posted April 4. https://newsroom.fb.com/news/2018/ 04/restricting-data-access.

Shane-Simpson, Christina, and Kristen Gillespie-Lynch. 2017. "Examining Potential Mechanisms Underlying the Wikipedia Gender Gap through a Collaborative Editing Task." *Computers in Human Behavior* 66 (January): 312–28. doi:10.1016/j.chb.2016.09.043.

Sharot, Tali. 2017. *The Influential Mind: What the Brain Reveals about Our Power to Change Others*. New York: Henry Holt.

Siemens, George. 2004. "Connectivism: A Learning Theory for the Digital Age." elearnspace. Posted December 12. www.elearnspace.org/Articles/connectivism .htm.

Statistica. 2018. "Most Famous Social Network Sites Worldwide as of July 2018, Ranked by Number of Active Users (in Millions)." Accessed October 2. www .statista.com/statistics/272014/global-social-networks-ranked-by-number-of -users.

Sullivan, M. Connor. 2018. "Why Librarians Can't Fight Fake News." *Journal of Librarianship and Information Science*, March 25. https://doi.org/10.1177/ 0961000618764258.

Tesich, Steve. 1992. "The Watergate Syndrome: A Government of Lies." *The Nation* (January): 12–14.

Tsipursky, Gleb. 2017. "From Post-Truth to Post-Lies: Using Behavioral Science to Fight 'Alternative Facts.'" *Psychology Today*, March 8. www.psychologytoday .com/blog/intentional-insights/201703/post-truth-postlies?destination =node/1100018.

Wardle, Claire, and Hossein Derakhshan. 2017. *Information Disorder: Toward an Interdisciplinary Framework for Research and Policymaking*. Cambridge, MA: Harvard Kennedy School, Shorenstein Center on Media, Politics, and Public

Policy. https://shorensteincenter.org/information-disorder-framework-for -research-and-policymaking.

Weingarten, Randi. 2017. "AFT President: Betsy DeVos and Donald Trump Are Dismantling Public Education." *Time*, "Ideas: Education," May 3. http://time .com/4765410/donald-trump-betsy-devos-atf-public-education.

Wineburg, Sam, Sarah McGrew, Joel Breakstone, and Teresa Ortega. 2016. "Evaluating Information: The Cornerstone of Civic Online Reasoning." Stanford Digital Repository. http://purl.stanford.edu/fv751yt5934.

MARC KOSCIEJEW

2

The Materiality of Metaliteracy

A Documentary Approach and
Perspective for Information and Literacy
Practices in the Post-Truth Era

Metaliteracy and documentation are intimately intertwined. Metaliteracy approaches often involve and depend upon documentation. When meta-literate learners actively and critically create, distribute, and evaluate diverse kinds of information, whether original, remixed, or repurposed content, they are directly dealing with documents. Although the metaliteracy framework implicitly recognizes the important roles played by documentation in facilitating and enabling various metaliterate practices, this chapter argues for a more explicit recognition and inclusion of these important roles within the broader metaliteracy framework. Documentation—that is, documents and our practices with them—is needed to materialize information into something tangible that individuals consume, produce, disseminate, interact with, and otherwise use.

A greater awareness and understanding of documentation that is implicitly recognized in the metaliteracy framework helps illuminate the centrality of documentation for most engagements with metaliteracy, metaliterate learning, and metaliterate practices. Although the metaliteracy framework currently features elements of documentation, they need to be more clearly emphasized to illuminate their significance. Indeed, a better and an explicit understanding of documentation, and the important roles it plays in metaliteracy, helps empower learners by raising their awareness of the affordances (what can and cannot be done with a particular document), implications, and effects of the documentation that they encounter, create, share, and use when they are dealing or are concerned with information. This greater, or more focused, awareness and improved understanding of documentation is particularly important in this post-truth era. There has been an alarming spread of dubious, misleading, and fake information and news featured in different digital documents that are at the center of most virtual interactions, social media networks, and online communities. Post-truth has become so powerful that Oxford Dictionaries (2018) declared it the 2016 International Word of the Year, defining it as "relating to or denoting circumstances in which objective facts are less influential in shaping public opinion than appeals to emotion and personal belief." The president of Oxford Dictionaries, Casper Grathwohl, notes that social media networks played a significant role in spreading and promoting fake information, explaining that post-truth has been "fuelled by the rise of social media as a news source and a growing distrust of facts offered up by the establishment" (Grathwohl, quoted in BBC [British Broadcasting Company] 2016). He further predicted that, because of its alarming expansion, post-truth could become "one of the defining words of our time" (Grathwohl, quoted in BBC 2016).

This chapter argues that the post-truth era's corrosive effects can be countered with a greater awareness and better understanding of the documentation involved. When learners and other individuals have a deeper awareness of the documents that they are creating, accessing, interpreting, evaluating, sharing, participating with, interacting with, and using, they can develop stronger ethical and responsible practices while gaining better understanding of their effects on information and other participants. This chapter therefore calls for a documentary-material literacy approach and perspective to be embedded in the metaliteracy framework to further advance metaliteracy theory and practice. In the metaliteracy framework, Mackey and Jacobson (2014) state that

> the core characteristics of the standard information literacy definition (determine, access, evaluate, understand, use, and incorporate) provide a foundation for related literacies. We expand the traditional definition of information literacy to include key elements needed for social media interaction (produce, collaborate, participate, and share). (68)

This chapter contributes a documentary-material literacy approach and perspective to this framework to help further illuminate documentation's centrality in creating, accessing, reading, interpreting, evaluating, sharing, incorporating, and otherwise using information. It presents a conceptual analysis of digital documentation and its importance for metaliteracy with its focus on social media networks and digital information environments, and it serves as a practical guide on how to develop, understand, and engage in a documentary-material literacy approach. The aim of this chapter is to help prepare metaliterate learners to become more aware of the materiality of the information they are dealing with and concerned about and how that materiality—that documentation—affects their behaviors, needs, and interactions with that information. Indeed, becoming a more active and engaged metaliterate learner in today's information environment requires a greater awareness and understanding of the documentation involved in metaliteracy and most other kinds of literacies.

DOCUMENTATION IN THE POST-TRUTH ERA

In today's post-truth era of fake information, which has been largely shaped by social media networks and other online communities, an expansion of metaliteracy to include an emphasis on documentation is vital. According to Farhad Manjoo (2016), "there is more reason to despair about truth in the online age. Why? Because if you study the dynamics of how information moves online today, pretty much everything conspires against truth." Social media networks and online communities, in particular, are being exploited and manipulated by diverse actors and agents spreading false and misleading information using various kinds of digital documentation that is ultimately undermining facts and truthful information. According to a recent study from the Massachusetts Institute of Technology on the spread of fake and true news across social media networks, lies spread faster than the truth. The researchers discovered that "falsehood diffused significantly farther, faster, deeper, and more broadly [on social media networks] than the truth in all categories of information" (Vosoughi, Roy, and Aral 2018, 1146).

This erosion of the truth threatens wider political, social, and cultural discourses and areas of life. This post-truth era of fake information has consequently begun to undermine collective grasps of objective truth; for example, in a recent Pew Research Center (2016) survey, 81 percent of respondents claimed that partisans not only differed about policies and plans but also about "basic facts." During the 2016 American presidential election campaign, Barack Obama, while still president of the United States, denounced fake information and its spread on social media. He warned that fake information threatened democracy, stating that "if we are not serious about facts and what's true and what's not, and particularly in an age of social media when so many people are getting their information in sound bites and off their phones, if we can't discriminate between serious arguments and propaganda, then we have problems" (Obama, quoted in Harris and Eddy 2016). He explained that "in an age where there's so much active misinformation and [it's] packaged very well and it looks the same when you see it on a Facebook page or you turn on your television . . . [i]f everything seems to be the same and no distinctions are made, then we won't know what to protect" (Obama, quoted in Harris and Eddy 2016).

The Russian government's (alleged and actual) interference in the 2016 American presidential election campaign is arguably one of the most controversial examples of the consumption, production, and dissemination of fake information, particularly through the exploitation of digital documentation on social media networks and the intended and resulting manipulation of their members, readers/viewers, the social networks of these members and readers/viewers, and, ultimately, the general public. The US Department of Justice, in fact, recently "charged 13 Russians and three companies . . . in a sprawling indictment that unveiled a sophisticated network designed to subvert the 2016 election and to support the [Republican presidential] campaign. It stretched from an office in St. Petersburg, Russia, into the social feeds of Americans and ultimately reached the streets of election battleground states" (Apuzzo and LaFraniere 2018). During the campaign, "the Russians repeatedly turned to Facebook and Instagram [and other social media networks], often using stolen identities to pose as Americans, to sow discord among the electorate by creating Facebook groups, distributing divisive ads and posting inflammatory images" (Frenkel and Benner 2018). These Kremlin-backed entities and agents, for instance, established Facebook pages dedicated to exacerbating contentious social issues including immigration, race, and religion through inflammatory, misleading, and fake coverage; created fake profiles or stole the identities of real American citizens to establish fake social media personas and accounts and to pose as political, social, or cultural activists; hacked and stole PayPal accounts to pay for divisive advertisements targeting specific political, social, cultural, religious, and racial communities across the country; organized emotionally charged political rallies; and sponsored controversial political exhibitions and events (Frenkel and Benner 2018). By the time of Election Day, around "150 million Americans had seen the Russian propaganda on [Facebook] and Instagram" (Frenkel and Benner 2018).

While Facebook and other social media and Internet companies are taking some steps to combat and prevent such exploitation of their services and products, manipulation of their members, and the spread of fake information, they nevertheless remain vulnerable to continued misuse and exploitation by malicious actors using different kinds of digital documentation. There remain "malicious forces [that] continue to use social media [and other online services] to sow discord and meddle in elections all over the world" (Roose 2018). But although these companies need to enact changes to their services and products to counter fake information and its spread across their networks, individuals also have a role to play in combating this scourge by becoming more vigilant about what is real and fake online. This vigilance can be realized through the adoption of the metaliteracy framework with an explicit emphasis on a documentary-material literacy approach to better understand this (digital) information. But often the materiality of this information is ignored, forgotten, or dismissed as irrelevant or unimportant. Let us now turn to a discussion on the importance of keeping information's materiality at the forefront of most considerations of and practices with information.

INFORMATION'S MATERIALITY

Information's materiality often tends to be either ignored or taken for granted. As Diana Coole and Samantha Frost (2010) argue, "for the most part we take . . . materiality for granted, or we assume that there is little of interest to say about it" (1). Many explorations of information often take for granted its materiality, particularly the very documentation that materializes it into tangible form. Information is often regarded as somehow indifferent to, even independent from, its documentation, as though this material basis and form is either interchangeable, disposable, or both. Information, in other words, is often (uncritically) seen as some kind of immaterial entity that is separate from any material considerations.

Regarding information as some immaterial entity seems to be encouraged and exacerbated by the increasing ubiquity of digital information, systems, infrastructures, and information and communication technologies (ICTs). Marlene Manoff (2013), for example, discusses how ICTs and the proliferation of digital information have helped foster "a widespread perception of the immateriality of the digital domain and the related assumption that it was somehow enabling us to transcend matter" (276). She argues for more materialist thinking regarding these ICTs and other related machines and technologies because of their material realities and their resulting effects and implications for real-world material environments. Further, a more materialist thinking regarding these technologies helps to show that the information itself is dependent upon its material instantiations. This seeming indifference to information's materiality is what makes a documentary-material literacy, embedded within a broader metaliteracy framework, crucial to more informed, and indeed aware, practices with information. A documentary approach to information, however, can foster a greater awareness and richer understanding of information and its many affordances, implications, and effects by shedding more light on its materiality by emphasizing its documentation. As this author notes elsewhere (Kosciejew 2017), for example, a documentary approach "cuts across the dual oppositions of document and information, giving special attention to matter by examining the materiality of documentation and the practices, processes, and assemblages involved in the materialization of information" (98). A documentary approach helps foreground the materiality of information to help (re)configure awareness, understandings, literacies, and uses of it as something that is material and tangible.

As Thomas Mackey and Trudi Jacobson (2016) note, an "emphasis of metaliteracy is understanding how information is packaged and delivered"; or, put differently, metaliterate learners must understand what documentation is involved in their information practices of consuming, producing, disseminating, and otherwise using information. Mackey and Jacobson (2016) explain that "packaging can be examined on a number of fronts. One is the medium used—is it text, photograph, video, cartoon, illustration or artwork? The other is how it is used—is the medium designed to appeal to our feelings? Does professional-looking design provide a level of credibility to the unsuspecting viewer?" A documentary approach extends this examination by asking, What is the document? For example, what kind of document is it—fiction, nonfiction, satire, news, political, religious, entertainment, or gossip? What are its components—textual, numerical, audio, visual, pictorial, a combination of each kind, or something else? What infrastructures does it belong and attach to—public, private, governmental, corporate, or other institution? What audiences does, could, or should it attract or repel—that is, is it published for a certain kind of individual or group in mind? What is its wider context?

Tim Gorichanaz and Kiersten Latham (2016), for example, ask, "Do documents exist? Or, perhaps more to the point: how do documents exist?" (1114). An object is a document when it furnishes some kind of information or, as Suzanne Briet famously describes it, proof of evidence. Michael Buckland (1997) presents Briet's classic definition of a document as being some kind of "evidence in support of a fact." A document, according to Briet, is "any physical or symbolic sign, preserved or recorded, intended to represent, to reconstruct, or to demonstrate a physical or conceptual phenomenon" (Briet, quoted in Buckland 1997). The implication is that documentation should not be viewed as being concerned only with texts but instead with access to evidence. In this sense, evidence is not only textual but comes in many forms, including digital, aural/audio, visual, imagery, pictorial, statuary, and more types. As Niels Windfeld Lund (2010) describes, a document is

> any results of human efforts to tell, instruct, demonstrate, teach or produce [information], in short to document, by using some means in some ways. In this way, the concept becomes extremely broad. Almost anything can be a document. At the same time, it can be very specific. All together, the concept of document may be a qualified alternative to the broad concept of text, avoiding the confusion about text as a distinctive concept for verbal expressions as well as a broad concept covering all kinds of expressions [in all kinds of forms and formats]. (743)

An object can be considered a document if it furnishes evidence of something. It is a document if it somehow instructs, proves, or shows something. Or, put differently, an object can be a document if it materializes information. It is important to emphasize, however, that the object's information does not necessarily have to be true to have evidentiary value. This emphasis is important to remember in this post-truth era of dubious, misleading, and fake information. The object's—the document's—information does not have to be accurate, correct, legitimate, trustworthy, or true to have evidentiary value; in fact, this evidence could be inaccurate, incorrect, illegitimate, untrustworthy, or false and still have evidentiary value. The alleged or actual truth-value of the information, in other words, does not diminish the object's status as a document. *neutrality* ✓ The object still serves as evidence of something, even if it is fake information, disinformation, misinformation, or propaganda. Indeed, whether the information is true or false, positive or negative, helpful or harmful, the document still materializes and constitutes it to be somehow informative and used. Or, put differently, a document materializes and constitutes information regardless of how factual or fake.

A documentary approach, particularly a documentary-material literacy embedded within and contributing to the metaliteracy framework, further extends this examination by asking what are the practices afforded, enabled, or required by the document? Different documents demand different practices. These differences are especially pronounced when documents are not the same in features, formats, forms, and functions. There are, for example, different kinds of practices involved in using a digital tablet compared to a clay tablet. A digital tablet, on the one hand, requires practices such as tapping, typing, and scrolling in addition to downloading, uploading, picture taking, audiovisual recording, and the use of diverse apps that themselves require different practices. A clay tablet, on the other hand, requires practices such as molding, inscribing, and reading. While there are admittedly a few similar practices that both kinds of documents share, such as reading textual or visual information, the differences between them are markedly pronounced.

These considerations of documentary practices are arguably more pronounced with the emergence of new kinds of (digital) documents in online environments that are increasingly pervasive, multisensory, participative, and immersive. Many new kinds of (digital) documents facilitate practices that are seemingly everywhere because they are multiplatform and multidevice; provide constant connection, communication, and recording (that is, documenting); allow direct, immediate, and even real-time interactions, contributions, and changes; and enable completely immersive experiences in which individuals not only use the information, whether for consumption, production, or dissemination, but also can fully sense and *live* that information. While many blog sites, for instance, permit space for lengthy textual information, often along with audiovisual, pictorial, and other kinds of information, Twitter allows space for only about 280 characters per tweet. The former permits more substantive information practices, particularly in terms of reading, writing, or otherwise using, while the latter allows for shorter and shallow engagement.

The important roles that are played by documentation in and for information are highlighted in Mackey and Jacobson's (2014) metaliteracy model. For instance, Mackey and Jacobson describe how the metaliteracy model "includes specific reference to several significant trends in open and online learning, including social media, Open Educational Resources (OERs), mobile technologies, and online communities. All of these evolving technologies and social environments mediate how we determine a specific need for information as well as how we access, evaluate, and understand information" (24). Documentation, particularly digital documentation, is at the center of these trends, technologies, and environments. It is the documentation that not only materializes and constitutes the needed information but also mediates—through its forms, formats, and functions—how to determine needs and access, evaluate, and understand information.

Metaliteracy should therefore be expanded to better understand the particular documentation involved in materializing and constituting information. Foregrounding information's materiality by illuminating its documentation helps to emphasize and show that metaliteracy theory and practice are not immaterial and intangible abstractions but instead are concerned with material and tangible objects. As Mackey and Jacobson (2011) argue, "information literacy is the metaliteracy for a digital age because it provides the higher order thinking required to engage with multiple document types through various media formats in collaborative environments" (70). This higher order thinking in part means that metaliterate learners must be aware of, recognize, and use diverse kinds of documentation in their various metaliteracy approaches and practices. A documentary-material literacy first involves placing the document at the center of attention and consideration before any substantial examination of its information. Second, a documentary-material literacy uses the document as a framing device to analyze and understand its wider context including its information. Third, a documentary-material literacy integrates the document in teaching, learning, and researching practices to then better guide information-related approaches to its information. The main goal of this kind of literacy is to help raise metaliterate learners' awareness of the documentation they are dealing with in order to develop better understanding of these documents and their practices with them.

why not use the word medium? media,

APPROACHING DIGITAL DOCUMENTATION

Presently, metaliteracy and many other information-related literacies, including digital, media, and visual, increasingly involve digital documentation. Creating, engaging, and interacting with digital information—from blogs and e-books to wikis and websites, to virtual reality environments, to podcasts—necessarily means engaging and interacting with some kind of digital documentation. Indeed, documentation is an essential component of the virtual realm by helping to materialize and constitute digital information in digital forms and formats to be accessed and used across diverse devices, platforms, networks, apps, and services. Digital documentation, in other words, plays important roles in facilitating and enabling digital information and, by extension, metaliteracy approaches and practices, not to mention other information, digital, and related literacies.

The aesthetics of digital documentation, for instance, help to configure and determine the affordances and usefulness of a document's digital information. Different digital documents will enable different kinds of practices for accessing, reading, interpreting, and otherwise using the documents' information. A wiki, for example, typically permits different kinds of interactions from those practices enabled and supported by an e-book. A wiki is typically a fluid digital document that can undergo constant alterations and edits, from additions and inclusions to deletions and reformats, that are often the result of ongoing collaborations and monitoring by a diverse community of contributors, writers, editors, readers, viewers, and other users. A wiki, moreover, often permits unlimited space and length in which to create, compose, and change its presented information. An e-book, meanwhile, is typically a more fixed digital document insofar as its content and formatting are concerned. An e-book does not usually undergo alterations and edits to its content or formatting. It enables only certain information practices, particularly reading and viewing, and other relatively minor formatting practices, such as text highlights (with italics, bold, and coloring options), note-taking features (usually in the margins or a section at the bottom of a digital page, the end of a chapter, or the book's end), and sometimes hyperlinks to other e-books or websites (if the device has Internet access). Beyond the practices of reading and viewing and a few formatting options, an e-book cannot be substantially changed. Thus, while both wikis and e-books are digital documents that materialize and constitute digital information, they nevertheless involve different kinds of practices and by extension have different experiences and effects for their users.

In another example, the practices enabled by virtual reality documents are different from those allowed by portable document format (PDF) digital documents, regular audiovisual videos, or conventional webpages. Virtual reality storytelling is an emerging trend in journalism. In 2015, the *New York Times* became a pioneer in this new kind of journalistic content creation, hiring the industry's first virtual reality editor; developing the industry's first virtual reality app, NYT VR; and producing and publishing the industry's first virtual reality stories, such as "Displaced," and series, such as "The Daily 360" (Hopkins 2017). "Displaced" helped to place "readers directly in the center of the real lives and experiences of three child refugees . . . [which helped the

New York Times] to reach readers on an emotional level and open up new ways to point out the terrible effects of war" (Tornoe 2017). "The Daily 360" is "a series that produces a 360-degree video from somewhere in the world every day" (Tornoe 2017). Since then, the *New York Times* and other newspapers and media organizations have introduced their own virtual reality documentation to present digital information via virtual 360-degree video to tell virtual stories.

The information practices involved with virtual reality documentation require more immersion than regular or typical practices, such as reading a relatively fixed and static PDF document or listening to or viewing a relatively stable audiovisual document on YouTube or elsewhere online. Consumers are not simply consuming this information; they are, in a way, sensing, even living, the information with their whole bodies, with all their perceptions. This immersive virtual documentation helps them to embody the information. Arguably, a new kind of culture of content/stories/information "is being developed and participants in these immersive experiences are living rather than consuming stories" (Hernandez 2017). Consuming this immersive virtual documentation "isn't simply consuming a piece of journalism [or other piece of work]; it's living through an experience prepared by the storyteller" that involves "embodiment and shapeshifting through" the stories—the information—which means that "in consuming this type of content, the participant experiences vulnerability and openness while living the story" (Hernandez 2017). Producing and disseminating this immersive virtual documentation, meanwhile, means that journalists and other creators must "re-examine [their] role as passive, 'fly on the wall' witnesses to become more active storytellers creating these highly influential experiences ethically and accurately" (Hernandez 2017). Whether blogs or social media posts, virtual reality stories or PDFs, different kinds of documents permit different kinds of practices and in turn have different kinds of effects.

The aesthetics of digital documentation consequently affect the diverse literacy practices of individuals and even impact our use of machines. Digital documentation, for instance, directs and influences the ways in which people access, evaluate, read, interpret, and otherwise use information through a range of technologies, devices, and services. Digital documentation therefore directly impacts and influences our understanding of digital information and related literacy practices. Yet, the seemingly dominant "emphasis on the technology of digital documents has impeded our understanding of digital documents as documents" (Buckland 1998). It is critical to have an awareness and understanding of the documentation involved in determining what kinds of documents are required when engaging with and creating digital information.

Further, being aware of and understanding the documentation involved is crucial in this post-truth era when fake information is composed, formatted, packaged, and presented (documented) in apparently or seemingly authoritative, credible, and legitimate kinds of documents, thereby imbuing the information with authority, credibility, and legitimacy. As Tim Gorichanaz (2016) notes, documents "have a long cultural history as sources of authority and trust" and, consequently, "when we encounter things that seem like documents—in that they exhibit some characteristics of things we already understand to be documents—we are likely to ascribe authority to those things" (302). Thus, "any given document gains authority by virtue of being a document (or being perceived as a document)" (Gorichanaz 2016, 300). It is often the trust in and of a document that usually determines its ultimate use. Often, for a document to be used, we need to "trust" and be "confident enough of [its] origin, lineage, version, and error rate" (Buckland 2015, 8). Gorichanaz (2016) recognizes how "trust and authority are, of course, not identical, but they are certainly linked. . . . [Authoritativeness is] the perception of trust. When we trust something, we imbue it with authority" (301). Applying a documentary-material literacy approach and perspective helps illuminate the information's authority, credibility, legitimacy, and truthfulness by asking, for example, if the document, including its form and function, indicates or proves that its information is real or fake.

Recall Mackey and Jacobson's (2016) discussion on how information's "packaging can be examined on a number of fronts" including on "how it is used—is the medium designed to appeal to our feelings? Does professional-looking design provide a level of credibility to the unsuspecting viewer?" The creators of fake information manipulate users' trust by producing documents that appear real, authoritative, and therefore trustworthy; for instance, they copy the same designs, features, and structures of long-standing respected newspapers, they mimic the same look of a friend's social media status update or tweet, or they infiltrate a wiki community and alter and edit the wikis or wiki entries to distort or include fake information.

What Is Digital Documentation?

While a documentary-material literacy, embedded within and contributing to a metaliteracy framework, is important to help raise this awareness and develop this understanding, it is first necessary to ask about documentation generally and digital documentation specifically. What exactly is digital documentation? Or, put differently, what is a digital document and what are the practices and literacies involved with it? What can, should, or must a digital document be and look like? What are the characteristics and components of digital documents? Are digital documents, for instance, fixed and stable or are they flexible and unstable; are they bounded and bordered or boundless and borderless; or are they permanent or impermanent? How are digital documents experienced? What are the distinctions between producers, consumers, authors, readers, observers, and participants in and with digital documentation? What kinds of information behaviors, expectations, and needs do digital documents demand or facilitate?

New digital technologies, devices, and services can further complicate these questions because they introduce and permit new kinds of documentation. Lund (2010) argues that "a digital document is a discrete unit of bits necessary to convey something meaningful in a digital environment" (742). A digital document—whether wiki or e-book, website or podcast, virtual reality environment or social media status update—is a discrete unit of bits, requiring a surrounding and supporting infrastructure of software and hardware, which cannot be separated from the digital technologies, programs, and devices upon which it depends. It cannot be held in one's hands as its own thing without its associated hardware and software infrastructure. It is not a discrete or separate object that is relatively independent of its surroundings, unlike most of its print and physical counterparts. Buckland (1998) similarly observes how "everything in digital technology is stored as a string of bits, so the usual [print or] physical form (on paper, on microfilm) no longer helps. In this sense, any distinctiveness of a document as a physical form is further diminished." He observes that

> when we refer to a paper document, a papyrus document, or a microfilmed document, the meaning is clear. However, the idea of a "digital document" is more difficult. We can recognize e-mail and a technical report generated by a word processor as digital documents, but beyond these simple examples the concept of a "document" becomes less clear. (Buckland 1998)

Is a software program a document? Or is an operating system a document? Their own constitutions necessarily involve digital documentation including codes, instructions, and algorithmic manuals; in other words, they are made up of digital documents and require specific kinds of human and machine practices with their use. Further, both software programs and operating systems are fundamental requirements for the virtual realm, generally, and for all digital documentation, specifically. Without these fundamental requirements, there could not be digital documentation let alone digital information. Software programs and operating systems should, at the very least, be considered as important components of all digital documentation, if not digital documentation in their own right (they are, after all, basically manuals that happen to be comprised of bits and bytes, codes, algorithms, and other kinds of digital instructions).

Different kinds of digital documents, moreover, have and require different kinds of surrounding and supporting software and hardware infrastructures and associated digital technologies, devices, and platforms. An e-book, as one example of a digital document, typically requires the EPUB file format (with the extension .epub) to be downloadable and operable on an electronic device, such as a smartphone, a tablet, an e-reader, a laptop, or a computer. An e-book also needs a chargeable battery and often a constant and reliable electrical source. It further usually requires the device to have Internet connectivity in order to find, access, and download it in the first place; moreover, if it has certain kinds of multimedia features (audio, video, hyperlinks, etc.), the Internet connectivity would always be required. The user then usually engages in relatively stationary practices, including reading, viewing, and possible highlighting and other note taking in nearly any kind of space, whether a lounge chair in a living room, a desk in a study hall, or a seat on a train.

A virtual reality environment, as an example of a different kind of digital document, typically requires a virtual reality headset (or some kind of headset or glasses with a live-camera feed). It often also requires a special physical space with lights, screens, projectors, props, and of course electricity and Internet connectivity. Users then usually engage in more physically active practices as they walk, gesture, and otherwise move around the space, sensing and experiencing the virtual reality environment with their whole bodies and perceptions, while realistic images, sounds, and other sensations appear to and around them. In other words, each kind of digital document, digital technology and device, and software and hardware infrastructure has different affordances and prohibitions. Different kinds of practices are therefore engaged in for these different digital documents based not only on their kind but also on the assemblages surrounding them. The assemblages for most virtual reality environments, for instance, involve special headsets, gaming and other programs, multiprojectors, props, and specific physical spaces in which they must be used; whereas the assemblages for most e-books involve digital devices, like e-readers, tablets, or smartphones, in addition to digital reading software programs and formats.

Buckland (1998) further notes that

> a paper document is distinguished, in part, by the fact that it is on paper. But that aspect, the technological medium, is less helpful with digital documents. An e-mail message and a technical report exist physically in a digital environment as a string of bits, but so does everything else in a physical environment. "Multimedia," which previously denoted multiple, physically-different media, is now of renewed interest, because, ironically, the multiple media can be reduced to the mono-medium of electronically stored bits.

Lund (2010) similarly observes how digital technologies and devices further complicate understandings of (digital) documents because

> when you can no longer hold a document in your hand, but only see it on the computer screen . . . [the] crucial quality of a document being a finite/discrete entity in a material sense is dissolved

> into a number of bits organized for a short period of time with the
> permanent risk of crash and disappearance. (740)

Or, put differently, where do or can digital documents begin and end? A digital document is a specific unit of bits existing within a large and complicated pool of different bits for diverse activities, reasons, and purposes. These bits must be specifically assembled together to form the digital document, for it to emerge and, in turn, materialize and constitute its information. Yet it remains unclear when, where, or if it has, or should have, strict or permanent borders and boundaries, like most of its print and physical counterparts.

Roswitha Skare and Niels W. Lund (2014), for example, ask if the popular social media network Facebook is a digital document. Is Facebook a book as it claims in its name or some other entirely different kind of document? Skare and Lund explore whether or not Facebook is a document and if it is a document what kind of document it purports or attempts to be. They examine, for instance, whether Facebook is bounded or has borders like a conventional print book. If it has borders, what or where are they? If it does not have borders, where does it begin and end? Buckland (1998), for instance, states that "it is not clear where the frontier between [digital] documents and non-documents should be." There is a lack of clarity about the borders or boundaries of a digital document comprised of bits that must be (temporarily) assembled together from a mass of other bits using specific digital technologies and devices, not to mention software and hardware infrastructures, in the virtual realm.

Skare and Lund (2010) refer to Facebook as "being a kind of worldwide document" (1) that is a complex digital document on its own, but one that also creates, embeds, facilitates, supports, shares, and extends a diverse range of other kinds of digital documents. Facebook can therefore be seen as a broad, complex, interactive, participatory, and immersive digital document. It offers more than a conventional book or e-book and has both similarities and differences with more established print and physical documents. This social media network, for instance, "has similarities with many classical documentation forms like literary books, telephone directories, annual [a]cademic [f]ace books, newspapers etc. and at the same time it is something completely new challenging hitherto used analytical conceptual tools" (Skare and Lund 2014, 3). One feature, for example, that makes Facebook a unique kind of (digital) document is its complex plethora of many documents that make up or are a part of it—such as pictures, videos, articles, stories, reports, e-books, blogs, links to other websites, interactive chat and video services, integration with other social media sites like Instagram, and so on—that render it seemingly borderless.

Facebook, as a unit of bits existing within a larger pool of bits that must be assembled together to establish its form, format, and function, is arguably borderless, at least in this material and technical way. Recall Lund's definition of a digital document as a discrete unit of bits necessary to convey something meaningful in a digital environment. Like Buckland, Lund (2014) states that "the problem of the digital world is that you can have a huge number of bits, but if you want to use them in a meaningful way, you have to select some of them and frame them as a document" (742). This selection and framing can lead to challenges in determining the borders or boundaries of what is or should be considered as the digital document. After all, a discrete unit of bits that when assembled together is considered a digital document is part of a complicated web of many different bits that are created and used for multiple different purposes and processes beyond those bits that make up the digital document.

Facebook can thus be regarded as a document without borders in terms of its material-technical constitution as a discrete unit of bits. It can also be considered borderless between the inside and outside of its documentary parameters (for example, you are either on Facebook in some capacity or not on it). It can further be considered borderless between it as a document itself and the documents it creates or facilitates (from pictures to videos to text), and between these documents and the documents that are considered outside of it (from linked websites and blogs to other social media postings).

Immersive, Participatory, and Pervasive Digital Documentation

Lyn Robinson extends these discussions and questions of digital documentation by illuminating the emergence of new kinds of immersive and participatory digital documentation. The metaliteracy framework's third goal of producing and sharing information in collaborative and participatory environments necessarily includes and involves many of these new kinds of digital documentation. For example, some objectives of this third goal include different kinds and uses of (new) digital documentation, such as seeing "oneself as a producer as well as consumer of information," sharing "knowledge accurately and effectively through the production of content using appropriate and evolving formats and platforms," translating "information presented in one manner to another in order to best meet the needs of a particular audience," and critically evaluating and verifying "user-generated content and appropriately apply[ing] in new knowledge creation" (Jacobson et al. 2018). Producing and consuming information necessarily involves producing and consuming documents. Sharing knowledge through the production of content using evolving formats and platforms means producing and sharing evolving document types. Translating information from one manner to another incorporates the changing, or adjusting, of document types for particular audiences and contexts. Evaluating and verifying user-generated content and applying it in new knowledge creation involves evaluating and verifying documentation and then adding, combining, or aligning it for new or other documents.

According to Robinson (2015), these new types arise "from a combination of rapidly developing technologies, particularly pervasive, networked information and multi-sensory interaction, when combined with participatory texts" (112). Robinson identifies three general technological trends that are contributing to new kinds of digital documents, namely, pervasive, multisensory, and participative features. The first technological trend affecting digital documents—when mobile becomes pervasive—involves ubiquitous networked information that diffuses focus away from specific information places and avoids the need for devices. The second technological trend—when multimedia becomes multisensory—extends augmented or virtual reality to include all the senses, thereby making engagement with these digital documents an even more immersive and convincing reality. The third technological trend—when interactive becomes participative—goes beyond interacting with a digital document to participating with and in it. An example of a participatory digital document is "*The Craftsman* (Portal Entertainment, 2013), in which events unfold in real time, engage the reader as part of the fiction, with texts, emails, calendar updates and phone messages from other characters within the plot, enhancing the main text" (Robinson 2015, 113). Practices become actively participatory in that individuals direct the flow of information instead of passively following fixed information. These participatory practices, further, become more richly immersive by their materialization and constitution across diverse digital technologies and devices.

As digital documentation becomes increasingly pervasive, multisensory, and participative, it is consequently becoming more immersive and all-encompassing. Robinson (2015) states that

> as these three trends develop and overlap, the feeling of being enveloped in information which is provided by a pervasive information environment, involving multi-sensory input, delivering a participative text, provides what may reasonably be described as an immersive experience. The record of such experiences is an immersive document. Both the "raw" text, and each experience of it, may be considered as a document, posing interesting issues for the organization and management of such documents. (113)

These immersive, participatory, and multisensory digital documents pose new challenges and opportunities for metaliteracy and indeed our understanding of most literacies because they directly affect and shape digital information. Engaging in practices with these documents, users are increasingly immersed within the all-encompassing information environments established, experiencing and sensing the information with their entire bodies, and participating in more complex, nuanced, and, in some cases, totalizing ways.

As Robinson (2015) states, "the most dramatic effects are to be seen in the use of such [digital] documents, active participation in an immersive reality being qualitatively different from passive reading of a conventional information resource" (114). Indeed, these new kinds of digital documents require new ways in which to create, access, interpret, understand, and use them, in addition to impacting individuals' information behaviors, practices, and needs across various digital technologies and devices.

Material, Mental, and Sociocultural Dimensions of Digital Documentation

Digital documentation is further shaped and influenced by enmeshed aspects of material, mental, and sociocultural dimensions. These intersecting and interconnecting dimensions must be accounted for in order to better understand digital documentation and, in turn, digital information and its associated literacies. A digital document, when approached and understood as a document, "must have both physical [material] and mental properties, but since the mental processes are culturally entangled with the social, the status of being a document also entails a social dimension indirectly through the mental" (Buckland 2016, 3).

The physical dimension of a document is its materiality. Buckland (2016) states that "a document is some entity regarded by someone as signifying something. It has to be a physical, material entity. One can discuss a text or a work in an abstract sense but texts and works can exist as documents only in some physical manifestation" (1). He further observes how "it is sometimes assumed or implied that electronic records ('the virtual') are somehow not physical, but this is an error because electronic systems are physical. They do not achieve much without, for example, magnetic chargers or electrical power" (63). A document's materiality means it has spatiotemporal features and occupies some kind of physical space.

Although materiality is an essential dimension of digital documentation, it is not fully sufficient for an object's documentary status. There must also be a mental dimension in which an object is intended and perceived to be a document. Buckland (2016) states that "someone must view [the object] as signifying (or potentially signifying) something, even if unsure of what the significance might be" (2). Since an object must be perceived to be a document, "status as a document . . . is an individual, personal mental judgment and therefore subjective. Such a perception occurs only in a living mind and, with any living, learning mind, the perception can change as what the individual knows changes" (Buckland 2017, 65). Contextual changes, in other words, can change a document's intentionality and phenomenological position.

A major contextual change confronting most digital documentation is the corrosive phenomenon of bit rot, that is, technological obsolescence. Bit rot "refers to the irrevocable degradation or loss of digital information when the infrastructure (the hardware and software) required to access, interpret, view, and use this information is no longer available or executable" (Kosciejew 2015, 21). Bit rot directly threatens the long-term stability, viability, and permanence of digital documentation as software, hardware, and other technological and infrastructural changes rapidly unfold. As Jennifer Gabrys (2011) argues, technological "obsolescence appears to be 'built-in' on multiple levels, from the actual decay of hardware, software, and content; to the economic requirement for continued innovation; to the way in which the pastness and the newness of electronic media and technology [and documentation] is narrated" (115). When a digital document can no longer be accessed, viewed, read, interpreted, evaluated, shared, and otherwise used, its information cannot be interacted with in any way.

For example, bit rot has affected and changed music and storage technologies, particularly compact discs (CDs) and CD players, over the past decade and a half. CDs and CD players

> are quickly vanishing. Many people no longer purchase CDs, either for music or storage. Music is now commonly purchased or pirated [or streamed] online through digital music services. People are accessing and listening to their favorite songs in MP3 format on their mobile devices instead of on CDs played in CD players. Information storage is now placed in so-called cloud computing services and transported via universal serial bus (USB) sticks—which, interestingly, are themselves slowly, perhaps still imperceptibly, becoming "rotten"—instead of burnt onto, stored, and carried on CDs. Many companies and retailers no longer produce or sell CDs or CD players. (Kosciejew 2015, 21–22)

In another example of bit rot, the information constituted within documents created and stored on a floppy disk can no longer be opened or supported, let alone interacted with, using contemporary digital technologies or devices, rendering that document, and by extension its information, inaccessible and unusable. This contextual change arguably alters the floppy disk's intention to be a document, and interacted with as such an object, in addition to the perception of it as being a document. It is now apparently simply a floppy disk, a technological artifact (which admittedly is its own kind of historical document, a discussion of which is beyond this chapter's scope or purview).

The social, or cultural, dimension of a document involves intersubjectivity. Buckland (2016) discusses how "an individual can make a subjective idea objectively perceptible by others" (2). Documentation helps make a subjective idea objectively perceptible. Buckland (2017) explains that

> a text may be authored through the mental efforts of a solitary individual but physical documents are ordinarily the result of actions of many different people. A printed book depends on

> paper manufacturers, printers, publishers, typesetters, binders, book retailers, and many others. Shared financial, transportation, and other infrastructures support all of their varied contributions, and a book would not be printed in the absence of readers. (67)

Digital documentation also depends upon a complex assemblage of diverse actors, infrastructures, institutions, systems, technologies, devices, and practices within sociocultural contexts.

Thus, while materiality is a necessary but not a sufficient condition for being a document, there must also be a mental angle, which, in turn, entails a sociocultural angle. The materiality of documentation is influenced by social controls. The inability of any one dimension to fully characterize a document explains the role of documents in the sociocultural construction of reality. To understand the nuances of a document, its materiality, cognitive, and cultural aspects need to be taken into account. A document is not only a material object; it is one that is intended, perceived, and treated as a document in intersubjective sociocultural contexts. These material, mental, and sociocultural dimensions—or intersubjective features—facilitate and involve a fusion among the digital document, practices, information, individual/user/participant, and the larger sociocultural context. These intersubjectivities are crucial in the metaliteracy framework, especially regarding metaliteracy approaches and practices involving, and understandings of, digital documentation as part of and within context-bound information environments and networked systems.

Documentation is a fundamental aspect of information and an important part of various information practices including consuming, producing, disseminating, and otherwise using information. An awareness and understanding of documentation, especially in how it materializes, constitutes, and enables information to emerge as something informative, would also assist metaliterate learners to engage in more nuanced metacognitive reflections about their own thinking, learning, and information practices and needs. This metacognitive reflection is particularly important in this post-truth era in which the authority, credibility, legitimacy, and trustworthiness of documents is blurred or blurring between real and fake, especially in social media networks where most documents either appear to be of the same value or are in many ways indistinguishable. It is therefore vital to be aware of and understand documentation to help better prepare metaliterate learners and other users of information to navigate and engage in increasingly complex information environments and post-truth contexts. A documentary-material literacy can help develop this preparation.

A DOCUMENTARY-MATERIAL LITERACY
APPROACH AND PERSPECTIVE FOR METALITERACY

Preparing active and engaged metaliterate learners requires an increased awareness and understanding of the specific documentation involved in our technology-mediated information environments. It appears that this deeper understanding of what a document is, and its many different forms and modalities, would only increase understanding, critical thinking, and the ability to actively participate in these environments. Mackey and Jacobson (2011) argue that metaliteracy, in many ways, is a process of learning how to learn and that

> information-literate individuals acquire the ability to understand information using different forms of technology. They apply information knowledge gained from a wide range of verbal, print, media, and online sources and continuously refine skills over time. This constitutes a practice of critical engagement with one's world as active and participatory learners. (70)

This practice of critical engagement with one's world often involves documentation. We are constantly creating, consulting, managing, engaging with, and otherwise using all kinds of documentation in our daily lives for diverse purposes and goals. After all, it is often with and through documentation that we deal with information to help construct, maintain, support, promote, extend, expand, and add to various aspects of our lives and world.

Critically engaging with a social media network like Facebook, in addition to other online communities and virtual environments, requires metaliterate learners and other users to employ various metaliteracy approaches and practices, of which a documentary-material literacy is a vital part. As Mackey and Jacobson (2014) state,

> metaliteracy has a role to play in how learners interact in social and visual networking environments such as Facebook and Pinterest. Metaliteracy challenges learners to analyze and use social spaces such as blogs and microblogs for self-publishing and sharing reusable content. . . . Since metaliteracy considers the relationship between technology and learning, a meta perspective recognizes emergent trends such as global mobility and prepares reflective creators and distributors of information in these settings. Metaliterate individuals adapt to changing technologies and think about their own learning in these spaces. This metacognitive emphasis prepares students to ask questions about how systems function and how to be active contributors as the social environments evolve. . . . Metaliteracy fosters active engagement online and provides learners with a means to develop the specific

competencies to produce, arrange, and communicate visual information in socially networked environments. (43)

Let us unpack this exploration of metaliteracy to illuminate the centrality of documentation for digital information and metaliterate practices. Recall that "documentation helps to show information's materiality and contextual contingencies that make it informing; without documents and documentary practices, information is dematerialized and thus decontextualized and in some cases rendered meaningless" (Kosciejew 2017, 110). First, analyzing and using social digital spaces for consuming, producing, and disseminating information necessarily involves documentation. One needs to create or use some kind of digital document, such as a blog, Word document, or social media platform, in order to create, consume, share, interact with, participate with, and otherwise use information, or what Mackey and Jacobson refer to here as "self-publishing and sharing reusable content."

Second, preparing reflective creators, consumers, and distributors of information in increasingly complex, networked, and mobile information environments necessarily means and involves creating, consuming, and distributing digital documents. It is this documentation that materializes and constitutes the digital information that is engaged with and used across digital technologies and devices. Creators, consumers, and distributors of digital information need to reflect upon the kinds of documents they are producing and using in order to better understand their possible effects on other people or consequences for their particular contexts. Digital information, after all, is not some immaterial abstraction or something that is indifferent to its documentation; instead, digital information is material phenomena instantiated and enabled by documentation. Individuals need a stronger appreciation for these material phenomena, especially since they are creating, consuming, and distributing them in multiple ways and venues every day.

Third, adapting to and learning about changing technologies, asking questions about how systems function, and being active contributors of information all involve digital documentation. It is important to develop a greater awareness and understanding of digital documentation's various forms, formats, and functions. This need for greater awareness and understanding is particularly significant as digital documentation becomes more pervasive, multisensory, participative, and immersive. Further, the necessity for greater awareness and understanding is critical in this post-truth era to learn and know how to interact with these technologies and devices in more reflective ways. Ultimately, greater awareness and understanding of digital documentation will help individuals become more proactive, informed, and responsible contributors and consumers of information.

Fourth, developing the specific competencies to produce, arrange, and communicate information necessarily involves documentation. It is documentation that materializes and constitutes the information that, in turn, is produced, arranged, and communicated, regardless of how factual or fake, subjective or objective, or helpful or harmful it may be. In this post-truth era, in which all information can appear to be of equal value, it is vital to be more cognizant of the forms, formats, and functions of the information's documentation to better determine its actual value. A greater awareness and understanding of documentation, in other words, is necessary in helping to develop these specific competencies and, of particular relevance for the post-truth era, in helping to determine the degree of the information's authority, credibility, legitimacy, and trustworthiness.

Indeed, as this author argues elsewhere (Kosciejew 2017), "documents are more than disposable 'things' that only serve to convey information. When one considers a document as a throwaway item of secondary—or no—importance, then information becomes decontextualized, slippery, unanchored" (104). It is only "once a document is identified, its roles defined and understood and its associated practices routinized and normalized, [that] information emerges [and materializes]" (Kosciejew 2017, 103). Metaliterate individuals must acquire the ability to understand different kinds of documentation to create, access, acquire, learn about, interpret, evaluate, incorporate, and otherwise use information. Learning how to learn, further, means learning about different kinds of documents as well as how and why to use them. Different documents, after all, have different purposes and effects. It therefore means learning about and considering documentation's various forms, formats, and functions, in addition to its other infrastructures, networks, components, contexts, and effects, to help discern its degree of truthfulness. This learning and consideration are urgent activities in this post-truth era when "the spread of misinformation on social media is an alarming phenomenon . . . [and that this misinformation and other] false claims are increasing online" (Aral 2018). When most individuals are unaware of the documents they are dealing with, focusing more on the information, they are likely to exercise less reflection on that information's authority, credibility, legitimacy, and trustworthiness.

Robinson (2015) advises that because digital documentation, especially the emerging pervasive, multisensory, participative, and immersive kinds, presents new forms, formats, and functions of documents "to handle, of potentially wide scope and significance[,] . . . [i]t would be wise to begin to consider these issues now, so that [we] can be well-prepared to deal with them, rather than struggling to catch up later, as has sometimes seemed to be the case with new digital formats" (113). A documentary-material literacy approach and perspective, embedded within and contributing to the metaliteracy framework, can help in this preparation by illuminating the centrality of documentation for information. This approach and perspective illuminates the conceptual components and considerations of what makes an object a document, which, in turn, helps inform individuals' practices when dealing with an object as a document for their information. This approach and perspective, for example, can help inform practices with information by foregrounding the information's materiality, including how it is materialized, constituted, produced, designed, formatted, shaped, presented, displayed, contained, and so forth. In other words, it helps show that information's materiality— its documentation—is not an incidental or unimportant consideration but instead a fundamental aspect in dealing with, in addition to understanding, information.

This author's documentary-material literacy approach and perspective responds to Mackey and Jacobson's (2014) argument for the need for "an expanded conception of information literacy as a metaliteracy to build on the information literacy foundation and to develop linkages with related literacy types" (44) by introducing a connection to the essential, yet often overlooked or undermined, roles played by documentation in materializing and constituting information. This connection contributes to the metaliteracy framework by illuminating information's materiality and, in so doing, showing how related literacy characteristics work together in a comprehensive way. This connection can indeed help strengthen this framework's unifying meta-approach to literacy in order to help avoid the proliferation of disconnected or disparate literacies, especially each time a new technology emerges. This documentary-material literacy approach and perspective thus starts an important conversation and useful contribution to the metaliteracy framework because it provides both a conceptual and practical guide for unifying literacies on the materiality of information.

This documentary-material literacy approach and perspective helps provide a way to explore "how documents relate to the material world and vice versa" (Kosciejew 2017, 97–98). Not all documents do the same thing or have the same purpose. As this author argues elsewhere, each kind of document, or documentary genre,

> has a specific set of inscriptions, formats, or signals that help determine the role a document is meant to play. . . . A document's particular genre helps in its identification. Once its genre is properly identified, then a document's roles emerge. The roles are further shaped by institutional disciplining methods of routinization and standardization that mandate, oblige, instruct. (Kosciejew 2017, 100)

Different documents have different forms, formats, and functions that determine both their affordances and the materialization and constitution of their information. A documentary-material literacy approach and perspective, complementing and embedded within a metaliteracy framework, helps to better inform and guide practices with information and other related literacies. The reason for this connection is because the ability to understand information using different forms of technologies, platforms, networks, devices, and services necessarily means interacting with and understanding different kinds of digital documentation. This approach and perspective is comprised of three main components or steps:

1. First, one places a specific document—or multiple documents or an object that is regarded as evidence of something—at the center of observation, study, and analysis. This centering of the document further helps to develop and refine documentary dialogues about and for it; in other words, it helps enable specific analyses of the document as the specific intention and focus. This centering, moreover, helps illuminate and determine the document's degree of value for the particular observation, study, or analysis.

2. Second, one uses the document itself to analyze and understand its wider context and its context's influences upon it. This contextual analysis can include the wider material, infrastructural, technical, institutional, organizational, sociocultural, economic, political, and environmental aspects affecting, shaping, and involved with the document as well as the document's affordances and influences of, involvement with, and effects on those other contextual aspects.

3. Third, one integrates the document in teaching, learning, and researching practices and literacies. This scrutiny can be conducted throughout when centering the document and using it to analyze its contextual contingencies, which can help determine or reveal its particular value or significance for the situation. The document is regarded, not as a disposable or unimportant item of secondary, incidental, or no significance to its information, but instead as an essential and important part of understanding information. Documentary approaches and perspectives are thus incorporated in teaching, researching, and applying information literacy and other related literacies, including digital, media, and visual literacies, in diverse kinds of practices and contexts.

These three components, or steps, align with three goals of the metaliteracy framework (Jacobson et al. 2018): first, to "actively evaluate content while also evaluating one's own biases"; second, to "engage with all intellectual property ethically and responsibly"; and, third, to "produce and share information in collaborative and participatory environments." Let us begin applying this documentary-material literacy approach and perspective to these metaliteracy goals.

Although Jacobson and colleagues (2018) do not directly refer to the need for a documentary-material literacy in the first goal, they nevertheless acknowledge its need by stating that actively evaluating content and one's own biases involves determining "how a source's purpose, document type, and delivery mode affect its value for a particular situation," in addition to critically assessing "information from all sources, including dynamic content that circulates online." Evaluating content critically, including dynamic, online content that changes and evolves, aligns with and involves the documentary-material literacy's first component of placing a document or documents at the center of observation, study, and analysis. This centering of dynamic online content's documentary forms, formats, and functions sheds more light on how the types and delivery modes of this information affect, impact, and shape the resulting information and various literacy practices with it. As Mackey and Jacobson (2014) argue, "when individuals need to be able to recognize information for what it is, and be able to synthesize disparate information formats to effectively meet their needs" (87), they become metaliterate. Or, put differently, when individuals can recognize information for what it is, including what it is materially as documentation, they are better able to synthesize disparate formats to effectively meet their needs. They are, for example, better able to compare, collate, compile, and consult information from different kinds of documents such as blogs, websites, e-books, newspapers, and articles. This recognition helps them determine if their information needs require certain kinds of technologies, platforms, or networks; if their information needs require multiplatform and/or multidevice interoperability and interactivity; and if their information needs require diverse kinds of documents, whether text-based, audio, visual, photographic, pictorial, or combinations of each.

Actively evaluating content also requires analyzing the document's wider context and how it, as a document that materializes and constitutes specific information, affects, impacts, and shapes that context. This examination also requires analyzing how the document's wider context also affects, impacts, and shapes the document, practices with it, and ultimately the information it materializes and constitutes. The political, economic, sociocultural, and historical circumstances in which the document is situated directly influence its documentary status, evidentiary value, and ways in which it is used. This analysis critically asks, for example, if the document is published by a known, reputable, or respected individual, group, organization, or institution, or are its origins unknown, unclear, questionable, or problematic in some way? For whom is the document intended—a particular group or a mass audience? Where is the document meant to circulate and impact—a particular place such as a specific country, region, city, institution, or some other place or organization? What is the document's date of creation and publication? What are the sociocultural, political, economic, religious, and legal circumstances bearing upon the document, and simultaneously, what sociocultural, political, economic, religious, and legal circumstances does the document aim to bear upon?

The second goal is to "engage with all intellectual property ethically and responsibly" (Jacobson et al. 2018). Again, although only implicitly recognized, some of this second goal's objectives necessarily involve documentation, including differentiating between producing original information and remix-ing openly licensed content, responsibly producing and sharing "original infor-mation and ethically remix[ing] and repurpose[ing] openly licensed content," distinguishing "between public and personal information and mak[ing] ethi-cal and informed decisions about appropriately sharing information online," and differentiating "between copyright, Creative Commons, and open licenses in both the creation and licensing of original and repurposed content" (Jacob-son et al. 2018). Indeed, metaliteracy can help "prepare learners to be active creators and distributors of information . . . [and to] [d]ifferentiate between the production of original information and remixing or re-purposing open resources" (Mackey and Jacobson 2014, 88). In other words, engaging with intellectual property (ethically and responsibly) often means engaging with documentation. This second goal aligns with a documentary analysis because it aims to better define and understand the kinds of documents that are cre-ated, evaluated, and used in matters of intellectual property.

The third goal argues for producing and sharing information in collabora-tive and participatory environments, recognizing that one is both "a producer as well as consumer of information" (Jacobson et al. 2018). While documen-tation is not explicitly highlighted, this goal's objectives are intimately inter-twined with documents and practices with them, including, for instance, sharing "knowledge accurately and effectively through the production of content using appropriate and evolving formats and platforms," translating "information presented in one manner to another in order to best meet the needs of a particular audience," critically evaluating and verifying "user-gen-erated content and appropriately apply[ing] in new knowledge creation," and recognizing "diverse cultural values and norms to create and share information for global audiences" (Jacobson et al. 2018). This approach therefore aligns with and involves all three components of the documentary-material literacy framework. It requires placing the document at the center of examination, analyzing its wider context, and integrating the document in the teaching, learning, and research practices involved with meeting this goal's objectives. Further, this method helps address some of this post-truth era's challenges of determining the authority, credibility, legitimacy, and trustworthiness of the information materialized in this plethora of documentation.

TOWARD A METALITERATE DOCUMENTARY-MATERIAL LITERACY

The current and emerging information environment is becoming increasingly complex with evermore dynamic, pervasive, multisensory, participatory, and immersive documentation to consume, produce, disseminate, and otherwise use diverse kinds of information. As this author states elsewhere,

> while a document is typically associated with printed texts, there is no theoretical or practical excuse as to why documentation should be limited to them; indeed, there are many other kinds of signifying objects in addition to printed texts. Examples of non-printed text-bearing documents include photographs, artwork, film, audiovisual recordings, digital recordings, web pages, and virtual signs. (Kosciejew 2017, 102)

Documents are therefore "important because they are considered as evidence, and so there are cognitive and cultural as well as physical [material] aspects to them" (Buckland 2017, 21). It is this material, mental, and sociocultural evidence—this documentation—that is at the center of information and an essential component of the metaliteracy framework because it is what materializes, constitutes, and mediates the information in question.

The metaliterate learner, after all, is concerned, dealing, and working with diverse kinds of documentation in his or her various activities and practices. The metaliterate learner is indeed an "engaged and active researcher capable of differentiating among a multitude of document types and modalities" (Mackey and Jacobson 2014, 92). Applying a documentary-material literacy involves the metaliterate learner placing a document at the center of observation, study, and analysis; using the document to analyze its wider context and vice versa; and integrating the document in teaching, learning, and researching practices and literacies. It further aligns with three of the primary goals of the metaliteracy framework: actively evaluating content while also critically evaluating one's biases, engaging with intellectual property ethically and responsibly, and producing and sharing information in collaborative and participatory information environments (Jacobson et al. 2018).

Thus, a documentary-material literacy approach and perspective, when combined and incorporated within the metaliteracy framework, helps expand awareness and enrich understanding of information. Greater awareness and improved understanding of information by analyzing its materiality through documentation helps counter the post-truth era's deleterious aspects of fake information eroding trust in many areas of life and society. This approach and perspective can help provide insight about how and why fake information spreads and can help develop strategies and interventions to halt and stop that spread. One such documentary intervention that could help stem the tide of falsity, for example, might involve "labeling news stories, in much the same way we label food, [which] could change the way people [reflect on and] consume and share it" (Aral 2018). Being aware of and understanding the documentation they are necessarily using, metaliterate learners can engage in better and more ethical and responsible practices including creating, accessing, interpreting, evaluating, sharing, participating with, interacting with, and using digital documentation.

CONCLUSION

This chapter argued that a documentary-material literacy approach and perspective, embedded within the metaliteracy framework, can help strengthen metaliterate learners' reflective and responsible information practices, including their consumption, production, dissemination, and other uses of information, in the post-truth era of fake information. This chapter presented a conceptual analysis of digital documentation to help illuminate its importance for metaliteracy and a practical guide on how to develop and engage in a documentary-material literacy approach to information and practices with it. This approach places the document at the center of observation, study, and analysis; uses the document to analyze and understand its wider context and its context's influences upon it; and integrates the document in teaching, learning, and researching information practices and literacies. This documentary-material literacy approach and perspective helps prepare metaliterate learners and other users of information to raise their awareness and improve their understanding of the materiality of the information they are concerned about and dealing with on social media networks, as part of online communities, and in other virtual places. This awareness and understanding of documentation further helps metaliterate learners to determine whether the information they are consuming, producing, or disseminating is real or fake.

REFERENCES

Apuzzo, Matt, and Sharon LaFraniere. 2018. "13 Russians Indicted as Mueller Reveals Effort to Aid Trump Campaign." *New York Times*, February 16. www.nytimes .com/2018/02/16/us/politics/russians-indicted-mueller-election-interference .html.

Aral, Sinan. 2018. "How Lies Spread Online." *New York Times*, March 8. www .nytimes.com/2018/03/08/opinion/sunday/truth-lies-spread-online.html.

BBC (British Broadcasting Corporation). 2016. "'Post-Truth' Declared Word of the Year by Oxford Dictionaries." *BBC News*, November 16. www.bbc.com/news/ uk-37995600.

Buckland, Michael. 1997. "What Is a Document?" School of Information Management and Systems, University of California, Berkeley. http://people.ischool.berkeley .edu/~buckland/whatdoc.html.

———. 1998. "What Is a 'Digital Document'?" School of Information Management and Systems, University of California, Berkeley. http://people.ischool.berkeley .edu/~buckland/digdoc.html.

———. 2015. "Document Theory: An Introduction." http://people.ischool.berkeley .edu/~buckland/zadardoctheory.pdf. Preprint (10 pp.), subsequently published in *Records, Archives and Memory: Selected Papers from the Conference and School on*

Records, Archives and Memory Studies, edited by Mirna Willer, Anne J. Gilliland, and Marijana Tomić, 223–37. Zadar, Croatia: University of Zadar.

———. 2016. "The Physical, Mental and Social Dimensions of Documents." *Proceedings from the Document Academy* 3(1): Article 4, 6 pp. http://ideaexchange .uakron.edu/docam/vol3/iss1/4.

———. 2017. *Information and Society.* Cambridge, MA: MIT Press.

Coole, Diana, and Samantha Frost. 2010. "Introducing the New Materialisms." In *New Materialisms: Ontology, Agency, and Politics*, edited by Diana Coole and Samantha Frost, pp. 1–43. Durham, NC: Duke University Press.

Frenkel, Sheera, and Katie Benner. 2018. "To Stir Discord in 2016, Russians Turned Most Often to Facebook." *New York Times*, February 17. www.nytimes .com/2018/02/17/technology/indictment-russian-tech-facebook.html.

Gabrys, Jennifer. 2011. *Digital Rubbish: A Natural History of Electronics.* Ann Arbor: University of Michigan Press.

Gorichanaz, Tim. 2016. "How the Document Got Its Authority." *Journal of Documentation* 72 (2): 299–305.

Gorichanaz, Tim, and Kiersten F. Latham. 2016. "Document Phenomenology: A Framework for Holistic Analysis." *Journal of Documentation* 72 (6): 1114–33.

Harris, Gardiner, and Melissa Eddy. 2016. "Obama, with Angela Merkel in Berlin, Assails Spread of Fake News." *New York Times*, November 17. www.nytimes .com/2016/11/18/world/europe/obama-angela-merkel-donald-trump.html.

Hernandez, Robert. 2017. "Virtual Reality: The Shift from Storytelling to 'Storyliving' Is Real." *Journalism 360*, June 29. https://medium.com/journalism360/virtual -reality-the-shift-from-storytelling-to-storyliving-is-real-ff465c220cc3.

Hopkins, Marcelle. 2017. "Pioneering Virtual Reality and New Video Technologies in Journalism." *New York Times*, October 18. www.nytimes.com/2017/10/18/ technology/personaltech/virtual-reality-video.html.

Jacobson, Trudi, Tom Mackey, Kelsey O'Brien, Michele Forte, and Emer O'Keefe. 2018. "Goals and Learning Objectives: Draft Revision (April 11, 2018)." Metaliteracy.org. https://metaliteracy.org/learning-objectives.

Kosciejew, Marc. 2015. "Digital Vellum and Other Cures for Bit Rot." *Information Management* 49 (3): 20–25. http://imm.arma.org/publication/frame.php?i=2570 26&p=31&pn=&ver=htm15.

———. 2017. "A Material-Documentary Literacy: Documents, Practices, and the Materialization of Information." *Minnesota Review* 2017 (88): 96–111.

Lund, Niels Windfeld. 2010. "Document, Text and Medium: Concepts, Theories and Disciplines." *Journal of Documentation* 66 (5): 734–49.

Mackey, Thomas P., and Trudi E. Jacobson. 2011. "Reframing Information Literacy as a Metaliteracy." *College and Research Libraries* 72 (1): 62–79.

———. 2014. *Metaliteracy: Reinventing Information Literacy to Empower Learners.* Chicago: ALA Neal-Schuman.

————. 2016. "How Can We Learn to Reject Fake News in the Digital World?" *The Conversation*, December 5. https://theconversation.com/how-can-we-learn-to-reject-fake-news-in-the-digital-world-69706.

Manjoo, Farhad. 2016. "How the Internet Is Loosening Our Grip on the Truth." *New York Times*, November 2. www.nytimes.com/2016/11/03/technology/how-the-internet-is-loosening-our-grip-on-the-truth.html.

Manoff, Marlene. 2013. "Unintended Consequences: New Materialist Perspectives on Library Technologies and the Digital Record." *Libraries and the Academy* 13 (3): 273–82.

Oxford Dictionaries. 2018. "Word of the Year 2016 Is . . ." https://en.oxforddiction aries.com/word-of-the-year/word-of-the-year-2016.

Pew Research Center. 2016. "In Presidential Contest, Voters Say 'Basic Facts,' Not Just Policies, Are in Dispute." *U.S. Politics and Policy*, October 14. www.people -press.org/2016/10/14/in-presidential-contest-voters-say-basic-facts-not-just -policies-are-in-dispute.

Robinson, Lyn. 2015. "Immersive Information Behaviour: Using the Documents of the Future." *New Library World* 116 (3/4): 112–21.

Roose, Kevin. 2018. "On Russia, Facebook Sends a Message It Wishes It Hadn't." *New York Times*, February 19. www.nytimes.com/2018/02/19/technology/russia-facebook-trump.html.

Skare, Roswitha, and Lund, Niels W. 2014. "Facebook—a Document without Borders?" *Proceedings of the Document Academy* 1 (1): Article 7, 9 pp. http://ideaexchange.uakron.edu/docam/vol1/iss1/7.

Tornoe, Rob. 2017. "Digital Publishing: Why the *New York Times* Continues to Invest in Virtual Reality." *Editor and Publisher*, January 18. www.editorandpublisher.com/columns/digital-publishing-why-the-new-york-times-continues-to-invest -in-virtual-reality.

Vosoughi, Soroush, Deb Roy, and Sinan Aral. 2018. "The Spread of True and False News Online." *Science* 359 (6380): 1146–51.

JOSH COMPTON

3

Inoculation Theory and Metaliterate Learning

Most persuasion theories explain how messages can be made more influential. But inoculation theory is unique in that its domain is *resistance* to other persuasive messages (Compton 2013; McGuire 1964)—a preemptive strike against future persuasive attempts that could lead to unhelpful attitudes, beliefs, or opinions. The theory is built on—and explained by—an analogy: Just as we can be made resistant to future viral threats through pre-exposure to weakened versions of a virus (consider a conventional annual flu shot), we can also be made resistant to future persuasive threats through pre-exposure to weakened versions of potentially persuasive attacks. The goal of an inoculation campaign, then, is to create a more robust, healthier immune response to that which could harm. In terms of metaliteracy, metaliterate learning, and a post-truth world, the hope is that inoculation—in conferring immunity to threats—is achieving such resistance through enhanced critical thinking, more dialogue, and deeper engagement with information environments.

Decades of research, in the lab (e.g., Ivanov et al. 2016) and in the field (e.g., Pfau et al. 2001), have confirmed inoculation's success in conferring resistance to influence (see Banas and Rains 2010, for a meta-analysis; see

Compton 2013, for a narrative review) in the contexts of politics (Compton and Ivanov 2013), health (Compton, Jackson, and Dimmock 2016), and other areas where making an existing belief more resistant to change is the goal. More recently, inoculation scholars have turned their focus to inoculation's efficacy in education, including efforts to improve classroom practices (preempting student technology frustrations by inoculating against them: Compton 2012; discouraging student plagiarism by inoculating against temptations/rationalizations: Compton and Pfau 2008) and students' classroom experiences (managing public speaking anxiety by inoculating against it: Jackson et al. 2017). Through this work, we are gaining a better understanding of the role inoculation might have in an educational setting. What is less known is how inoculation theory might be connected to learning, in general, and to metaliteracy, in particular.

What we do know is encouraging. Scholars working in science communication, for example, have found support for using inoculation strategies to teach people to be better, critical consumers of climate change arguments (Cook, Lewandowsky, and Ecker 2017; van der Linden et al. 2017), and some work in political communication suggests that inoculation can enhance political knowledge (Pfau et al. 2001). Still, many questions remain unanswered about how inoculation messaging might be connected to larger processes of learning.

This chapter draws on the four domains of metaliteracy learning (Jacobson et al. 2018) to outline how inoculation theory might inform—and be informed by—the key areas of behavioral, cognitive, affective, and metacognitive learning objectives, especially in a post-truth world. As Cooke (2017) observes:

> The acquisition and implementation of metaliteracy skills is a long-term and integral part of addressing the reach and influence of fake news and nonpolitical misinformation and disinformation. ... The end goal is to produce proactive critical thinkers, researchers, and information consumers who can sidestep false information and its deleterious effects. (219)

But before considering how inoculation theory might be a vibrant way of thinking of and theorizing about metaliteracy—to produce such "proactive critical thinkers, researchers, and information consumers" (Cooke 2017, 219)—it is important to consider what we know of inoculation theory, including how scholars think inoculation works and to what effects.

INOCULATION THEORY: RESISTANCE TO INFLUENCE

William McGuire introduced inoculation theory in the early 1960s as a theory of resistance to influence. The main idea was that attitudinal (or belief) inoculation functions much like a medical inoculation: Early exposure to weak attacks motivates processes of resistance to protect against later exposure to strong attacks. A conventional flu shot, for example, contains a weak version of the flu virus itself—purposefully injected to trigger protective mechanisms that, ideally, help to ward off stronger flu viruses encountered later. Persuasion inoculation works the same way. A persuasion inoculation message contains weak versions of potentially harmful arguments—purposefully presented to trigger protective mechanisms that, ideally, help to ward off stronger arguments encountered later (see Compton 2013; McGuire 1964).

The two components of resistance that have received the most attention in inoculation scholarship are threat and counterarguing. Threat in inoculation can be thought of as "recognized vulnerability, a perception that an existing position, once thought safe from change, may be at risk" (Compton 2013, 222). A person experiencing threat might think, "I was confident in my position on this, but now I'm beginning to wonder if I'd be able to defend my position if challenged."

Threat can be triggered in two main ways during inoculation: a response to the presence of threatening, or counterattitudinal, content in the inoculation message (i.e., the weakened persuasion arguments); and/or a response to the presence of an explicit forewarning that a held position will be attacked (McGuire 1964). Inoculation scholars now regularly use forewarnings when crafting inoculation messages for their research to try to motivate audiences to think carefully about their positions (see Banas and Richards 2017). These forewarnings are often worded along these lines: "You have the right position on this issue now, but there are people who will try to change your mind, and their arguments are so strong, you might, indeed, actually change your mind." Regardless of the source, threat motivates more attention to the now vulnerable position, and this "more attention," including counterarguing, is what makes the position more robust.

Counterarguing plays an important role in inoculation—as a rhetorical strategy and as a process of critical thinking. First, as a rhetorical strategy, the inoculation message itself contains examples of counterarguing. Counterarguments are raised and refuted, paralleling how viruses are altered—rendered into weakened forms—in medical inoculations. This two-sided message format has become the prototypical inoculation message format (Compton 2013). Usually, two to three counterarguments are raised and then refuted, converting the potentially strong and effective counterargument into something weaker, less virulent. Consider, for example, an inoculation message designed to keep someone committed to a new exercise program. After a general forewarning that commitment to the exercise program might be challenged in the future, an inoculation message would then raise and refute some specific challenges that could thwart efforts to stick with the new program, such as a perceived lack of time or peer pressure to engage in social activities instead of exercising (see Compton and Ivanov 2018). "Your friends might try to convince you that it would be more fun to go out for drinks after work than to hit the gym," an inoculation message could warn. "But these experiences are short-term. Think of the longer-term benefits you'll enjoy—for years to come—from a healthier mind and body." This format—a counterargument followed by a refutation—reflects the counterarguing process.

Second, the inoculation message motivates more internal counterarguing by the message recipient. Upon encountering the counterarguing process modeled in the inoculation treatment message, people think up additional counterarguments and refutations, motivated by threat (McGuire 1964), forming "an arsenal of argumentation for the individual" (Compton and Pfau 2004). Scholars have pointed to this feature of inoculation to explain how an inoculation treatment message confers protection against not only the counterarguments raised and refuted in the treatment message but also novel, not previously refuted counterarguments (Pfau and Kenski 1990). That is, if the inoculation treatment's efficacy were limited to simply memorizing a refutation to a specific counterargument, inoculation would not be able to protect against attacks that were not raised and refuted in the inoculation message. But research shows that inoculation can protect against these new counterarguments (Banas and Rains 2010), suggesting that something more complex than rote memory is at work. Returning to the previous example, raising and refuting a counterargument based on peer pressure could also protect against other challenges to exercise commitment, such as low motivation or frustration with how long it takes to see results.

Third, more recent theorizing (Compton and Pfau 2009)—backed up by empirical investigations (Ivanov et al. 2012)—has demonstrated that inoculation also leads to more verbal, external dialogue. Those inoculated are more likely to talk about the issue with friends and family, engaging in powerful, consequential postinoculation talk (Ivanov et al. 2012). We know from existing research that the more people talk about the issue, postinoculation, the stronger their resistance to subsequent stronger attacks on that position (Ivanov et al. 2012). Others have theorized, too, that if this postinoculation talk contains both counterarguments and refutations, then this talk could also be spreading inoculation along social networks or, at minimum, spreading information about the issue (Compton and Pfau 2009).

Much of our understanding of inoculation messages comes from research that seeks to protect individuals from specific counterarguments against specific attitudes toward specific policies, like legalizing marijuana or restricting depictions of violence on television (e.g., Pfau et al. 2004). In a typical inoculation study, some participants receive an inoculation message tailored to strengthen an existing position toward a policy, while others do not receive such a message. Later, all participants encounter a persuasive message designed to change their mind (e.g., an editorial, an advertisement). Those who were inoculated are more able to resist. They experienced more threat (i.e., perceived vulnerability to their position) and generated more thoughts about their position (i.e., they engaged in internal and/or external counterarguing). In short, they became more motivated and more thoughtful.

More recently, inoculation scholars have tested inoculation messages designed to help individuals work through forms (or modes) of counterarguments, such as media visuals (e.g., Pfau et al. 2008) or verbal, negative criticism offered by an individual (Jackson et al. 2015). Another recent development is evidence that inoculation can affect feelings, including fear (Jackson et al. 2017), and other theoretical work has considered whether inoculation might combat frustration with technology during digital learning activities in the classroom (Compton 2012).

Inoculation—by definition, by analogy, by its theory, and by its practice— has been viewed mostly as a prophylactic intervention—a way to preemptively confer resistance to attacks. More recently, however, scholars have been testing inoculation's effects on those who have a different position from what is being advocated in the inoculation message, and they have found that inoculation can function as a persuasive message, shifting attitudes in the advocated direction (e.g., Wood 2007), and can even function as an inoculation message (e.g., van der Linden et al. 2017). These findings seem to challenge the very foundation of inoculation theory. One cannot usually be inoculated against a virus if the virus already infects the person. But the qualifier "usually" is important here. Medical science has studied therapeutic vaccines— treatments that heal *and* confer resistance to future attacks (e.g., Hildesheim et al. 2007). As we move forward with inoculation theorizing and research, then, it is important to clarify that conventional inoculations are preemptive, but that new insight into therapeutic inoculation is testing the boundaries of conventional theorizing (Compton 2017) and holds exciting promise.

Inoculation theory, then, can be seen as a messaging strategy and a theoretical explanation for resistance to influence. It shows how considering multiple perspectives (e.g., a two-sided message) can make an existing idea stronger, or more resistant to subsequent challenges. Inoculation also offers an explanation for how this resistance works: threat motivates more attention to the issue (e.g., counterarguing), which creates a better defense against future attacks. This is the basic model of inoculation—introducing both a messaging format and a theoretical framework for understanding resistance.

INOCULATION MESSAGING IN A COURSE SYLLABUS

To this point, this chapter argues that extant research suggests that inoculation is a messaging strategy used to prepare learners to actively work through challenges—not to eliminate those challenges or to ignore them, but to engage with and to actively work through these challenges, motivated by threat and refutational preemption. It is an important clarification: an inoculation message is not intended to *eliminate* challenges. As I note in my proposal to inoculate against frustrations with technology during digital learning projects (Compton 2012), some challenges are helpful and a crucial part of the learning process. Indeed, teachers regularly monitor this balance of that which is welcoming and that which is challenging when talking with students about their courses (Thompson 2007). It is also important to clarify that some "attacks" should *not* be resisted but, instead, incorporated into a learner's position, knowledge, or beliefs.

Nevertheless, when inoculation messages offer the potential to protect against unproductive "attacks," one forum for inoculation messaging might be the course syllabus. As a preface to a class (Matejka and Kurke 1994), the syllabus serves to "prime" students in key ways that can affect their learning (Haigh 2013). I pointed out in an earlier work that the syllabus is an ideal forum for introducing to students proactive means of working through digital learning challenges (Compton 2012). Indeed, and consistent with our consideration of inoculation-informed strategies in a syllabus, consider Matejka and Kurke's (1994) argument that a syllabus can be "an exercise in preventive medicine" (116).

A course syllabus can affect, in ways positive or negative, student experience in the classroom. As Mark Canada (2013) put it, "A well-crafted syllabus can be the beginning of a promise fulfilled and part of the difference between just another course and one that changes lives" (37). Jeanne Slattery and Janet Carlson (2005) note that "a strong syllabus facilitates teaching and learning" (159), and Richmond and colleagues (2016) found that a more learner-centered syllabus—that which approaches course content from the perspective of the learners, offering learners choices, for example—creates a more favorable impression than a teacher-centered syllabus. A course syllabus, then, can have powerful effects. Might it also have powerful inoculative effects that encourage a more robust approach to learning?

Some professors already offer comments on a syllabus or in discussions about a syllabus that fit within the parameters of inoculation theory—comments that raise or acknowledge future challenges and offer different ways of thinking about such challenges. Thompson's (2007) study of how syllabi communicate finds that professors help their students to anticipate and overcome challenges, including "fears they might have regarding the course based on the syllabus" (59). One professor, cited in Thompson's (2007) study, recalled, "I remind them over half of the graded material is stuff over which they have total control" (59). In some syllabi, then, the ingredients are already in place for inoculation-informed messaging: a reference to upcoming challenges and a preemptive refutation of some specific challenges. Indeed, the syllabus is well positioned to preempt challenges—it is usually one of the first parts of a class. Using a syllabus to anticipate and preempt challenges is recommended in teaching scholarship (Matejka and Kurke 1994); inoculation theory provides a theory-informed, evidence-based approach to such preemption.

Consider, then, how inoculation-informed messaging might be incorporated into assignment/project rationale—a feature recommended to be included in course syllabi (Appling et al. 2015). Project rationale might be preceded by acknowledgment of likely, unhelpful initial perceptions of an assignment. For example, I incorporate a declamation assignment (a brief speech recited from memory) in my public speaking class—a class that is built on principles of dialogic public speaking and, for nearly all of the term, a class that rejects a memorization approach to public speaking. I precede my declamation assignment description with a message such as this:

> At first glance, we might consider memorization to be antithetical to a dialogue model of public speaking. And in many ways, it is. But in this activity, we are going to be memorizing and reciting content as a way to compare memorized content with more flexible modes of delivery (e.g., extemporaneous), to further refine our understanding of dialogue.

This brief segment contains a counterargument ("Memorization is antithetical to a dialogue model of public speaking") and a refutation ("Memorization can serve as a useful contrast for understanding dialogue").

Consider, too, syllabus content that encourages effective learning behaviors, such as utilizing a college library (see Haigh 2013). Syllabi can do more than provide practical information on the library or even list assignments of library activities. Syllabi content might also raise and refute potential challenges to library use before those challenges arise. Consider, for example, how inoculation-informed messaging could try to lessen "library anxiety" (Jiao, Onwuegbuzie, and Lichtenstein 1996)—"a psychological barrier to academic success among college students" (151)—by raising and addressing common concerns that discourage library use. Imagine a brief message that made this counterpoint/point:

> Many college students think that they'd be bothering library staff if they were to ask for help, so they don't. But it's no bother at all! Our library staff want you to ask your questions—any questions—so that they can help you with your projects.

More perceived barriers to working with librarians are to be found in a number of places, including extant literature (e.g., Black 2016; Fagan 2002; Green 1994) and directly from student comments. Such work could also help to enhance student perceptions of their information-seeking self-efficacy (Clark 2017), as inoculation has established success in boosting perceptions of efficacy in other contexts (Jackson et al. 2015).

In some ways, such an application of inoculation theory to encourage library use is similar to a recommendation a colleague and I made about using inoculation theory to encourage gym use—to raise and preempt anxieties about going to the gym before they occur (Compton and Ivanov 2018). We also have reason for optimism from the results of the study by Jackson and colleagues (2017) that found inoculation messaging helps with fears of public speaking. Work in these areas could meet calls for more attention to social psychological strategies to encourage better library use (e.g., Black 2016).

Inoculation strategies might also emerge in introductions of grading philosophies and practices, as described in syllabi. Canada's (2013) advice for constructing a more welcoming, effective syllabus encourages professors to preface grading practices by putting the grading approach in context. In his example, he compares grades in a class to going to the gym or playing the piano—things done for enjoyment, not primarily for a quantitative ranking—followed by a clear articulation of what will guide his assessments of student learning. Canada describes this approach as a way to "combat . . . suspicion" (41) that grades are determined through unclear procedures. In this application, the suspicion might function as the counterargument or counterpoint in an inoculation-informed message, and the analogic extensions might function as refutations, weakening the counterargument (suspicion) to function as inoculation.

Inoculation, then, is well-suited as an early strategy to prepare students for upcoming challenges. But as I propose in the next section, inoculation messages do more than instill resistance to challenges. Inoculation messages change how people think and even feel about challenges to their positions, encouraging a more thoughtful, more dialogic relationship with arguments and evidence. Such an approach to learning is particularly healthy in a post-truth world, as inoculation messaging aims to enhance more thinking about issues, more dialogue about issues, more discernment of persuasive efforts—in short, more engagement with one's environment.

In the remainder of this chapter, we will look at additional features of inoculation in the context of the four domains of metaliteracy learning, to see how inoculation might be used as a theoretical lens for better understanding metaliteracy learning and, perhaps, to design messaging strategies to better encourage metaliteracy learning. Mackey and Jacobson (2011) call for learners who have "a comprehensive understanding of information to critically evaluate, share, and produce content in multiple forms" (62), and some effects of inoculation research seem to support all of these dimensions.

FOUR DOMAINS OF METALITERACY

Mackey and Jacobson (2014), working with the Metaliteracy Learning Collaborative, introduced the four domains of metaliteracy learning: behavioral, cognitive, affective, and metacognitive (Jacobson et al. 2018). In this section, I will show how inoculation theory has both direct and indirect connections to these four domains, suggesting that inoculation theory provides a useful lens through which to study, practice, and inform metaliteracy.

Behavioral

A good deal of research indicates that inoculation does more than strengthen attitudes. Inoculation also influences behaviors. Political inoculation theory research points to inoculation's effects on "participatory attitudes and behaviors, which underpin democracy" (Compton and Pfau 2005, 119), something particularly important in a post-truth world. Consider, for example, the finding by Pfau and colleagues (2001) that inoculation can, under some conditions, increase likelihood of voting in an election. Likewise, in another context, Compton and Pfau's (2004) work suggests that inoculation treatments can lead to increased intentions of young adults to pay down their credit card debt. More recently, as mentioned previously, inoculation scholars have revealed effects of inoculation on word-of-mouth communication. As theorized by Compton and Pfau (2009), then confirmed by empirical investigations (Ivanov et al. 2012), inoculation messages lead to more talk about the issue of the message—and this talk strengthens resistance to future influence. An earlier study suggested that inoculation messaging can even support increased talk about opinions that are in the minority (Lin and Pfau 2007), promoting more robust, more complete dialogue.

It seems possible—likely, even—that inoculation messaging might affect additional behaviors, including specific behaviors proposed in metaliteracy learning outcomes. My earlier case (Compton 2012) for inoculation as a "frustration vaccination" against technology obstacles would promote a goal to "adapt to and understand new technologies and the impact they have on learning" (Jacobson et al. 2018). Compton and Pfau's (2008) finding that inoculation can help inform how students think about issues of academic misconduct supports a goal to "identify and follow the specific intellectual property attribution expectations in the setting in which you are working" (Jacobson et al. 2018). Inoculation's proven efficacy for motivating more talk about issues (Compton and Pfau 2009; Ivanov et al. 2012) would seem to promote goals to "effectively communicate and collaborate in shared spaces to learn from multiple perspectives" (Jacobson et al. 2018). A host of other metaliterate learning behaviors may prove consistent with inoculation theory's assumptions and boundary conditions once studied.

Cognitive

Evidence suggests that inoculation leads to a knowledge-based resistance to influence. For example, a study by Pfau and colleagues (2001) found that inoculation campaigns enhanced voters' knowledge of political candidates and the candidates' positions on key issues. In a more general sense, a traditional explanation for how inoculation confers resistance rests on an assumption of learning—that those inoculated gain new knowledge, from multiple perspectives, and this new knowledge promotes resistance (Compton 2013; McGuire

1964). Some work has found that inoculation can prepare people to better identify and interpret sources of information (Pfau et al. 2007), and work in climate science communication seeks to create more critical consumers of science argumentation (Cook, Lewandowsky, and Ecker, 2017; van der Linden et al. 2017), consistent with my earlier idea of Aristotelian inoculation (Compton 2005), or inoculation that enhances critical thinking. For example, Cook, Lewandowsky, and Ecker's (2017) work looks to confer resistance to climate change misinformation. Instead of raising and refuting explicit arguments, as is typical in an inoculation message, Cook and his colleagues designed inoculation messages that attempted to expose faulty reasoning. They note, "The purpose of this type of intervention is to stimulate critical thinking through the explanation of argumentative techniques, thus encouraging people to move beyond shallow heuristic-driven processing and engage in deeper, more strategic scrutinizing of the presented information" (Cook, Lewandowsky, and Ecker 2017, 15). Such inoculation approaches highlight the potential to lead to better, more careful thinking.

These effects of inoculation seem promising to help meet metaliterate learning outcomes. One of the most important features of inoculation is its ability to prepare. This idea of preparation—instead of, or in addition to, reaction, postencounter—emerges in contemporary discussions of fake news. It is critical, in a post-truth world, to *preempt* misleading influences when we can. Consider, for example, Mackey and Jacobson's (2016) focus: "The question then is: Can we better prepare ourselves to challenge and reject fabrications that may easily circulate as untruthful texts and images in the online world?" (para. 6). One approach might be to use inoculation messaging to boost evaluation skills. Cooke (2017) has noted that

> the bulk of disinformation on the Internet could be combated with basic evaluation skills. If consumers of information would take time to make a few simple assessments, disinformation would not be so prevalent or insidious. To become critical consumers of media information, users should question the recency of date of the information (or lack thereof), carefully examine the site's URL, consider the language being used . . . , consider the plausibility of the information, and consider the reputation and leanings of the website providing the information . . . (217)

An inoculation message could aim for these (and other) results—not just to provide metrics through which to evaluate information, but also to point to specific challenges that might thwart the use of such metrics. A key objective of metaliterate learning is to "recognize that critical thinking depends upon knowledge of a subject and actively pursue deeper understanding through inquiry and research" (Jacobson et al. 2018), and inoculation could help to achieve these aims. Consistent with the principles of metaliteracy in general, and the cognitive domain in particular, an inoculation message could encourage ways of thinking and not simply transmitting what to think.

For example, consider an inoculation message that was intended to protect against accepting outdated information when newer information would offer better understanding. Such a message could read as follows:

> When we read news online, it's tempting to assume that what we're reading is the most up-to-date, current information available. But upon further thought, we might discover that the information is outdated and now inaccurate based on more recent data. So it's a good idea to stop and check when information was posted—and to explore more recent findings—as a step toward finding the best information available.

In this simple message, a counterargument is raised and then refuted—and the refutation also provides a useful heuristic to use when evaluating information, as suggested by Cooke (2017).

Affective

Perhaps no area has seen more growth and development in inoculation scholarship than the role(s) of affect in inoculation-conferred resistance to influence, including new insight into inoculating *with* (e.g., Miller et al. 2013) and *against* (e.g., Jackson et al. 2017) affect. Work that explores inoculation's efficacy in building confidence seems particularly applicable to metaliteracy learning objectives, including findings that inoculation decreases pressures of negative anxiety (Jackson et al. 2017) and increases self-efficacy (Jackson et al. 2015).

Consider, for example, how fear and anxiety can disrupt optimum learning, including (as mentioned previously in this chapter) library anxiety. Jackson and colleagues (2017) have established that inoculation can help students reduce negative anxiety about public speaking and, furthermore, rechannel remaining anxiety into more productive motivations. Might a similar message—one that raises and refutes the things that make students anxious or fearful about using the library—work to inoculate college students for more, and more effective, library usage? What about anxiety toward research in general, outside the library? Perhaps inoculation, too, might help to address other research perception issues, such as overconfidence in one's expertise.

We might also find inoculation messages particularly well-suited to help boost student perception of their efficacy and investigate how these perceptions can help them to achieve affective metaliteracy learning objectives. Extant work in inoculation does find that inoculation boosts perceptions of efficacy in the face of verbal criticism, for example (Jackson et al. 2015). Might inoculation-informed messages also help to boost perceptions of efficacy in terms of collaborative learning, helping to meet the goal for students to "participate conscientiously and ethically in collaborative environments" (Jacobson et al. 2018)? Such an approach could benefit from extant research on interesting connections among self-regulation and academic self-efficacy and collaboration in an educational setting, like that of Fernández-Rio and colleagues (2017).

Metacognitive

Metacognition is embedded in many features of inoculation theory and, perhaps most notably, in its assumption that recipients of inoculation messages engage in intrapersonal processes of refutational preemption, or internal counterarguing, and consider multiple perspectives on issues (Compton 2013). That is, upon exposure to an inoculation message—a message that raises counterperspectives and responses to these counterperspectives—people generate additional thoughts about the issue. While these metacognitive elements have been guiding assumptions of inoculation theory since its introduction (McGuire 1964), metacognitive features of inoculation research, as a specific or an explicit focus, are rare. Here we find a particularly promising area of work that would enhance both metaliteracy and inoculation theory development. Might inoculation, as a pedagogical messaging approach, lead to not just more thinking about an issue but *better* thinking about an issue? Does exposure to an inoculation message motivate more, and better, research? Might exposure to counterperspectives cause inoculation message recipients to seek out additional counterperspectives, perhaps consulting information sources that might otherwise be ignored? Quite simply, does inoculation messaging lead to better thinking?

Such inquiries parallel nicely one of the distinguishing features of metaliteracy—that it motivates a search for more information when encountering new information (Mackey and Jacobson 2016). Some of this "search" is, as noted earlier, in the form of social engagement during the process of inoculation, suggesting that inoculation might be a way to promote "learners learning from each other," which is "a hallmark of metaliteracy learning goals and objectives" (O'Brien et al. 2016, 21), including the objective that students "recognize that learners are also teachers" (Jacobson et al. 2018). We know from extant inoculation research that inoculation messaging generates more thought, more talk, more feelings (Compton 2013); a metaliteracy focus might help to reveal under what conditions inoculation messaging leads to better thinking and better research. If inoculation messaging can lead to a search for more information—including through increased dialogue with others, including others who hold different opinions (Ivanov et al. 2015; Lin and Pfau 2007)—it could be an antidote to some of the negative effects of a post-truth world. That is, inoculation messaging might make it more likely that upon encountering conflicting or incomplete information, the next step would be more inquiry—more dialogue, more learning from others—instead of accepting or dismissing the information without deliberation.

CONCLUSION

As I have argued in this chapter, one of the most important features of inoculation is how it can enable a proactive approach to metaliterate learning—preparation for deliberation and dialogue. My hope is that inoculation theory encourages metaliteracy in a post-truth world "to produce proactive critical thinkers, researchers, and information consumers who can sidestep false information and its deleterious effects" (Cooke 2017, 219). Of course, inoculation messaging will not always promote and foster metaliterate learning. When extreme beliefs have set in, it is probably too late for inoculation, just as someone already sick with the flu would not benefit from a flu shot. But there is the potential for it to help. As mentioned previously, some research is finding that inoculation messages can generate more thinking and attitude change even when an attitude is based on suspect information (e.g., van der Linden et al. 2017).

As we move forward in considering how inoculation and metaliteracy are complementary, some key questions about inoculation will need to be answered, too, including whether, at least under some circumstances, an inoculation treatment message might give the illusion of deliberate thought and critical reasoning, a type of "thoughtfulness heuristic" (Barden and Petty 2008, 489), but not actually increase critical thought. Future investigations should continue to test whether inoculation is leading to the type of robust thinking we think that it might foster, because in our effort to encourage more robust learning in a post-truth world, the illusion of learning, or a type of pseudo-learning, would be counterproductive.

Inoculation and metaliteracy research can each inform the other. Further investigation is needed among researchers and practitioners to explore the promising connections discussed here—and beyond. Increased attention to this resistance messaging strategy as a tool to encourage deeper learning should uncover a number of strategies that offer a proactive approach to theorize about and apply metaliteracy.

REFERENCES

Appling, Jeffrey, Andrew Dippre, Ellen Gregory, Megan Hembree, Kaitlyn Kooi, Kyle Pazzo, Sarah Carson, and Avery Shawen. 2015. "General Education and ePortfolios: Syllabi and the Role of Faculty." *International Journal of ePortfolio* 5 (1): 55–62.

Banas, John A., and Stephen A. Rains. 2010. "A Meta-analysis of Research on Inoculation Theory." *Communication Monographs* 77 (3): 281–311.

Banas, John A., and Adam S. Richards. 2017. "Apprehension or Motivation to Defend Attitudes? Exploring the Underlying Threat Mechanism in Inoculation-Induced Resistance to Persuasion." *Communication Monographs* 84 (2): 164–78.

Barden, Jamie, and Richard E. Petty. 2008. "The Mere Perception of Elaboration Creates Attitude Certainty: Exploring the Thoughtfulness Heuristic." *Journal of Personality and Social Psychology* 95 (3): 489–509.

Black, Steve. 2016. "Psychosocial Reasons Why Patrons Avoid Seeking Help from Librarians: A Literature Review." *The Reference Librarian* 57 (1): 35–56.

Canada, Mark. 2013. "The Syllabus: A Place to Engage Students' Egos." *New Directions for Teaching and Learning*, no. 135: 37–42.

Clark, Melissa. 2017. "Imposed-Inquiry Information-Seeking Self-Efficacy and Performance of College Students: A Review of the Literature." *The Journal of Academic Librarianship* 43 (5): 417–22.

Compton, Josh. 2005. "Comparison, Contrast, and Synthesis of Aristotelian Rationality and Inoculation." *STAM Journal* 35: 1–23.

———. 2012. "Frustration Vaccination? Inoculation Theory and Digital Learning." In *Teaching, Learning and the Net Generation: Concepts and Tools for Reaching Digital Learners*, edited by S. P. Ferris, 61–73. Hershey, PA: IGI Global.

———. 2013. "Inoculation Theory." In *The Sage Handbook of Persuasion*, edited by James P. Dillard and Lijiang Shen, 220–36. Thousand Oaks, CA: Sage.

———. 2017. "Prophylactic versus Therapeutic Inoculation Treatments for Resistance to Influence." Presentation, Annual Convention of the National Communication Association, Dallas, TX, November 16–19.

Compton, Josh, and Bobi Ivanov. 2013. "Vaccinating Voters: Surveying Political Campaign Inoculation Scholarship." In *Communication Yearbook* 37, edited by Elisia L. Cohen, 250–83. New York: Routledge.

———. 2018. "Inoculation Messaging." In *Persuasion and Communication in Sport, Exercise, and Physical Activity*, edited by Ben Jackson, James Dimmock, and Josh Compton, 73–90. Abington, UK: Routledge.

Compton, Josh, Ben Jackson, and James A. Dimmock. 2016. "Persuading Others to Avoid Persuasion: Inoculation Theory and Resistant Health Attitudes." *Frontiers in Psychology* 7 (122). http://journal.frontiersin.org/article/10.3389/fpsyg.2016.00122/full.

Compton, Josh, and Michael Pfau. 2004. "Use of Inoculation to Foster Resistance to Credit Card Marketing Targeting College Students." *Journal of Applied Communication Research* 32 (4): 343–64.

———. 2005. "Inoculation Theory of Resistance to Influence at Maturity: Recent Progress in Theory Development and Application and Suggestions for Future Research." In *Communication Yearbook* 29, edited by Pamela J. Kalbfleisch, 97–146. Mahwah, NJ: Lawrence Erlbaum.

———. 2008. "Inoculating against Pro-plagiarism Justifications: Rational and Affective Strategies." *Journal of Applied Communication Research* 36 (1): 98–119.

———. 2009. "Spreading Inoculation: Inoculation, Resistance to Influence, and Word-of-Mouth Communication." *Communication Theory* 19 (1): 9–28.

Cook, John, Stephan Lewandowsky, and Ullrich K. H. Ecker. 2017. "Neutralizing Misinformation through Inoculation: Exposing Misleading Argumentation Techniques Reduces Their Influence." *PLOS ONE* 12 (5): e0175799.

Cooke, Nicole A. 2017. "Posttruth, Truthiness, and Alternative Facts: Information Behavior and Critical Information Consumption for a New Age." *Library Quarterly: Information, Community, Policy* 87 (3): 211–21.

Fagan, Jody. 2002. "Students' Perceptions of Academic Librarians." *The Reference Librarian* 37 (78): 131–48.

Fernández-Rio, Javier, José A. Cecchini, Antonio Méndez-Giménez, David Méndez-Alonso, and José A. Prieto. 2017. "Self-Regulation, Cooperative Learning, and Academic Self-Efficacy: Interactions to Prevent School Failure." *Frontiers in Psychology* 8 (22). doi:10.3389/fpyg.2017.00022.

Green, Tracey. 1994. "Images and Perceptions as Barriers to the Use of Library Staff and Services." *New Library World* 95 (7): 19–24.

Haigh, Adam E. 2013. "You Can Lead Students to the Library, but Can You Make Them Do Research? The Effect of Syllabus Design and Content on Undergraduates' Perceptions and Use of the Academic Library." *Journal of Business and Finance Librarianship* 18 (1): 33–48.

Hildesheim, Allan, Rolando Herrero, Sholom Wacholder, Ana C. Rodriguez, Diane Solomon, M. Concepcion Bratti, John T. Schiller, Paula Gonzalez, Gary Dubin, Carolina Porras, et al. 2007. "Effect of Human Papillomavirus 16/18 L1 Viruslike Particle Vaccine among Young Women with Preexisting Infection: A Randomized Trial." *JAMA* 298 (7): 743–53.

Ivanov, Bobi, William J. Burns, Timothy L. Sellnow, Elizabeth L. Petrun Sayers, Shari R. Veil, and Marcus W. Mayorga. 2016. "Using an Inoculation Message Approach to Promote Public Confidence in Protective Agencies." *Journal of Applied Communication Research* 44 (4): 381–98.

Ivanov, Bobi, Claude H. Miller, Josh Compton, Joshua M. Averbeck, Kylie J. Harrison, Jeanetta D. Sims, Kimberly A. Parker, and James L. Parker. 2012. "Effects of Postinoculation Talk on Resistance to Influence." *Journal of Communication* 62 (4): 701–18.

Ivanov, Bobi, Jeanetta D. Sims, Josh Compton, Claude H. Miller, Kimberly A. Parker, James L. Parker, Kylie J. Harrison, and Joshua M. Averbeck. 2015. "The General Content of Postinoculation Talk: Recalled Issue-Specific Conversations following Inoculation Treatments." *Western Journal of Communication* 79 (2): 218–38.

Jackson, Ben, Josh Compton, Ashleigh L. Thornton, and James A. Dimmock. 2017. "Re-thinking Anxiety: Using Inoculation Messages to Reduce and Reinterpret Public Speaking Fears." *PLOS ONE*, no. 1: e0169972.

Jackson, Ben, Josh Compton, Ryan Whiddett, David R. Anthony, and James A. Dimmock. 2015. "Preempting Performance Challenges: The Effects of Inoculation Messaging on Attacks to Task Self-Efficacy." *PLOS ONE* 10 (4): e0124886.

Jacobson, Trudi, Tom Mackey, Kelsey O'Brien, Michele Forte, and Emer O'Keeffe. 2018. "Goals and Learning Objectives." Metaliteracy.org. Accessed August 22. https://metaliteracy.org/learning-objectives.

Jiao, Qun G., Anthony J. Onwuegbuzie, and Art A. Lichtenstein. 1996. "Library Anxiety: Characteristics of 'At-Risk' College Students." *Library and Information Science Research* 18 (2): 151–63.

Lin, Wei-Kuo, and Michael Pfau. 2007. "Can Inoculation Work against the Spiral of Silence? A Study of Public Opinion on the Future of Taiwan." *International Journal of Public Opinion Research* 19 (2): 155–72.

Mackey, Thomas P., and Trudi E. Jacobson. 2011. "Reframing Information Literacy as a Metaliteracy." *College and Research Libraries* 72 (1): 62–78.

———. 2014. *Metaliteracy: Reinventing Information Literacy to Empower Learners*. Chicago: ALA Neal-Schuman.

———. 2016. "How Can We Learn to Reject Fake News in the Digital World?" *The Conversation*, December 5. http://theconversation.com/how-can-we-learn-to -reject-fake-news-in-the-digital-world-69706.

Matejka, Ken, and Lance B. Kurke. 1994. "Designing a Great Syllabus." *College Teaching* 42 (3): 115–17.

McGuire, William J. 1964. "Inducing Resistance to Persuasion: Some Contemporary Approaches." In *Advances in Experimental Social Psychology*, edited by Leonard Berkowitz, 191–229. New York: Academic Press.

Miller, Claude H., Bobi Ivanov, Jeanetta Sims, Josh Compton, Kylie J. Harrison, Kimberly A. Parker, James L. Parker, and Joshua M. Averbeck. 2013. "Boosting the Potency of Resistance: Combining the Motivational Forces of Inoculation and Psychological Reactance." *Human Communication Research* 39 (1): 127–55.

O'Brien, Kelsey L., Michele Forte, Thomas P. Mackey, and Trudi E. Jacobson. 2017. "Metaliteracy as Pedagogical Framework for Learner-Centered Design in Three MOOC Platforms: Connectivist, Coursera and Canvas." *Open Praxis* 9, no. 3. https://doi.org/10.5944/openpraxis.9.3.553.

Pfau, Michael, Josh Compton, Kimberly A. Parker, Elaine M. Wittenberg, Chasu An, Monica Ferguson, Heather Horton, and Yuri Malyshev. 2004. "The Traditional Explanation for Resistance versus Attitude Accessibility." *Human Communication Research* 30 (3): 329–60.

Pfau, Michael, Michel M. Haigh, Theresa Shannon, Toni Tones, Deborah Mercurio, Raina Williams, Blanca Binstock, Carlos Diaz, Constance Dillard, Margaret Browne, Clarence Elder, Sherri Reed, Adam Eggers, and Juan Melendez. 2008. "The Influence of Television News Depictions on the Images of War on Viewers." *Journal of Broadcasting and Electronic Media* 52 (2): 303–22.

Pfau, Michael, Michel M. Haigh, Jeanetta Sims, and Shelley Wigley. 2007. "The Influence of Corporate Front-Group Stealth Campaigns." *Communication Research* 34 (1): 73–99.

Pfau, Michael, and Henry C. Kenski. 1990. *Attack Politics: Strategy and Defense.* New York: Praeger.

Pfau, Michael, David Park, R. Lance Holbert, and Jaeho Cho. 2001. "The Effects of Party- and PAC-Sponsored Issue Advertising and the Potential of Inoculation to Combat Its Impact on the Democratic Process." *American Behavioral Scientist* 44 (12): 2379–97.

Richmond, Aaron S., Jeanne M. Slattery, Nathanael Mitchell, Robin K. Morgan, and Jared Becknell. 2016. "Can a Learner-Centered Syllabus Change Students' Perceptions of Student–Professor Rapport and Master Teacher Behaviors?" *Scholarship of Teaching and Learning in Psychology* 2 (3): 159–68.

Slattery, Jeanne M., and Janet F. Carlson. 2005. "Preparing an Effective Syllabus: Current Best Practices." *College Teaching* 53 (4): 159–164.

Thompson, Blair. 2007. "The Syllabus as a Communication Document: Constructing and Presenting the Syllabus." *Communication Education* 56 (1): 54–71.

van der Linden, Sander, Anthony Leiserowitz, Seth Rosenthal, and Edward Maibach. 2017. "Inoculating the Public against Misinformation about Climate Change." *Global Challenges* 1 (2). http://onlinelibrary.wiley.com/doi/10.1002/gch2.201600008/full.

Wood, Michelle L. M. 2007. "Rethinking the Inoculation Analogy: Effects on Subjects with Differing Preexisting Attitudes." *Human Communication Research* 33 (3): 357–78.

ALLISON B. BRUNGARD and
KRISTIN KLUCEVSEK

4

Constructing Scientific Literacy through Metaliteracy

Implications for Learning in a Post-Truth World

Scientists and the entire academic community are being challenged by a post-truth world that emphasizes emotion as well as personal, political, or religious affiliations over evidence. This environment makes it more difficult than ever before to address the disparities in scientific literacy among learners. Incorporating other literacies and encouraging the transfer of literacy competencies across disciplines may address the solutions to these concerns. Numerous relevant studies address the roles of scientific literacy and information literacy in higher education (Klucevsek 2017; Norris and Phillips 2003; Porter et al. 2010; Yore, Pimm, and Tuan 2007). However, there is a need to examine the connection between scientific literacy and metaliteracy. Because our post-truth era has emerged through the digital environment, including social media, it is essential that we explore how metaliteracy can construct stronger scientific literacy.

Metaliteracy recognizes common characteristics of related literacies, such as visual, media, digital, and critical, with foundational information literacy at the core, to create a critical thinking and reflective framework (Mackey and Jacobson 2014). In today's post-truth world, the connection to scientific literacy is especially relevant. Metaliterate learners critically reflect on their own literacy to enhance learning and continuously adapt to new technologies and information situations. They also collaborate with others to learn, adapting to content in new formats in an ever-changing digital environment. The four domains of metaliteracy—*behavioral*, *cognitive*, *affective*, and *metacognitive*—help define a metaliterate learner's ability to succeed in a range of information environments (Jacobson et al. 2018).

In *Metaliteracy: Reinventing Information Literacy to Empower Learners*, Mackey and Jacobson (2014) compare discrete and combined literacies with metaliteracy (table 3.1, 67). This list includes health literacy, which has a functional relationship to scientific literacy, as scientific evidence supports health initiatives. Some core information literacy competencies in health literacy are also crucial to scientific literacy, such as the ability to find, evaluate, and use science and health information to make decisions. Mackey and Jacobson (2014) discuss these competencies in a digital age: "At the same time, however, these basic competencies do not go far enough for today's social media environment and must be repurposed to include the creation and distribution of digital documents in collaborative networks" (66). This is also true of scientific literacy, which would benefit from a metaliterate frame to understand the current challenges.

Consumers of scientific content need information literacy skills to find and evaluate scientific information, but this is more challenging in a digital environment. Science exists in a wider range of contexts online than is offered by the traditional one-way conversation of journal articles meant only for an audience of scientists. For example, scientific information can be found through Google searches and presented through YouTube videos, Flickr images, and the user-generated community of *Wikipedia*, which often cites these journal articles. This information is shared through Facebook posts and other social media platforms, such as Twitter and Instagram. The user needs to be a critical consumer of this varied information. As Mackey and Jacobson (2011) write, consumers "must contextualize this information within a decentered environment that connects the professional and novice and makes accessible both formal and informal sources of information" (73). After analyzing content and context, the consumer has the ability to produce new scientific information online, allowing an opportunity for creation as well as a potential for bias and misinterpretation. The *metacognitive* aspects of metaliteracy address these challenges by recognizing the need for consumers and learners to reflect on what they discover as they create and participate in social online environments.

In this chapter, we offer a holistic approach to enhancing scientific literacy through metaliteracy as a means of improving critical engagement through research, collaborative learning, and scholarly communication in the digital environment. Furthermore, we examine the use of social media in enhancing learning through connections with scientific research and the real world. We also discuss the metaliterate role of scientists and consumers in this process. In a digital age, scientists must learn to communicate with the public, translate and teach their research, and participate in nontraditional formats, such as social media, citizen science projects, and open-access resources. Consumers, traditionally learners of scientific content, can now have participant and creator roles as they interact with scientific content digitally. Here, we discuss how both scientists and learners must engage in metaliteracy to reflect on their responsibility to broaden scientific literacy in a post-truth world.

EXAMINING SCIENTIFIC LITERACY THROUGH A METALITERATE LENS

Scientific literacy has been partially inhibited by the lack of a simple definition, but most contemporary definitions recognize scientific literacy as more than a *cognitive* ability. Science education and science communication researchers argue that literacy itself may have different meanings for different groups or be completely unattainable in the optimal sense (Feinstein 2015; Lewenstein 2015; Norris and Phillips 2003; Yore, Bisanz, and Hand 2003; Roberts 2007). For example, some have argued that the literacy component of scientific literacy, in terms of reading and writing, is as essential to the definition as any concepts or facts one might retain from a science course, especially in a digital age (Norris and Phillips 2003; Yore, Pimm, and Tuan 2007; Turiman et al. 2012). Yore and colleagues (2007) call for a scientific literacy definition that includes cognition and metacognition, inquiry, and critical thinking, among other fundamental and overarching goals of science. In addition, the sciences do not agree with a term for literacy, as historically both science literacy or scientific literacy have been used by different groups (Roberts 2007; Roberts and Bybee 2014). Visual science literacy could also be tied into scientific literacy in terms of cognition, as people may be more familiar with images than terminology (Bucchi and Saracino 2016), which may be even more relevant in a digital age.

Organizational definitions of scientific literacy touch on some of the components of information and metaliteracy, even if the numerous benchmarks and outcomes that support them sometimes differ. The *National Science Education Standards* state that scientific literacy

> means that a person can ask, find, or determine answers to questions derived from curiosity about everyday experiences. . . . Scientific literacy entails being able to read with understanding articles about science in the popular press and to engage in social conversation about the validity of the conclusions. . . . A literate citizen should be able to evaluate the quality of scientific information

on the basis of its source and the methods used to generate it.
(National Research Council 1996, 22)

Project 2061, an initiative of the American Association for the Advancement of Science (AAAS), includes in their *Benchmarks for Science Literacy* a benchmark called Habits of Mind, which strives to move students from what they should know to what they should do with their knowledge and encourages students to make connections by reflecting on the material (Project 2061 2009). For a broader, international perspective, the Programme for International Student Assessment's (PISA) 2015 framework defines scientific literacy as "the ability to engage with science-related issues, and with the ideas of science, as a reflective citizen" (OECD 2013, 7). Together, these organizations recognize reflection and metacognition, as well as information, as part of the definition of scientific literacy. This supports the role of metaliteracy in scientific literacy. Because the definitions for scientific literacy are so diverse, it may help to examine a definition that uses the metaliteracy domains.

In practice, most scientists and educators today would probably agree that understanding and analyzing science as a process is a fundamental part of scientific literacy. This inherently includes some knowledge, but also reading, writing, and collaboration. For the purpose of understanding scientific literacy for this chapter, we also define science as an iterative process. The scientific method, though often misrepresented as a linear process, is completely reflective. This process involves forming a hypothesis based on the literature, designing and implementing an experiment, collecting and analyzing data, comparing that data to the hypothesis and published literature, and sharing data in a scholarly community. These steps often involve a metacognitive "feedback loop" so that the scientist must return to earlier steps and repeat or reanalyze based on results, conversations with colleagues, and new publications. In practice, the scientific process has reflective qualities that it shares with metaliteracy domains (see table 4.1).

Though table 4.1 separates steps of the scientific process into distinct domains for the purpose of comparing literacies, the iterative process of science means that these steps are not discrete. For example, asking questions is a *behavioral* step because it is something all scientists should be able to do, but their ability to ask questions is also affected by what else they know (*cognitive*). Questions are also influenced by the processes of reflecting on how results fit into other research and personal biases (*affective* and *metacognitive*). A single experiment never exists alone. It is situated between the original hypothesis or objective and similar research. Related to the *affective* domain, scientists analyzing their data must ask if their research is what they expected and if the research contradicts or agrees with other experiments. For example, if a scientist hypothesized one result but uncovers something different, the scientist will undergo an *affective* change as the scientist reflects on the data through

TABLE 4.1

Aligning the Metaliteracy Domains to the Scientific Process

METALITERACY DOMAIN	DESCRIPTION	SCIENTIFIC PROCESS
Behavioral	Students' skills, or what they should be able to do	• Asking questions • Creating hypotheses • Finding sources • Evaluating sources • Analyzing data
Cognitive	Students' comprehension, or what they should know	• Understanding basic scientific concepts and methods
Affective	Changes in students' emotions or attitudes	• Considering how data compares to beliefs and current issues • Comparing data to existing scholarship
Metacognitive	Students' reflections on their own learning	• Reflecting on data in light of the hypothesis and published data • Asking new questions • Participating in a collaborative environment

metacognition. The scientist may decide to find and read additional literature, repeat an experiment, include a different control, use another method, or design another hypothesis. In essence, what we produce as part of the scientific process exhibits culminating effects of the *cognitive* and *behavioral* domains of metaliteracy. The *affective* and *metacognitive* domains substantially enhance our definition of scientific literacy as they help scientists put data in the context of their original questions and the existing scholarship. This allows scientists to ask new questions, create new hypotheses, and continue the iterative process of research and exploration.

To help consumers become more scientifically literate, the *affective* and *metacognitive* domains of metaliteracy can be achieved through several of the metaliteracy learning objectives (Jacobson et al. 2018; Mackey and Jacobson 2014). Here, consumers as participants should be encouraged to reflect on scientific content in the context of other knowledge. For example, consumers must learn to critically evaluate contributions from different sources, including social media, and they must understand their role in both consuming and producing new information. This includes reflecting on their own knowledge and any potential biases that might affect their understanding and translation and recognizing when they need additional sources before creating new content. Consumers who become creators must also recognize the ethical necessity to cite the scientists who performed the research as they distribute information and become collaborators in a digital environment.

UPDATING SCIENTIFIC LITERACY
IN A DIGITAL ENVIRONMENT

Scientific literacy also converges with metaliteracy in emphasizing digital formats. By nature, scientists are engaged in using new technologies, such as computer, biomedical, mechanical, or nanotechnology. The modes of producing and sharing information, be they experiments, patents, new drugs, inventions, computer programs, or mobile apps, have been influenced by a changing digital environment. This digital growth of science has undoubtedly led to more collaborations, large-scale experiments, open data sources, and powerful applications to analyze and visualize data. The Association of College & Research Libraries is developing an information literacy framework specifically focused on science and technology to address these rapid changes in the digital environment and to make a stronger connection between formats of information and engagement. The *Framework for Science Information Literacy for Higher Education* will list specific outcomes and assessment techniques related to science information literacy (ACRL 2018).

These changes in a digital environment can bring both benefits as well as challenges to scientific literacy. For example, the online social environment has given everyone the opportunity to search for information on scientific issues or scroll through science news on a social media account. The scientific process, however, is indiscernible in a tweet, far removed from the news we read and view on social media. If members of the public rarely participate in science as a reflective process in a research setting or classroom, they may not know how to engage with this content. This is also further complicated by the fact that scientific literacy, in terms of critical thinking and analysis, is difficult to measure in the public sphere. Scientific literacy in terms of knowledge is easier to measure, making a fact-based quiz a common, albeit inaccurate, way to assess scientific literacy and opinions on controversial issues.

The public does not have the same access to scientific literature as scientists do, nor the training or expertise to evaluate it. How can we encourage learners who encounter science news online to evaluate sources as active researchers, and how do we address changes in searching behaviors and available resources? Information acquired through social media may be more passive than active, with less likelihood that individuals will think critically or effectively analyze content. Social media platforms do, however, allow learners to participate in ongoing dialogues. This gives everyone the opportunity to add to conversations in the form of comments, tags, forwards, and shares. Learners can become producers online, where their opinions are published and may be easily linked to the original or related sources.

The solution to scientific literacy for nonscientists may be teaching them to seek and evaluate news through a metaliterate frame. Mackey and Jacobson (2011) describe an information-literate researcher as one who must "review this dynamic content critically as part of the evaluation process" (74).

Metaliteracy could help all learners participate in the online dissemination of scientific findings through metacognition and transfer. Learners can consume and translate research or scientific news to social media, YouTube videos, and blogs, becoming new authors of scientific content that they produce and share. This makes them participants in scientific communication but requires them first to critically reflect on what they have learned, where it has come from, and how they could add it to a collaborative environment or a global network (Mackey and Jacobson 2014).

THE EFFECTS OF POST-TRUTHS ON SCIENTIFIC LITERACY

It is widely known that we now live in a post-truth world where people readily accept information that aligns with their personal beliefs and appeals to their emotions as opposed to looking for more objective or factual information (Cooke 2017). Several compounding problems of the post-truth movement affect scientific literacy. For example, social media feeds are often curated by users who choose to follow and share content they already agree with from personal "filter bubbles" (Cooke 2017). This type of filter imparts a bias to the information received and distributed. In addition, content is not always read and fully digested before being shared. Some may choose to read only a headline from an article before sharing, posting, or retweeting because the headline may say enough to align with their personal beliefs. These approaches pose a threat to scientific literacy because they essentially ignore the *affective* domain of metaliteracy by avoiding any scientific data that opposes an opinion.

Bias has always been a barrier to effective scientific communication on controversial subjects. Students' background and environment largely shape their beliefs and the way they acquire and process knowledge. Logic and reasoning evolve, yet cognitive biases are still present. Adding to this problem, the post-truth era has risen out of counterclaims and spin and is at the forefront of public discourse. The ability of social and news media to perpetuate alternative facts means that bias becomes a more pervasive issue.

Post-truisms build upon these biases and must be addressed, as learners may not even be aware of such predispositions. The Implicit Associations Test (IAT), developed by researchers at Harvard's Project Implicit (https://implicit. harvard.edu/implicit/index.jsp), is a way to assess one's own hidden or unconscious biases. Researchers report that female respondents are sometimes surprised by their results. For example, both men and women indicate that they feel men are more associated with the sciences than women and that women are more associated with the liberal arts and family roles (Nosek, Banaji, and Greenwald 2002). Gender bias is just one example that illustrates the challenges of merging our social beliefs with facts and data.

Climate change is a prime example of an issue that has become controversial and polarized in the post-truth era. For example, scientific documents on climate change are perceived as less credible by readers than are scientific documents on noncontroversial topics (Bromme et al. 2015). Interestingly, opinion on climate change does not correlate with scientific literacy (defined by basic knowledge and math skills). Those with high scientific literacy have a more polarizing response to climate change—either being more accepting of climate change data or more strongly against it—likely a collective result of personal influences (Kahan et al. 2012). This further supports a presence of bias that masks scientific data and reasoning. Some have investigated how we might frame scientific research to help gain more public support despite this deep-rooted bias. Myers and colleagues (2016) investigated whether priming public participants with questions about general science would improve opinion of the climate science research of federal governments. It did not. Rather, for those with more conservative political views, asking participants about climate science research actually lowered their trust in science overall, biasing them against other scientific research.

Political partisanship is a bias that can strongly influence one's views, even in scientific matters. Consumers must be in the habit of evaluating the website, language, and political leanings of the source and triangulating the news with other sources (Cooke 2017). Nisbet and Markowitz (2014) analyzed the influence of political beliefs and science-related schema on the US public's support and level of federal funding for embryonic stem cell research from 2002–2010. They found that both Republicans and Independents were less likely than Democrats to favor embryonic stem cell research, and the difference was even greater when education was a factor. Republicans with a higher level of education tended to have more reservations about stem cell research than Republicans with less education. Their findings show that "it is the best educated among this group who are likely to be the most opposed to advances in biomedical research, the most receptive to the arguments made by political opponents to such research, and the most dismissive of those advocating on behalf of research" (11). The authors suggest that scientists can deter politically biased views of biomedical research by addressing ethical concerns in direct and indirect ways, such as partnering with organizations, leaders, and institutions which the public trusts and which share similar values and beliefs.

Political partisanship has become even more relevant since the 2016 US presidential election, when the spread of fake news about the candidates and related issues was reportedly a factor in the outcome of the election. A scientific study of Americans' exposure to fake news in the months surrounding the 2016 election was published in January 2018 (Guess, Nyhan, and Reifler, 2018). The authors found that approximately one in four Americans visited a fake news website between October 7 and November 14, 2016, and that the fake news was disseminated primarily through Facebook. Furthermore, readers of fake news failed to fact-check or take note of other articles specifically discrediting the misinformation they had just consumed.

FactCheck.org along with Snopes and PolitiFact are well-known, credible online sources dedicated to debunking partisan claims and inaccuracies. Sci-Check, part of FactCheck.org, was launched in January 2015 to focus specifically on identifying misleading scientific claims that are made by politicians to influence the public. In 2017, politicians' false or inaccurate statements about science-related topics permeated the news, including CO_2 emissions, air quality, insecticides, obesity, autism, and the opioid addiction crisis (Schipani, 2017). Post-truths in the form of fake news and personal and political biases affect our scientific literacy. We need to help consumers navigate this content, preparing them to understand context. We also need to help consumers ethically evaluate and share accurate scientific content by integrating the *affective* and *behavioral* domains of metaliteracy so that the consumer is an effective communicator, translator, and producer of information (Mackey and Jacobson 2014).

THE ROLE OF SCIENTISTS IN THE POST-TRUTH ERA

In response to post-truths and bias, public trust in scientists may also change. People may believe that scientists are following their own agenda to obtain governmental funding, to collaborate with medical, pharmaceutical, and new energy companies, and to hide public health risks. Recognizing these issues, scientists may wonder how they can obtain public trust and communicate without sounding elitist. Typical science publications, primarily in the form of peer-reviewed, subscription-based journal articles, are not accessible or appealing to the general public. To complicate matters, the rise of predatory publishers (Shen and Björk 2015), the increasing number of retractions (McCook 2016), and the exposure of fake peer reviews involving one of the largest academic publishers (Ferguson, Marcus, and Oransky 2014) could cause even seasoned experts to distrust the peer review and publication process. The traditional method of publishing is changing, as more articles and journals become open access, but formal scholarship must convey a different feeling from that of science news. Scientists and consumers may have different metaliterate responses to these research articles. In respect to the *cognitive*, *affective*, and *metacognitive* domains, scientists know that science is a process of mounting experimental evidence, which means that guidelines and recommendations can change with new experiments, a process that could result in confusion and contradictions for the public. Additionally, open participation in an online environment creates a new dynamic for scientific research, allowing for an open conversation for collaborative commenting and sharing. This contrasts deeply with the one-way reporting of traditional publications.

Scientists must now think about how to communicate research to a broader audience in a digital space, which affords scientists more opportunities to participate in conversations with the public.

As participants in a discipline that depends on evidence, scientists have begun to take on more roles in social media in response to an environment of alternative facts. In January 2017, new alternative social media accounts (alt-government) multiplied across social media platforms in response to concerns that federal government accounts could not control their own scientific content, especially on matters of climate change. They included alternative accounts for the National Park Service, NASA (National Aeronautics and Space Administration), the U.S. Forest Service, the Environmental Protection Agency, and the Agriculture and Health and Human Services Departments. These groups, such as Alt National Park Service and Alt NASA, are collective, yet anonymous. Though the alt-government science events began as a grassroots movement to disseminate procured scientific information to the public, the implications of going to these alternative places for trustworthy information may be further reaching. What is at stake when so-called normal publishing outlets turn to unconventional ways to get their message out? In another 2017 event, the Penn Library Data Refuge project by scientists and other professionals endeavored to combat post-truths and ensure open access to information. Librarians, along with faculty and scientists, led efforts to collect and preserve federal climate and environmental data that was at risk of being deleted from government websites as a sort of socially positive "hacking" event (Allen, Stewart, and Wright 2017).

Scientists have also investigated how to use social media to overcome bias and advance health and science initiatives. In a unique effort, scientists are using Facebook to identify ideal candidates to vaccinate to prevent disease outbreaks (Mones et al. 2018). Vaccinations have been a controversial issue due to a lack of scientific literacy and personal bias. Through computer modeling, certain individuals are classified as being central to their digital network and, thus, according to the researchers, a real-life network as well. Vaccinating these central individuals, or targeted vaccination, would protect against diseases such as influenza because these individuals come into contact with the greatest number of people (Mones et al. 2018).

While scientists have been using social media to combat post-truths and biases within the sciences, this effort needs to extend to a more collaborative conversation online if scientists are to influence the *affective* domain of metaliteracy and ask consumers to assess their own reactions. Social media can be a place for scientists to share opinions and articles as well as to engage with various scientific and public communities (Bik and Goldstein 2013). In a *Science Friday* interview, Sue Desmond-Hellmann (2017), CEO and scientist for the Bill & Melinda Gates Foundation, discusses the challenges for scientists communicating their results in a post-truth era:

> Science is under threat. . . . Post-truth being the Word of the Year [in 2016] meant that the public is now relying on emotion and personal belief more than scientific facts. And so what my call to action to scientists is if we aren't part of that dialogue—if we aren't part of shaping public perception and personal belief, then our science, frankly, won't matter.

To better engage with the public in a post-truth era, scientists need communication education and training. Science communication tools and courses are becoming more popular for scientists, encouraging them to connect with their communities through outreach and media. The European Science Communication Network, for example, created twelve teaching modules for scientific communication and training (Miller and Fahy 2009). These training modules include communicating with the public on controversial issues and communicating with media outlets. Modules like this serve as an important step in enhancing scientific communication skills of scientists, but they need updating in the wake of changes in social media.

Though scientists use Facebook and Twitter the most of all social media platforms, many choose to use only Twitter for their own scientific discourse or outreach (Collins, Shiffman, and Rock 2016). Often, scientists choose not to use Facebook as a platform to discuss science or to address controversial issues, even though they likely have more followers on Facebook than on other social media platforms (McClain 2017; Collins, Shiffman, and Rock 2016). This may be because they see Facebook more as a personal space than a professional one. McClain (2017) advocates for scientists to be "Nerds of Trust" on Facebook to engage with their personal communities. Metaliterate scientists can participate in social media conversations to teach and communicate science. Scientists can also use Facebook, as well as other types of social media, to counteract inaccurate scientific claims shared online by friends and families in their networks. The goal is to encourage *affective* change in the learners in their networks, who will need to address inherent bias when presented with scientific evidence. A scientist friend whom a learner sees as trustworthy could be better at promoting this change.

Indeed, scientists need to consider using diverse social media outlets that represent the different ways consumers obtain scientific news. A recent Pew Research Center survey found that most social media users have Facebook accounts, and 66 percent of users state that they learn news from Facebook (Gottfried and Shearer 2016). Another Pew Research Center survey reported that only 28 percent of adults aged eighteen to twenty-nine get news from Twitter, with Snapchat and LinkedIn being other popular ways to obtain news (Shearer and Gottfried 2017). The Pew Research Center also found that 67 percent of Americans get at least some of their news on social media—with 26 percent getting their news from two or more sites (Shearer and Gottfried

2017). More research that looks at social media use is under way, but it is difficult to compare changes due to the rapid nature of new tools coming onto the scene and changes in users' behaviors and preferences. Project Information Literacy (2018) has partnered with Northeastern University and Wellesley College to study how young adults from high schools and colleges consume and interact with news online. This research could help scientists and communicators better engage with students in the digital environment.

Social media communication is a translation skill that scientists need to improve scientific literacy within the field and among the broader population. Through social media, scientists can participate in conversations to promote issues important to scientific literacy. In this scenario, scientists act as translators of scientific information to a wider audience with less expertise but curious about the world. In metaliteracy, the role of the translator is to synthesize and adapt information for a different audience (Mackey and Jacobson 2014, 89–90). In this case, the content that scientists produce for sharing must incorporate an understanding of their audience, whether it be other scientists or the general public. A social media course for scientists at the California Institute of Technology is an example of academia's efforts to bring together interdisciplinary faculty to prepare a new generation of scientists for professional and social communication online (Wilkins, Davis, and Mojarad 2017). This type of course can help scientists engage with a variety of audiences, paying attention to their style, clarity, and accuracy. Scientific conferences are now dedicating discussions and presentations to social media use (Bert 2014). These courses and training modules for scientists would benefit from building upon metaliteracy learning goals, such as sharing information, collaborating in a variety of online environments, and connecting research strategies with their scientific findings (Mackey and Jacobson 2014). It is important for this training also to encourage scientists to make their research strategies clear to a more public audience as part of their social communication.

In addition to social media training and communication education, scientists have been using citizen science to bring scientists and the public together on collaborative projects. Citizen science, a relatively new trend, encourages the general public to participate in scientific research, usually related to an issue of societal concern, such as health, technology, or the environment. Citizen science can have the symbiotic impact of improving scientific literacy in a community as well as adding to scientific knowledge through collaboration and participation. Different types of citizen science projects can have varying objectives, collaborations, and outcomes. Not all citizen science projects are designed to result in scientific learning objectives for the citizens involved; some projects focus more on data collection and analysis for scientists than on metacognition for the participants (Bonney et al. 2016). However, with careful design, citizen science can engage a local community or a class in a project and encourage participants to reflect on scientific responsibility and scientific process (Bonney et al. 2016; Haywood and Besley 2013). Citizen science may be most effective when it combines student, teacher, and scientist in a collaborative project to model, practice, and mentor the scientific process. Here, the processes of metacognition and self-regulation are just as important as training and data collection (Hiller and Kitsantas 2015). Excitement and enthusiasm for authentic science happens, too, which could potentially encourage learners to take a more active and reflective role in science even when the project has ended.

Citizen science projects combine several components of metaliteracy in the development of metaliterate learner characteristics. Citizen science encourages participants to be active, collaborative members of a scientific initiative. They become researchers and producers of new knowledge in the scientific community who must also communicate their findings to their group, which includes scientists. Citizen science endeavors can be further encouraged through the sharing of data and analysis in online environments and communities. For example, an ongoing citizen science project, Coastal Observation and Seabird Survey Team, uses volunteers to document the seabird population. In a recent study, the volunteers of the project reported personal outcomes of their participation, such as greater awareness of and appreciation for nature, learning, community, and contribution to science (Haywood 2016). This practice could also engage other literacies, including information literacy and visual literacy, to enhance metaliteracy. Citizen science projects might be further bolstered by an online presence, such as through Facebook groups and Snapchat, to provide a venue for additional discussion, promotion and motivation, and sharing related resources. Participants can become teachers and translators of both the results and the overall implications of scientific findings to their friends and families, expanding the impact of the research to combat post-truths beyond personal *affective* responses. In this way, scientists and citizen science participants could engage with their communities both physically and digitally to challenge preconceptions and post-truths, especially on controversial issues such as climate change.

TEACHING LEARNERS TO PARTICIPATE IN SCIENCE THROUGH METALITERACY

Teachers and facilitators must empower learners with the critical thinking abilities they need to make informed and sophisticated decisions. It is crucial to help students develop the metacognitive processes necessary to discern fact from fiction, based on evidence and reasoning. This is important to all disciplines, but it is especially important that our science students, as scientists in training, understand how this affects their own professional development as well as their scientific communication. One way to accomplish this is to invite students to join the discussion and engage them in inquiry, discourse, and critical reflection.

Students are continuously immersed in the digital environment. They have trouble distinguishing where the information they encounter is coming from, with "the Internet" being a popular response versus a more specific format, such as an online newspaper article, a personal blog, a conference paper, a politicized Facebook post, and so forth. Kalker (2016) found that students may know how to be consumers of information, but this does not mean they understand the process that goes into this content, let alone how to create it. More important, students do not recognize whether or not the information is trustworthy, making it impossible for students to evaluate it. So while they may be participating in science by way of sharing or discussing ideas on social media, they are not necessarily comprehending or learning on a more *meta-cognitive* level.

EVALUATING SCIENTIFIC INFORMATION

Critique and reasoning, important elements when examining scientific claims, are even more important in a post-truth era. We must consider what *evidence* means to a nonscientist. In science, evidence simply cannot be information in the sense of what people find and read. To scientists, evidence arises from data, calculations, analysis, controls, and well-designed experiments. Scientific evidence produces far-reaching outcomes in health and medicine, the environment, and engineering, including new experiments, theories, standards, and policies. We must critically evaluate information more now than ever before. Questioning is not only acceptable; it is necessary.

Learning to argue, as a skill, is lacking in science education, where science is often presented as a series of accepted theories and facts, or successes. Less often, students encounter failed experiments or hypotheses, thus depriving them of opportunities to develop these argumentation skills. Encouraging students to engage in argumentation or collaborative discourse can enhance their understanding and scientific reasoning (Osborne 2010). Science faculty identified a gap in science students' ability to evaluate scholarly material, especially in the digital environment (Perry 2017). Faculty reported a concern that students believe everything they read. In the same survey, the professors identified undergraduates' inability to establish a level of skepticism as an important issue to tackle. Faculty postulated that students did not feel qualified to question research or researchers (Perry 2017). By broadening students' knowledge about scientific discourse, they may become better able to evaluate scientific information from their position as laypersons (Bromme et al. 2015). By engaging in argumentation and scientific discourse, a metaliterate learner demonstrates curiosity and thinks critically in context, adapting new information. The transfer of critical thinking to new learning is a goal of metaliteracy (Jacobson et al. 2018).

Emphasizing the *metacognitive* domain of metaliteracy is a solution to the post-truth issues facing scientific literacy. Cooke (2017) states:

> Becoming metaliterate in a way that is especially effective in the online domain takes practice and diligence, and it begins with learning in the classroom and in libraries. The end goal is to produce proactive critical thinkers, researchers, and information consumers who can sidestep false information and its deleterious effects. (219)

To support metacognitive development, we can encourage students to reflect on how they use social media for scientific news. For example, they can analyze hashtags to reflect on social media conversations and understand the collective discussion in an online space (Witek and Grettano 2016). Reflection is an essential part of metacognition in writing and research. The Council of Writing Program Administrators' (WPA) framework connects college writing and creativity, arguing that we should encourage students to reflect on the consequences of their creative content (WPA, NCTE, and NWP 2011). This is also true in a digital environment. Students should be encouraged to reflect on the effects of their creation and participation online. They must learn to critically analyze content before sharing something that may be inaccurate. To promote understanding, they should be encouraged to translate and create new content rather than simply retweet. In this way, they contribute to the online conversation as active and ethical participants.

Active-learning activities informed by metaliteracy can combat post-truths and pseudoscience. Some strategies include these:

- Engage students in a fake news lesson in a writing-intensive course.
- Review an online news media article or other secondary source and trace the primary research.
- Critically evaluate vetted sites, such as *Retraction Watch* (a blog), SciCheck, and Snopes.com, and discuss potential reasons for any misinformation (e.g., bias, conflict of interest, intent to mislead, poorly designed study).
- Involve students in an authentic peer review project for which student reviewers post comments and revisions to a live feed or blog.

To enhance scientific literacy of the scientific process, learners should also become creators. Here, learners practice communicating and evaluating scientific evidence to produce new content. Students can practice writing news articles from recent scientific research, modeling strategies that nonscientist journalists may use to search for content, find credible sources, fact-check, and write for the appropriate context (Polman et al. 2014). This supports the metaliteracy learning goal to share information and collaborate in different environments, adapting information across formats (Jacobson et al. 2018). Through data preservation events, students can also identify and archive existing data by reproducing it in new digital formats to increase discoverability for future audiences. Learners can become collaborative producers and communicators of scientific research in citizen science projects. We can also ask learners to create communities of discussion on social media to teach and share scientific findings. Another way to create could be through digital storytelling, whereby a metaliterate learner would combine narrative and scientific evidence to combat a controversial issue or post-truth (Mackey and Jacobson 2014).

We can also engage learners outside the traditional classroom through MOOCs. In the framework of metaliteracy, MOOCs promote self-regulation, creation, and reflection to enhance learning (O'Brien et al. 2017). Working in small groups also promotes more active learning online. These MOOCs could also be a solution to teaching scientific literacy in terms of process, by asking users to find, read, discuss, and reflect on scientific research in an online discussion. This would also allow learners to share research from several related areas and publishing outlets so that they can reflect on how one publication fits into the larger scheme of scientific scholarship and science as a process, a key theme of metacognition in scientific literacy (table 4.1). By creating a MOOC where users collaborate to teach one another about a scientific concept, learners would become producers as they contribute to a collaborative, digital space. This nontraditional classroom would serve as a space where metaliteracy learning objectives (Mackey and Jacobson 2014) could flourish to support scientific literacy.

As they create and produce, consumers need to self-direct their own learning and see themselves as both learners and teachers. The production pieces could be text, visuals, and/or audio, allowing the creativity of consumers to translate scientific research. The consumer could also undergo metacognitive reflection to understand how his or her own learning has changed. In a post-truth world, collaborative projects or MOOCs that specifically focus on combatting common scientific misconception could also be a way to encourage *affective* change through asking learners to collaboratively investigate a relevant or controversial issue.

CONCLUSION AND FUTURE IMPLICATIONS

Scientific literacy draws on an understanding of science as it relates to the real world. Science informs decisions about concerns that affect our daily lives, such as climate change, alternative fuels, organic foods, pesticides, and vaccinations. Science deals with problems that need to be solved. Yet, it has been difficult to define what a scientifically literate person should know or do, a process made even more difficult by the digital environment and a rise in the prevalence of post-truths. Metaliteracy and metacognitive approaches to education by both scientists and consumers provide a holistic approach to improving scientific information literacy in a post-truth world.

There has been an increasing movement among scientists toward sharing and translating their research to online environments. Social media platforms present an opportunity to enhance learning by making connections between scientific research and the real world. However, learners must approach information with a critical lens, particularly in our post-truth era. Learners must also be encouraged to create and produce scientific content on their own and with scientists, furthering collaboration and understanding. These objectives particularly focus on the *affective* and *metacognitive* domains of metaliteracy. We must encourage scientists and consumers to reflect on scientific evidence and on how this reflection is key to science as an iterative process and therefore scientific literacy.

Metaliteracy has shared goals with scientific literacy and literacies in other disciplines and thus needs to expand beyond librarians and libraries. Recently, the coverage of metacognition in science education literature has grown significantly. It is crucial that faculty design teaching strategies to help develop students' metacognitive abilities. However, a gap in science education must be filled in order to effectively bring about a pedagogical shift (Zohar and Barzilai 2013). As lifelong learners, faculty must be metaliterate as well and reflect on their own teaching and participatory learning. They can update pedagogical approaches to incorporate the use of digital and interactive technologies to enhance critical thinking and collaborative learning. Teachers can reimagine a course to increase scientific literacy either in the classroom, in the library, in an open environment, or in the real world, with the goals of metaliteracy in mind.

As colleges and universities revise their core curricula, student learning outcomes, and disciplinary programs designed to meet accreditation requirements, metaliteracy can be emphasized in liberal studies courses, such as critical thinking and writing, or in digital citizenship, as a multidisciplinary approach. When linked with scientific literacy, metaliteracy can be infused in a course in scientific communication or writing to increase engagement and strengthen learning through reflection across various science and other STEM disciplines. Students will ultimately benefit from any course that incorporates structured content aligned with metaliteracy goals and learning objectives to support scientific literacy.

REFERENCES

ACRL (Association of College & Research Libraries). 2018. "ACRL/STS Information Literacy Framework Task Force." American Library Association. Accessed August 23. www.ala.org/acrl/sts/acr-ststfil.

Allen, Laurie, Claire Stewart, and Stephanie Wright. 2017. "Strategic Open Data Preservation: Roles and Opportunities for Broader Engagement by Librarians and the Public." *College and Research Libraries News* 78 (9): 482.

Bert, Alison. 2014. "How to Use Social Media for Science." *Elsevier Connect*, February 25. www.elsevier.com/connect/how-to-use-social-media-for-science.

Bik, Holly M., and Miriam C. Goldstein. 2013. "An Introduction to Social Media for Scientists." *PLOS Biology* 11 (4): e1001535. doi:10.1371/journal.pbi0.1001535.

Bonney, Rick, Tina B. Phillips, Heidi L. Ballard, and Jody W. Enck. 2016. "Can Citizen Science Enhance Public Understanding of Science?" *Public Understanding of Science* 25 (1): 2–16.

Bromme, Rainer, Lisa Scharrer, Marc Stadtler, Johanna Hömberg, and Ronja Torspecken. 2015. "Is It Believable When It's Scientific? How Scientific Discourse Style Influences Laypeople's Resolution of Conflicts." *Journal of Research in Science Teaching* 52 (1): 36–57. doi:10.1002/tea.21172.

Bucchi, Massimiano, and Barbara Saracino. 2016. "Visual Science Literacy: Images and Public Understanding of Science in the Digital Age." *Science Communication* 38 (6): 812–819. doi:10.1177/1075547016677833.

Collins, Kimberley, David Shiffman, and Jenny Rock. 2016. "How Are Scientists Using Social Media in the Workplace?" *PloS One* 11 (10): e0162680.

Cooke, Nicole A. 2017. "Posttruth, Truthiness, and Alternative Facts: Information Behavior and Critical Information Consumption for a New Age." *The Library Quarterly* 87 (3): 211–21.

Desmond-Hellmann, Sue. 2017. "Defending Science in a 'Post-Truth' Era." Interview with Ira Flatow; produced by Christopher Intagliata. *Science Friday*, November 3. www.sciencefriday.com/segments/defending-science-in-a-post-truth-era.

Feinstein, Noah Weeth. 2015. "Education, Communication, and Science in the Public Sphere." *Journal of Research in Science Teaching* 52 (2): 145–63. doi:10.1002/tea.21192.

Ferguson, Cat, Adam Marcus, and Ivan Oransky. 2014. "The Peer-Review Scam." *Nature* 515 (7528): 480.

Gottfried, Jeffrey, and Elisa Shearer. 2016. "News Use across Social Media Platforms 2016." Pew Research Center, Journalism and Media: Analysis, May 26. www .journalism.org/2016/05/26/news-use-across-social-media-platforms-2016.

Guess, Andrew, Brendan Nyhan, and Jason Reifler. 2018. "Selective Exposure to Misinformation: Evidence from the Consumption of Fake News during the 2016 US Presidential Campaign." Unpublished manuscript. www.dartmouth .edu/~nyhan/fake-news-2016.pdf.

Haywood, Benjamin K. 2016. "Beyond Data Points and Research Contributions: The Personal Meaning and Value Associated with Public Participation in Scientific Research." *International Journal of Science Education, Part B* 6 (3): 239–62.

Haywood, Benjamin K., and John C. Besley. 2013. "Education, Outreach, and Inclusive Engagement: Towards Integrated Indicators of Successful Program Outcomes in Participatory Science." *Public Understanding of Science* 23 (1): 92–106. doi:10.1177/0963662513494560.

Hiller, Suzanne E., and Anastasia Kitsantas. 2015. "Fostering Student Metacognition and Motivation in STEM through Citizen Science Programs." In *Metacognition: Fundaments, Applications, and Trends*, edited by Alejandro Peña-Ayala, 193–221. Cham, Switzerland: Springer.

Jacobson, Trudi, Tom Mackey, Kelsey O'Brien, Michele Forte, and Emer O'Keeffe. 2018. "Goals and Learning Objectives." Metaliteracy.org. Accessed August 22. https://metaliteracy.org/learning-objectives.

Kahan, Dan M., Ellen Peters, Maggie Wittlin, Paul Slovic, Lisa Larrimore Ouellette, Donald Braman, and Gregory Mandel. 2012. "The Polarizing Impact of Science Literacy and Numeracy on Perceived Climate Change Risks." *Nature Climate Change* 2 (10): 732–735.

Kalker, Felicia. 2016. "Digital/Critical: Reimagining Digital Information Literacy Assignments around the ACRL Framework." In *The Future Scholar: Researching and Teaching the Frameworks for Writing and Information Literacy*, edited by Randall McClure and James P. Purdy, 205–22. Medford, NJ: Information Today.

Klucevsek, Kristin. 2017. "The Intersection of Information and Science Literacy." *Communications in Information Literacy* 11 (2): 354–65.

Lewenstein, Bruce V. 2015. "Identifying What Matters: Science Education, Science Communication, and Democracy." *Journal of Research in Science Teaching* 52 (2): 253–62. doi:10.1002/tea.21201.

Mackey, Thomas P., and Trudi E. Jacobson. 2011. "Reframing Information Literacy as a Metaliteracy." *College and Research Libraries* 72 (1): 62–78.

———. 2014. *Metaliteracy: Reinventing Information Literacy to Empower Learners*. Chicago: ALA Neal-Schuman.

McClain, Craig R. 2017. "Practices and Promises of Facebook for Science Outreach: Becoming a 'Nerd of Trust.'" *PLoS Biology* 15 (6): e2002020.

McCook, Allison. 2016. "Retractions Rise to Nearly 700 in Fiscal Year 2015." *Retraction Watch* (blog), March 24. https://retractionwatch.com/2016/03/24/ retractions-rise-to-nearly-700-in-fiscal-year-2015-and-psst-this-is-our -3000th-post.

Miller, Steve, and Declan Fahy. 2009. "Can Science Communication Workshops Train Scientists for Reflexive Public Engagement? The ESConet Experience." *Science Communication* 31 (1): 116–26. doi:10.1177/1075547009339048.

Mones, Enys, Arkadiusz Stopczynski, Nathaniel Hupert, and Sune Lehmann. 2018. "Optimizing Targeted Vaccination across Cyber-physical Networks: An Empirically Based Mathematical Simulation Study." *Journal of the Royal Society Interface* 15 (138): e20170783.

Myers, Teresa A., John Kotcher, Neil Stenhouse, Ashley A. Anderson, Edward Maibach, Lindsey Beall, and Anthony Leiserowitz. 2016. "Predictors of Trust in the General Science and Climate Science Research of US Federal Agencies." *Public Understanding of Science* 26 (7): 843–60. doi:10.1177/0963662516636040.

National Research Council. 1996. *National Science Education Standards*. Washington, DC: The National Academies Press. http://doi.org/10.172264962.

Nisbet, Matthew, and Ezra M. Markowitz. 2014. "Understanding Public Opinion in Debates over Biomedical Research: Looking Beyond Political Partisanship to Focus on Beliefs about Science and Society." *PloS One* 9 (2): e88473.

Norris, Stephen P, and Linda M. Phillips. 2003. "How Literacy in Its Fundamental Sense Is Central to Scientific Literacy." *Science Education* 87 (2): 224–40.

Nosek, Brian A., Mahzarin R. Banaji, and Anthony G. Greenwald. 2002. "Harvesting Implicit Group Attitudes and Beliefs from a Demonstration Web Site." *Group Dynamics: Theory, Research, and Practice* 6 (1): 101.

O'Brien, Kelsey L., Michele Forte, Thomas P. Mackey, and Trudi E. Jacobson. 2017. "Metaliteracy as Pedagogical Framework for Learner-Centered Design in Three MOOC Platforms: Connectivist, Coursera and Canvas." *Open Praxis* 9 (3): 267–86.

OECD (Organisation for Economic Co-operation and Development). 2013. "PISA 2015 Draft Science Framework." www.oecd.org/pisa/pisaproducts/Draft%20 PISA%202015%20Science%20Framework%20.pdf.

Osborne, Jonathan. 2010. "Arguing to Learn in Science: The Role of Collaborative, Critical Discourse." *Science* 328 (5977): 463–66.

Perry, Heather Brodie. 2017. "Information Literacy in the Sciences: Faculty Perception of Undergraduate Student Skill." *College and Research Libraries* 7 (7): 964–77.

Polman, Joseph L., Alan Newman, Ellen Wendy Saul, and Cathy Farrar. 2014. "Adapting Practices of Science Journalism to Foster Science Literacy." *Science Education* 98 (5): 766–91. doi:10.1002/sce.21114.

Porter, Jason A., Kevin C. Wolbach, Catherine B. Purzycki, Leslie A. Bowman, Eva Agbada, and Alison M. Mostrom. 2010. "Integration of Information and Scientific Literacy: Promoting Literacy in Undergraduates." *CBE-Life Sciences Education* 9 (4): 536–42.

Project Information Literacy. 2018. "How Do Students Consume News?" Last modified August 16. www.projectinfolit.org/news_study.html.

Project 2061. 2006. *Benchmarks for Science Literacy*. New York: American Association for the Advancement of Science.

Roberts, Douglas, A. 2007. "Scientific Literacy/Science Literacy." In *Handbook of Research on Science Education*, edited by Sandra K. Abell and Norman G. Lederman, 729–80. Mahwah, NJ: Lawrence Erlbaum.

Roberts, Douglas A., and Rodger W. Bybee. 2014. "Scientific Literacy, Science Literacy, and Science Education." In *Handbook of Research on Science Education*, vol. II, edited by Norman G. Lederman and Sandra K. Abell, 545–558. New York: Routledge.

Schipani, Vanessa. 2017. "FactChecking Science Claims in 2017." *The Wire*, December 21. www.factcheck.org/2017/12/factchecking-science-claims-2017.

Shearer, Elisa, and Jeffrey Gottfried. 2017. "News Use across Social Media Platforms 2017." Pew Research Center, Journalism and Media: Analysis, September 7.

Shen, Cenyu, and Bo-Christer Björk. 2015. "'Predatory' Open Access: A Longitudinal Study of Article Volumes and Market Characteristics." *BMC Medicine* 13 (1): 230.

Turiman, Punia, Jizah Omar, Adzliana Mohd Daud, and Kamisah Osman. 2012. "Fostering the 21st Century Skills through Scientific Literacy and Science Process Skills." *Procedia—Social and Behavioral Sciences* 59: 110–16. doi:http://dx.doi.org/10.1016/j.sbspr0.2012.09.253.

Wilkins, Olivia, Mark E. Davis, and Sarah Mojarad. 2017. "Tweet, for Science! A Social Media Course for Scientists at Caltech Tackling Inreach and Outreach Online." Presented at the 253rd American Chemical Society National Meeting and Exposition, San Francisco, CA, April 2–6.

Witek, Donna, and Teresa Grettano. 2016. "Revising for Metaliteracy: Flexible Course Design to Support Social Media Pedagogy." In *Metaliteracy in Practice*, edited by Trudi E. Jacobson and Thomas P. Mackey, 1–22. Chicago: ALA Neal-Schuman.

WPA (Council of Writing Program Administrators), NCTE (National Council of Teachers of English), and NWP (National Writing Project). 2011. *Framework for Success in Postsecondary Writing*. WPACouncil.org. http://wpacouncil.org/files/framework-for-success-postsecondary-writing.pdf.

Yore, Larry, Gay L. Bisanz, and Brian M. Hand. 2003. "Examining the Literacy Component of Science Literacy: 25 Years of Language Arts and Science Research." *International Journal of Science Education* 25 (6): 689–725.

Yore, Larry D., David Pimm, and Hsiao-Lin Tuan. 2007. "The Literacy Component of Mathematical and Scientific Literacy." *International Journal of Science and Mathematics Education* 5 (4): 559–89. doi:10.1007/s10763-007-9089-4.

Zohar, Anat, and Sarit Barzilai. 2013. "A Review of Research on Metacognition in Science Education: Current and Future Directions." *Studies in Science Education* 49 (2): 121–69.

THOMAS PALMER

5

When Stories and Pictures Lie Together—and You Do Not Even Know It

Walking down the aisles of our neighborhood supermarket, we cast our eyes from one label to the next, trusting that the food we buy and ingest in the comfort of our homes will be what the packaging promises. This relationship between consumer and retailer hinges on trust—and woe to the company that falsely sells us a flawed product under the guise of a safe, nutritious meal. Lives are truly in the balance. Much in the same way, the consumers of news can be said to wager their well-being on the information they cull from sources in the media that inform their worldview. Our faithful follower of the news trusts that the text and imagery that make up a story present a reflection of reality—not a false scenario manufactured out of misrepresented pieces of information.

Presented accurately, text and image affirm each other, and together they convey, at minimum, the essence of what a journalist observed. Yet as this chapter shows, images and text can be linked in misleading ways. This can arise out of innocent error, but it can also emerge from devious intentions. As the Internet has expanded and become such a vital part of our lives by encompassing the transmission of all of our data, the chances for error have grown in tandem and so, too, have the opportunities for deception on a massive scale.

A practice exists in online news and social media publishing whereby the text and photo together may create a false story narrative. This phenomenon is called the *intersemiotic contextual misrepresentation of photojournalism* (Palmer 2015g). The range of offenders includes fake news sites, online-only news organizations, and even some traditional print-based newsrooms that now publish online. The consequences are far-reaching. Several visual and textual examples in this chapter will reveal how

- legitimate photojournalism is being misappropriated by fake news site operators to promote social and political propaganda;
- citizens' identities and photographed activities may be misrepresented to support false narratives in online stories and social media;
- the mere inclusion of a picture with a statement can "inflate truthiness"—even when the contextual premise is false;
- US foreign policy decisions may be adversely influenced by deceptive actors;
- citizens without a metaliteracy learning foundation are susceptible to spreading fake news through social media; and
- metaliterate learners can identify and take action to counter malicious social media campaigns that are based on such deviancy.

As a media critic and educator, the author of this chapter created the *Picture Prosecutor* blog to target news outlets' text–image malpractices through "case" analyses (Palmer, 2015h). Some of these exposures have caused news organizations to correct the misuse (Palmer, 2015b). This blog is an effective resource for University at Albany journalism students who use it for related assignments to apply metaliterate learning. This blog also informs the illustrative examples provided in this chapter.

DEMONSTRATING CONTEXTUAL MISREPRESENTATION IN A JOURNALISTIC FRAMEWORK

How One News Aggregator Created a False Narrative

Let us examine the first image in this chapter (figure 5.1). The loving and relieved reunion between US presidential candidate Mitt Romney and wife, Ann, after her frightening flight experience, never happened. The picture is real. The screaming words in the sensational headline are correct. But the event that these words and picture convey together did not occur; the Drudge Report's framing of the headline around a month-old Associated Press photo suggests this, though, through the ways readers negotiate semantic relationships with

FIGURE 5.1
False Narrative Conveyed by Text and Image

text and image (see figure 5.1). Presidential candidate Romney was actually campaigning in Nevada when his wife's plane landed at Denver International Airport on September 21, 2012. News outlets did not photograph Ann Romney disembarking the aircraft (Stokols 2012). The deliberate juxtaposition of the headline and photo on the Drudge Report (2012) website delivered a false narrative to readers. This is how text and pictures lie together. The semantic cues of text and image ease the gullible reader into a cognitive snare—completely unaware. The author has termed this broadly as intersemiotic contextual misrepresentation. Its relevance in social semiotic analysis is examined later in this chapter.

Inappropriate imaging manipulations in photojournalism through the use of Adobe Photoshop (as self-contained modes of deception) have triggered intense ethics and policy reactions in journalism, but contextual misrepresentation has persisted off the radar of our collective understanding. According to David Sutherland, associate professor of the S. I. Newhouse School of Public Communications, "This misuse affects the credibility of pictures just as surely as changing content with Photoshop" (e-mail to author, January 7, 2018). Metaliterate learners develop an awareness that the meaning of a picture may be significantly altered by the influence of adjacent text—typically captions.

Life with the "X Factor"—Before Contextual Misrepresentation

The combined impact of photographic imagery put together with text was well-known long before the emergence of online sites. Wilson Hicks (1952), executive editor of *Life* magazine, explained it in *Words and Pictures: An Introduction to Photojournalism*. *Life*'s staff had pioneered the "photographic essay," noted first in the fledgling magazine's index in 1937. Text-based story narratives were not solely the "vital means of communication," proclaimed *Life* founder Henry Luce, "but what is vital is the photographic essay" (Elson and Prendergast 1968). The effectiveness of *Life*'s storytelling, including picture magazines inspired by it, was based on the photograph's ability to deliver principal narrative details to readers. However, the connotative nature of photography partnered with the denotative sharpening of text expands the power of this bimodal communication form for readers.

In his book, Hicks (1952) describes this relationship of carefully integrated photographs with text for inducing a cognitive effect he termed the "X factor" (6–7). He makes three points about this text–image fusion becoming "greater than the sum of its parts":

- "This phenomenon is caused by the addition of an 'X factor' to the joint impression made on the reader's mind by the mediums [picture and words] acting in concert—the X factor being the reader's own contribution to the communicative chemistry" (6).
- "Appealed to through eye and ear, his emotional or intellectual reaction doubly stimulated, the reader supplies material from memory and imagination to round out and enrich what is being conveyed to him" (6).
- "Produced by a basic unit of one picture with words, this imaginative 'plus' is multiplied, in a picture story, far beyond the arithmetical limits of the number of photographs and words actually involved" (7).

In the context of news publishing, the X factor is a presemiotic, cognitive-processing description that must be fully researched today, given how fake news site operators have weaponized its effects to spread disinformation. The disciplines related to this study include, but are not limited to, social semiotics, sociolinguistics, cognitive psychology, neurology, and metaliteracy. Social semiotics provides analyses for understanding the meanings formed by a combination of modal content elements, specifically image and text in this chapter. Sociolinguistics encompasses the intermixing of cultures with systems of text–image relations. These systems include logico-semantic relations and the relative status of text and image (Martinec and Salway 2005). Findings in cognitive psychology studies in recent decades provide insights about human behavior through multimodal sensory input and processing. Findings in neurology address differences in perceptual processing between an image, as a nondiscursive mode, and text, as a discursive mode; pictures, as visual forms, do not present their details successively like text but simultaneously, in milliseconds, during a single act of viewing (Langer 1942, 75; Trafton 2014). Metaliterate learning promotes not only the understanding of images in publishing contexts but also the responsible creating or gathering of images for private communication and social media.

Now for a reexamination of the first image (figure 5.1) through Hicks's X factor (see figure 5.2): The image on the Drudge Report website was taken by Charles Dharapak, an Associated Press photographer, during a Romney campaign event in Jacksonville, Florida, on September 21, 2012. According to the original photo caption, Romney embraced his wife before boarding a charter plane (Dharapak 2012).

Only readers who digest the full story will discover that Romney was a couple of states away during the incident and subsequent landing of the aircraft at Denver International Airport. The Romney airfield reunion is not an isolated example of these phenomena. What Hicks (1952) does not address in *Words and Pictures* is contextual misuse—the antithesis of the X factor. At the height of Hicks's career, such misuse was probably unimaginable to

WORDS: "Campaign scare: Ann Romney plane makes emergency landing."

PICTURE: The photograph showed the couple embracing with concerned gestures.

= X FACTOR (Stimulated reader adds imaginative "plus" to round out and enrich). The "joint impression" conveyed that candidate Romney is reunited with his wife after a dangerous event. Readers, recalling memories of their own travel experiences and possibly other scenarios, feel an emotional response.

FIGURE 5.2
Wilson Hicks's X Factor Construct

editors who sought accurate story portrayal through effective text–image relationships.

Furthermore, the decades-old protocol of copyediting and picture editing from the print era is essentially absent in many online publishing models. A copydesk chief in a twentieth-century newsroom, for instance, would strike down such nonsense of selecting a picture that is not relevant to the story. But today's typical online staff bears only a slight resemblance to the layers of thoughtful editing that typified newspapers and magazines in recent decades. These once vital layers were an essential part of the publishing process but have since retired, been ignored, or even laid off and have been replaced by digital-first publishing expediency. Instead, online producers who lack an education in journalistic principles or traditional newsroom mentoring may be the new meaning makers. Moreover, this workforce is joined by an increasing wave of citizen journalists and social media users who create and publish multimodal content.

As a result, the keys to meaning making with text, image, and other online modes are available for all, and now everyone participates as soon as a mobile device is removed from its box and set up—no license required and no traditional editorial filters available. The potential for reckless publishing, leading to a crash in credibility, arrives with no insurance or editorial processes for protecting an unsuspecting public from contextual misrepresentation.

HOW METALITERACY CAN EMPOWER LEARNERS TO DETECT AND COUNTER THE CONTEXTUAL MISREPRESENTATION OF PHOTOJOURNALISM

Metaliteracy empowers news consumers with a framework to discern the credibility of news stories and the websites that publish them. Despite gaps in journalism research that would provide a more comprehensive understanding of multimodal cognition, metaliteracy learning makes possible the skills of detection, assessment, and critical thinking necessary to react to narrative deceptions. Specifically, this section examines in detail how metaliteracy learning corresponds to metaliteracy domains (Mackey and Jacobson 2014, 85–86) with the modalities of text and picture in online news story dissemination.

Through the behavioral domain, metaliterate learners engage in deconstruction of the modal relationships that form the whole of integrated meaning. They should be able to detect or directly identify the conditions for contextual misrepresentation. This is based on a wide range of techniques explained in the *Picture Prosecutor* blog and through additional study of the metaliteracy literature. Detection originates at observational and engagement levels.

Jake ?

At the observational level, metaliteracy goal 1, and its related learning objectives, calls for metaliterate learners to "actively evaluate content" (Jacobson et al. 2018). To ensure success at the observational level, the reader needs to be sufficiently literate in world and US history and have knowledge of current events concerning subject matter within a picture. This includes, but is not limited to, global geopolitics, economics, gender and race studies, psychology, advertising, the arts, religion, science and technology, entertainment, sports, and communications. Following the initial impression of a picture, triggered by visual dominance processing, the learner negotiates its meaning through exposure to other modes. For example, a learner encountering a picture may react to it and then begin to examine how the story narrative is interwoven with the picture or expanded beyond the scope of detail contained in the picture. Next, the learner deconstructs the modes, in concert, that have formed the meaning of the story narrative by examining the following:

1. The relationship of the picture and text:

   a. Does the picture contain any details that contradict the full textual narrative? If so, this is a red flag (raises a credibility alarm).

   b. Does the story or caption text refer to details that are not included in the picture? This is a yellow flag (requires a cautionary stance) because it is a common writing technique for directing a reader's attention from the picture to the story text.

   c. Given that photographs, by nature, represent exact times, places, and circumstances, does the integration of the story narrative sync with all aspects depicted by the image? This is a yellow flag—with exceptions including clearly marked archive pictures or authenticated handout or reference images.

   d. Regarding image reproduction characteristics, does the picture reveal physical properties to suggest a time of origin that is out of sync with the story, or does the quality of the picture call its origins into question? Any such problem is a yellow flag. For instance, a black-and-white or color photo showing the silver halide granularity of film would not denote a breaking news event in 2018. A low-resolution, low-contrast image accompanying a news story may indicate that it was created and cropped from a personal computer screen shot of a YouTube video. A careful study of an image's characteristics may reveal additional inconsistencies.

   e. Do a caption and a credit accompany the photograph in close proximity, or are these absent or placed at the end of the story? It is a red flag when the caption is absent or placed at the end of a story. Metaliteracy goal 2 calls for learners, as content creators, to "identify and follow the specific intellectual property attribution expectations in the setting in which you are working" (Jacobson et al. 2018). By extension, learners may critically observe how these combinations of modes are edited by others.

    f. In the absence of a caption, is the headline acting as a default caption to provide a meaning for the picture? This is a red flag.

2. Structure and content of the news story text in a semantic relationship with photojournalism (requires some familiarity with journalistic story-writing styles such as those common to the *New York Times*, *Wall Street Journal*, and Associated Press):

    a. Does the story have a byline with the name of the reporter who wrote the story? If not, this is a red flag. Authorship is a source of pride in journalism.

    b. Does the byline include a link to the reporter's biography or contact information? If not, this is a red flag. Reporters seek contact with the public for story tips, feedback, and ideas.

    c. Does the story lead use active (instead of passive) tense? Passive tense is a yellow flag (though, stylistically, it is effective in certain uses).

    d. Are the story lead and its supporting paragraphs filled with adverbs such as "very" or other superlatives for injecting drama? Such embellishments are a red flag. Journalists avoid "very." Sensational writing is absent from credible news sources.

    e. Does attribution to an official or a key person referenced in the story occur within the first three paragraphs of the story? If not, it earns a yellow flag. Feature news stories exhibit more stylistic techniques, but be wary of attributions buried paragraphs deep. One's initial attraction to a story's content may lead to confirmation bias, long before the source is identified and examined by the reader for veracity.

    f. Do claims in the story list the sources? No sources is a red flag.

    g. Do anonymous sources establish the premise of the story? If so, this is a yellow flag because the sources are speaking on the condition of anonymity; it may end up as a red flag if corroboration or verification do not follow in a timely manner.

    h. Are redundancies (repetition of details) and grammatical sloppiness apparent? Such problems are a red flag. Experienced journalists write tightly to minimize or eliminate redundancies.

The observational level may be sufficient for readers to discern the credibility of pictures integrated with news stories. If so, the evaluation can end here.

But if concerns persist, readers need to try a different engagement level, such as that included as a learning objective under metaliteracy goal 1, which calls for the metaliterate learner to "evaluate user-generated information" as an active researcher (Jacobson et al. 2018). At this engagement level, readers could use search engines to locate news stories that corroborate events—even if the reporting varies to some degree.

New search tools help readers determine the sources of images for authentication purposes. Using such tools readers can determine whether a picture was lifted from a legitimate news site to support a contextually false narrative. These tools will also reveal when editors have chosen generic images from a stock image agency to portray a news story. In many cases, this research may reveal an unacceptable deviation from journalistic principles for faithful storytelling. As such, we need a deeper awareness of the tools, as summarized here:

1. Search engines for comparing different accounts of a news event: for example, Google, Bing, and Yahoo! Search.
2. Reverse-image search engine tools: Results vary. The author uses all three of the following options, and more may be forthcoming, but these sites cannot access for evaluation pictures from protected data services, those from certain subscription-based providers, or ones that have not been published previously. The latter includes, for example, an exclusive handout photo related to an investigation given by law enforcement to a news organization. Note that the frequent updating of these sites means they may include features that are not listed here:

   a. TinEye (https://tineye.com): This Toronto-based company offers an array of interfaces, browser extensions, and filters that allow the reader to discover a list of URLs of websites posting the image and filter results by date ranges, stock images, and agency collections.

   b. Google Images (https://images.google.com): This service, owned by Google Inc. and a subsidiary of Alphabet Inc., also lists the URLs of websites posting an image. It includes a selection of visually similar images that may be helpful for exposing an image that has been intentionally cropped or altered in an effort to conceal its origin.

   c. Bing (www.bing.com/images): Microsoft's search engine is similar functionally to Google Images, even with its different user experience design.

The cognitive domain of metaliteracy is evident in metaliteracy goal 1's learning objective that calls for learners to "determine how a source's purpose, document type, and delivery mode affect its value for a particular situation" (Jacobson et al. 2018). In this domain, learners must evaluate and make a judgment about the story source in question. Mindful that the story is just one among many from the news organization, learners must assess whether or not the contextual misrepresentation is systemic in the organization's publishing mission.

If learners determine that a story is not credible at the behavioral domain level, this may not prove that the entire news site is corrupt. If a news site contains a staff directory, a corrections and ethics policy, a thorough "About Us" company section, and a reader-representative or an ombudsman, then that site has all the hallmarks of a legitimate news organization. A decision to proceed with the evaluation of a second or third story may depend on the organization's history, in its community's context, for providing consistently trustworthy reportage. This may be the case with a news website that is associated with a traditional newspaper but employs an online staff that is not managed directly by the newsroom, which can lead to irregularities in news judgment.

It is through the affective domain of metaliteracy that readers will gain a level of discernment that may, in turn, lead to them taking certain actions, such as disregarding malformed journalistic content by excluding it from their research, preventing its sharing on social platforms, alerting others to the corrupt practice, or countering the deception through criticism. Metaliteracy goal 3 calls for metaliterate learners to "recognize that learners are also teachers and teach what you know or learn in collaborative settings" (Jacobson et al. 2018). By "teaching," the affective domain affords activism by learners to counter malicious social media campaigns as they develop.

An example of how metaliterate learners can protect the public trust occurred during the opening of the *Black Panther* movie in February 2018. Racist trolls published a range of tweets, including one that displayed the photo of a bloodied white woman with text claiming that she had been assaulted by African Americans at a theater. But discerning social media users suspected this was an instance of contextual misuse and countered with online reverse-image search tools to expose this fraud. This misappropriated picture, it turns out, was a teenager who had been assaulted a month earlier at a bar in Sweden (Silverman 2018). The connection to the *Black Panther* movie debut was blatantly false. News outlets quickly followed up with online stories, but the first wave of debunking was initiated by intrepid social media users. This phenomenon, with social media users investigating and publishing before journalists, expands upon three crowd-powered collaboration models that journalists have used to acquire reader-generated content (Briggs [2010, 2013] 2015, 91–92). These models include pro-am journalism (participatory publishing), crowdsourcing, and open-source reporting. These social media users and metaliteracy learners are now capable of connecting with the public independently and beyond the authority of newsroom-based paradigms.

Levels of engagement in the affective domain can be designated as a range of active and passive responses. Responses may be a blend, depending on the nature of the false content and the available time and resources to communicate with others, as summarized here:

1. An *active response* to the identification of fake news content may protect the learner, the learner's community of relationships, news consumers connected by social platforms, and those who may be harmed by the spreading of false or malicious content.

   a. The learner may use social media tools such as hashtags and different apps to counter false media content.

   b. The learner records details about the site, including its stated purpose in the "About" section and sponsors or advertisers posting on the site.

   c. The learner may contact the site operators to make them aware of the false content. This may also include advertisers who post.

   d. The learner contacts a reporter at a reputable news organization to share about the false content, including media criticism sites such as Snopes.

   e. The learner contacts the hosting company of the bogus news site to make a complaint.

   f. The learner alerts friends, family members, professionals, or other associates directly.

   g. The learner contacts people or members of a community in a picture who have been contextually misrepresented through identity reassignment or other false portrayals.

2. A *passive response* to the identification of a deceptive online news source may protect the learner but not others who are deceived by its content. This would be the opposite of the itemized action points previously outlined.

It is through the metacognitive domain of metaliteracy that readers comprehend with reflective thinking. Through this domain, learners reflect on the following:

1. How the contextual misrepresentation of photojournalism is a deviant form of multimodal communication through social semiotic systems: Metaliterate learners understand how different combinations of modalities, including linguistic and nonlinguistic forms, create new meanings—and thus messages. The progression from mode to meaning is articulated through theoretical frameworks by Ferdinand de Saussure, Roland Barthes, Gunther Kress, Theo van Leeuwen, Michael Halliday, and others (Kress and Van Leeuwen 1996, 5).

2. How surreptitious social and political propaganda campaigns through this misuse may propel social division, including ethnocentrism, racism, bigotry, stereotyping, and misogyny: Metaliterate learners, through introspection, may identify personal biases or ideologies to question and change. Metaliteracy goal 4 underscores this attribute:

"Engage in informed, self-directed learning that encourages a broader worldview through the global reach of today's social media environment" (Jacobson et al. 2018).

3. How contextual misrepresentation may disparage individuals within the picture: This inaccurate portrayal or identity reassignment may adversely affect their personal lives, relationships with others, public images, and professional reputations. Metaliterate learners gain an understanding about how entire communities and nations may be affected the same way.

4. How the average citizen, lacking a sufficient interdisciplinary education and foundation in metaliteracy learning, is subject to manipulations by surreptitious media campaigns that exploit his or her physiological and perceptual attributes as a human being: Metaliterate learners understand, for instance, how visual dominance in the cognitive process may be leveraged for the purposes of persuasion. Clotaire Rapaille, a social psychologist and marketing consultant, says that conclusions are based on these momentary, visual assessments—a pathway he calls the "reptilian mind": "My theory is very simple," he says. "The reptilian always wins. I don't care what you're going to tell me intellectually. I don't care. Give me the reptilian. Why? Because the reptilian always wins" (quoted in Apkon 2013, 141).

By exercising the behavioral, cognitive, affective, and metacognitive domains through critical thinking, metaliterate learners gain the empowerment to protect themselves and members of their communities from the wiles of contextual misrepresentation and other deviant forms of fake news publishing. Their discernment, engagement, and activism to achieve these ends draw upon the heritage of traditional news organizations whose charge has been to protect the public trust. The next section examines how the news outlets and journalism educators fumbled twentieth-century achievements and are now challenged in the digital age to master the communication modalities that have perplexed them for decades.

TRACING CONTEXTUAL MISREPRESENTATION

How the Silos of Picture Flow and Word Flow in News Organizations Stunted Pedagogy in Journalism Education over Decades

Now that we have examined all four domains of metaliterate learning in relation to the text and image modalities of online news story dissemination, let us take a closer look at the Hicks (1952) model of text–image relationships. This is relevant to this discussion for two reasons.

First of all, few scholarly initiatives by journalism programs in the United States have built upon Hicks's (1952) prescient insights. His landmark book opened the gateway for more research by academics outside of journalism, and this opportunity still awaits. Seminal textbooks such as *Visual Impact in Print* (Hurley and McDougall [1971] 1975), *Photojournalism: Principles and Practices* (Edom [1976] 1980), *Photojournalism: The Professionals' Approach* (Kobré [1980, 1983, 1995, 2000, 2004, 2008] 2017), and *Journalism Next* (Briggs [2010, 2013] 2015) have been lauded by educators teaching the craft of photojournalism and video. However, these books focus primarily on the front end of picture and video creation, postprocessing, special-topic multimedia presentations, and ethical issues—instead of the majority of news content publishing by online producers, copydesk/layout editors, and news editors. The potential for effective visual communication or deviancy through contextual misuse often occurs in this final phase of multimodal meaning making. As an example, Adriane Ohanesian's exemplary photojournalism of South Sudanese children in her Reuters special project was misappropriated years later to portray a fake story about a cannibal restaurant in Nigeria (Palmer 2015d). These malpractices, and an understanding of the semiotic and cognitive principles behind these deceptions, have exceeded the scope of journalistic oversight at this time.

Life magazine still sets one of the highest editorial standards for sequencing photographs with text in narrative and essay-style storytelling (Priit Vesilind, e-mail to author, January 8, 2018). But some other high-circulation publications, including newspapers, have often worked against the principle. Priit Vesilind, former *National Geographic* writer and editor, describes in his e-mail to the author a 1980s conversation with a *National Geographic* director of photography, who reflected on how the magazine works with two separate silos: the picture flow and the word flow. Vesilind questions the value of this system: "If you are watching a movie, with its forward timeline characteristic—and you hear sound—would you not expect this sound to be in sync with the pictures? Well, of course you would" (e-mail to author, January 8, 2018). To stitch the words and pictures together in the magazine, *National Geographic* employed "legend writers," whose job it was to ensure that each page reconciled the semantic narrative misalignment of body text and photographs. In today's leanly staffed online-only newsrooms or even legacy-based news organizations, this attention to the cohesiveness of text and visual content will remain a dream of yesteryear until corporate and editorial leadership embrace multimodality workflows from story concept to multiplatform dissemination.

This reference to the silos of the picture flow and the word flow also represents the intense infighting present in newsrooms across the United States. Mario Garcia, CEO of Garcia Media, has engaged with issues concerning "word people versus the visual people" for more than three decades (e-mail to author, January 14, 2018). This news design visionary, author, and teacher has worked with more than 700 news organizations globally through redesigns to integrate variations of his Writing/Editing/Design (WED) and iWED storytelling foundations for optimizing the integration of words and visuals in print and on mobile devices (Garcia, e-mail to author, January 14, 2018). Noting that "these two camps remained quite separate, each proud of what it considered the 'integrity' of the craft," Garcia describes the challenges of teaching this divided culture:

> We used to do seminars at the Poynter Institute in the 1980s and would do parodies of the word people (always in gray suits, like a Perry Mason black and white episode), while the visual people would be more fun (in Carmen Miranda tutti frutti hats). The newsroom people in attendance at these seminars laughed, but they knew that it was not a joke, that there was, indeed, a separation. (e-mail to author, January 14, 2018)

This cultural divide in the news publishing industry for two generations has stunted the development of a meaningful taxonomy of text–image relationships, despite *Life*'s efforts to propel photojournalism to great heights during the twentieth century. Consequently, a major issue arises: Without lexical terms and semantic examples to identify wide-ranging relationships among words and images, the foundation for pedagogy, discourse, and literacy becomes elusive, if not unattainable. Serious implications face the Fourth Estate, given its fault lines, as it navigates further into the twenty-first century's digital Wild West.

The second reason that this chapter highlights Hicks's (1952) model is to recognize the growing body of research by social semioticians, neuroscientists, cognitive psychologists, and linguists who are boosting cross-disciplinary and metaliteracy learning opportunities. The leadership in journalism programs must reach across collegiate divisions to initiate more scholarship, following the models by Mario Garcia (www.garciamedia.com), Nieman Journalism Lab (www.niemanlab.org), and other innovators.

How Contextual Misrepresentation Can Be Understood through Social Semiotic Analysis

Multimodal, social semiotic principles promote effective frameworks for developing a taxonomy of text–image relationships relevant to multimodal news publishing and the education of future journalists. Semiotics, the study of signs, provides an effective denominator for analyzing communication modes that are comprehended differently through cognitive processing (Bateman 2014, 5–6). For example, the brain begins to categorize and make sense of a picture in as little as a few milliseconds. In contrast, text comprehension, measured in seconds, lags behind. However, these different modes have one characteristic in common: meaning. Two pictures, as signs, can be placed together to change a meaning, also known as "the signified" in semiotics terms

(Silverman and Rader 2012, 7). Text, as a sign, may be placed with a picture, as a sign, to change an existing meaning or create an entirely new meaning.

Thus, social semiotics levels the playing field so that all communication modes, including photography and text, can be understood, selected for their potential, and designed to optimize the multimedia news report. John Kroll (2014), a digital journalist and educator at Kent State University in Ohio, has already begun preparing his students to be "jacks of all modes." His mission is to break the kind of cultural silos of words and images that Garcia has described (e-mail to author, January 14, 2018).

Modal elements for "making meaning," as described by linguist Gunther Kress (2010), include "image, writing, layout, music, gesture, speech, moving image, soundtrack, and 3D objects" (79). In terms of multimodal discourse, intersemiotic contextual misrepresentation in news communication is even broader than this chapter's focus on text–image relationships. Contextual misrepresentation may occur in any combination of modes to compromise effective communication. Thus, intersemiotic contextual misrepresentation is an inclusive term that covers deviants of meaning, intended or unintended, of combinations of modal elements for all news communication platforms.

Social semiotics is the third movement of its type in the past century to research linguistical (textual) along with nonlinguistical (including visual) communication modes. Its principals include Gunther Kress, Theo van Leeuwen, Michael Halliday, Robert Hodge, and Michael O'Toole (Kress and van Leeuwen 1996, 5). Helen Caple, a senior lecturer in journalism at the University of New South Wales and a photojournalist, is the notable new exemplar in this research. In *Photojournalism: A Social Semiotic Approach*, her articulation of the multisemiotic news story and news values has created a bridge to bring semiotic analysis to journalism (Caple 2013). Her innovative concepts correspond with the emergence of metaliteracy, transliteracy, and multimodal literacy frameworks examined in Mackey and Jacobson's (2014) book *Metaliteracy: Reinventing Information Literacy to Empower Learners*. Mackey and Jacobson note how "the postmodern era of multimedia and networked learning has demanded a pedagogical shift from a linear perspective to a multidimensional one that is based on multiplicity and associative ways of viewing one's world and perhaps oneself" (19). Caple's (2013) research comes at a time when news organizations must distinguish their multimodal journalistic content in the post-truth era. News organizations must incorporate storytelling workflows that integrate the full range of modalities in publishing and for journalistic pedagogy in education.

Caple (2013) names three terms in her book that lay the framework for understanding the nature of intersemiotic contextual misrepresentation:

1. Intersemiotic repetition: Photographs and text (typically captions) "enter a relationship of *elaboration* because they offer more precise details about each other rather than adding something new" (156).

2. Intersemiotic expansion: "Words and image enter a conjunctive relationship of *extension* with each other since they both bring something
new (but related) to the story" (156).

3. Intersemiotic deviation: "No relation between words and image" (156).

In practice, the author's students applied these concepts in his Visual Culture
journalism course by examining how *intersemiotic deviation* may include *identifiable* or *unidentifiable* instances, depending on the subject content. One of
his students, Eve Brewer (e-mail to author, October 2, 2015), reported about
a bimodal example of *identifiable intersemiotic deviation* (outside of still images
and text) in Immortal's music video of "Wintermoon" overlayed with the
soundtrack for "Yakety Sax" (Darkwave22 2009). The video imagery of this
heavy metal band in the rural ruins of an abbey includes fire breathing, the
wearing of corpse paint, and ancient weapons. Even if readers do not access
this video, many will be able to imagine the incongruence of the band's video
combined with a whimsical musical score, based on given social-construct
meanings. Thus, the expectation of a viewer would be for the video imagery
to correspond with a heavy metal style of music. The integration of the video
with a different musical style would likely be perceived as *intersemiotic deviation* in the viewer's expectation; however, this reaction would be based on
modal content meanings that the viewer learns through prior associations in
his or her educational or cultural experiences.

The author has also extended Caple's (2013) framework to include
intersemiotic contextual misrepresentation as a branch of *intersemiotic deviation*.
Intersemiotic contexual misrepresentation concerns imperceptible text–image
misuse on the part of the reader. This chapter focuses on the identification
and response to this malpractice in photojournalism in the post-truth era.
Its characteristics may include *intersemiotic expansion*, such as the effect produced in the portrayal of the Anne Romney plane incident described earlier.
In the absence of a caption, readers will likely negotiate the meaning of the
false Romney reunion narrative through its close proximity with the bold
stack headline and secondary headlines on the left (see figure 5.1). Had an
accurate caption accompanied the Romney reunion photo explaining the date
and location, it would have provided *intersemiotic repetition* with the image. At
this juncture, a reader would have questioned the online producer's decision
to include a month-old photo with this breaking news story. The result: a text–
image corruption that compromises editorial accuracy on the Drudge Report
website—but the reader is unaware of this effect.

An example of *intersemiotic contextual misrepresentation* in filmmaking
is evident in the editing and production of Katie Couric's 2016 shooting-
violence documentary *Under the Gun*. Kress (2010), one of the leading principals in social semiotics research, has explained that time is a semiotic entity
(81, 107). In this case, time was manipulated inappropriately, changing the

meaning of what actually took place during an interview with members of a Virginia gun rights group in April 2015. Couric asks this question: "If there are no background checks, how do you prevent . . . I know how you all are going to answer this, but I'm asking anyway. If there are no background checks for gun purchasers, how do you prevent felons or terrorists from walking into, say[,] a licensed gun dealer and purchasing a gun?" (*Washington Free Beacon* 2016; Folkenflik 2016). One of the members replied immediately to her question, but during the editing, about nine seconds of additional cuts and camera angles showing members looking down or away were added to extend the interview scene. These extra shots, known as B-roll, may be used appropriately by filmmakers to ensure the continuity of a given scene. But the contextual misrepresentation, in this case, occurred through the improper extension of time. The semiotic meaning effect for audiences was that Couric's stunning question caught the gun rights advocates off guard, leading to a dismayed period of silence. This is how *time*—as a semiotic entity—may be used to misrepresent participants during an interview.

Couric was apparently unaware that a member of the group had made a recording of the interview, shredding the documentary's credibility in regard to this scene. As the controversy erupted, Couric (2016) issued a statement to "take responsibility for a decision that misrepresented" her exchange with the gun rights group. David Folkenflik, an NPR (National Public Radio) media correspondent, notes in his commentary on the situation, "This manipulation—and that's what it was—would not pass muster at NPR under its principles for fairness in handling interviews" (Folkenflik 2016).

In *Controversies in Media Ethics*, A. David Gordon, John M. Kittross, and Carol Reuss (1996) recall how a New York television station "pretended to be providing daily pictorial coverage" of the Vietnam War "but was merely using stock footage," noting that "file footage might be broadcast or printed without attribution or with a dishonest provenance" (290). Thus, the inclusion of stock footage that does not depict the actual news story is another example of contextual misrepresentation.

Readers may have no assurance that online daily news reports are not using stock-image photos to portray news stories. For example, Odyssey (2018) is a news organization that relies frequently on copyright-free images from sources including, but not limited to, StockSnap, Startup Stock Photos, Unsplash, Wikimedia, Flickr Creative Commons, Pexels, Pixabay, FreeGreat-Picture.com, and SplitShire. According to former contributing writer Katie Lembo, a journalist at the *Spotlight* (Delmar, NY), reporters are required to post images and may use their personal photography, too; but, she said, many select from these free sources to illustrate stories (interview with author, Albany, NY, March 14, 2018).

This reliance on free sources for images may invite conditions for contextual misrepresentation. For instance, Tyra Christina's (2017) story in *Odyssey*

Online, "Gender Inequality in Hollywood and Mass Media," uses a rights-free photo from Unsplash by photographer Clem Onojeghou from London Fashion Week 2017 to illustrate this Hollywood, gender-based story (see figure 5.3). The photographers depicted on this London street would recognize themselves capturing Milan-based model Patricia Manfield on September 17, 2017 (Vierig 2017). Manfield, cofounder of the Atelier fashion website (Wilson 2016), does not match the story's focus about gender inequality. The back view of Manfield, who is walking toward photographers, would likely make her identifiable to those who follow street style fashion. The use of this image brings up concerns about journalistic accuracy and transparency. A caption is conveniently absent from Christina's (2017) story; thus, the headline becomes the de facto caption. Only a photo credit link to Onojeghou's image on Unsplash is located at the end of the story—as if to minimize the chances that readers will discover Manfield's unrelated picture.

A perusal of the authors on the *Odyssey Online* site reveals many college students who are publishing stories. Reporting and publishing are necessary to advance in the field of journalism; however, it calls into question whether these students will learn the value of photojournalism while they hunt for stock images. What practices will carry into their journalism careers? Readers will find the same image of Manfield on fertility expert Marc Sklar's website, where it is integrated into his blog page titled "How Celebrities Deal with Infertility" (Sklar 2018). No caption is present to denote anything else.

Photo by Clem Onojeghou on Unsplash

FIGURE 5.3
Rights-Free Image

Readers may make assumptions about the image based entirely upon the context in which it is presented.

For purposes unrelated to journalistic contexts, open-source or free images may be integrated successfully in multimodal storytelling, process descriptions, and various forms of training, to name a few. This depends on the context and purpose behind creating content. Metaliteracy goal 2, in its learning objectives, calls for learners to "ethically remix and repurpose openly licensed content" (Jacobson et al. 2018). The metaliteracy framework offers fine guidance for learners considering Creative Commons licensing in their goals to create and disseminate content (Mackey and Jacobson 2014, 38). For example, a Wiccan who publishes a blog about her community's activities in New York's Hudson Valley might create an article page about histories related to certain crystals. Open-source images provide avenues for integrating text and image modes in the creation of meaningful content.

How Contextual Misrepresentation Relates to Media Ethics

In journalism, the contextual misrepresentation of editorial content is contrary to the four main principles outlined in the Society of Professional Journalists' (SPJ 2014) "Code of Ethics." The ethics committee explains:

> The SPJ Code of Ethics is a statement of abiding principles supported by explanations and position papers that address changing journalistic practices. It is not a set of rules, rather a guide that encourages all who engage in journalism to take responsibility for the information they provide, regardless of medium.

The following principles are explained in depth on the SPJ website:

1. Seek the truth and report it.
2. Minimize harm.
3. Act independently.
4. Be accountable and transparent.

Within the framework of journalism ethics, the entry of Adobe Photoshop into the photography production process triggered a flashpoint of debates, introspection, and disciplinary policy changes within the industry (Irby 2003). Inappropriate Adobe Photoshop manipulations that changed the meaning of photographic content were identified as *the threat* to journalistic credibility more than two decades ago. David Sutherland cites notable examples that included Allan Detrich's *Toledo Blade* photo in April 2007, from which legs and feet had been removed, and Brian Walski's *Los Angeles Times* photo in April 2003, which combined parts of two pictures (e-mail to author, January 7, 2018).

Paul Martin Lester (1989), media ethics author and clinical professor of the School of Arts, Technology, and Emerging Communication at the University of Texas at Dallas, asserts:

> Photographs, particularly those used as accurate and trustworthy accounts, . . . are our best hedge against the threat of devious editors and special interest groups who want to change truth and history. If the manipulation of photographs is accepted for any image, the public will naturally doubt all photographs and text within all publications. (41)

But Sutherland says the journalism community has been slow to recognize the threat of contextual misrepresentation, "which can be just as damaging to credibility" as an inappropriate Photoshop alteration. He has observed over the past decade how "pictures are often used to 'illustrate' news stories that they have no connection to," explaining how producers select images of ISIS soldiers that may be several weeks or months old and republish them to denote a current news story. "The public notices these inappropriate uses," he says (e-mail to author, January 7, 2018).

Sutherland also identifies a form of modal manipulation in photojournalism that is akin to the creation of content that does not exist. This, too, can be classified as contextual misrepresentation. News photographers have been known to direct people in order to create scenes that would not exist in a natural context. They may even ask subjects to repeat their activities in instances when they missed the shot the first time. He recalls a *St. Petersburg Times* and *Evening Independent* photographer who was captured in the act by another photographer: "He wrote 'Yea Eckerd' on the bare feet of an Eckerd College fan at a baseball tournament and then photographed the feet for a photo that appeared two days later in the *Independent*. The photographer was immediately Fired" (e-mail to the author, January 7, 2018).

John Michael Kittross, media ethicist and educator, delivered a shocking declaration about photographic credibility two decades ago in *Controversies in Media Ethics*:

> I advocate that we take a Kantian view: The public should not trust pictures. They should look at all pictures through a veil of suspicion, without any presumption that they are truthful. That is the bottom line. If no picture is trusted, then the public shouldn't easily be harmed by a doctored one. True, this would reduce the communication value of pictures to the public and lower the photographer, artist, or editor in terms of public esteem, but it may be the price we have to pay. (Gordon, Kittross, and Reuss 1996, 293)

Kittross also brazenly called for photographers (as creators of images) to "certify the authenticity" of their work. "If the creator won't or can't so certify, then the publisher or station license is rendered vulnerable to legal action brought by anyone affected by the doctored picture, and the public may be trained to dismiss the unacknowledged image" (Gordon, Kittross, and Reuss 1996, 292). In 1996, the year Kittross's ethics book was first published, the dissemination of journalistic content online in the digital Wild West was gathering momentum—at a pace that would soon eclipse any effort to realize this passionate notion. The reason: contextual misrepresentation corrupts the picture's meaning through aberrant captioning in print or online, even if the photographer certifies the image; so a photographer would have no recourse in this scenario unless he or she was notified to check all future uses of the picture.

Why We Should Care How Pictures Affect Us

The image is the juggernaut in the perceptual process. Story text is not. News designers, online producers, editors, citizen journalists, and other meaning makers must learn to respect the power of the image because of its instantaneous command of attention. To underestimate the picture's effect is reckless in the post-truth era. Stephen Apkon (2013) explains why in the *Age of the Image*: "Communicating with images is quicker than with words. Images hit the brain in a shockingly brief sequence of events. . . . speed is part of the reason images tend to hit us in the gut quicker and more consistently than the written word" (75). This is affirmed by MIT neuroscientists who discovered that the "human brain can process entire images that the eye sees for as little as 13 milliseconds" (Trafton 2014).

James H. Neely, professor and director of the Cognition Psychology PhD program at the University at Albany in New York, explains that "visual dominance is so powerful that visual input preempts all other sensory inputs" (Palmer 2018). Cognition study findings show that a picture likely engages more than 85 percent of the functional capabilities of the brain (Apkon 2013, 75). "Pictures beat text as well, in part because reading is so inefficient for us," claims John J. Medina (2018), developmental molecular biologist and author of *Brain Rules*. Medina (2018) notes that the "brain sees words as lots of tiny pictures, and we have to identify certain features in the letters to be able to read them. That takes time."

Dirk Remley (2015) integrates models from neurobiological research and multimodal rhetoric in his book *How the Brain Processes Multimodal Technical Instructions*, which has relevancy in the fusion of photos and text in news publishing. He writes, "Neurobiology scholarship finds an attention-related preference for visual information. If visual information exists along with other stimuli, then the visual will draw attention no matter what other stimuli are involved" (43).

The first eye-tracking research by Garcia and Stark (1991) for the Poynter Institute for Media Studies affirmed in news publishing that artwork and photos "dominate processing (that is, the number of elements actually 'looked at')" (70). In a variety of photographic sizes, from a thumbnail-size mugshot to nearly full-page widths, processing ranged, respectively, from 44 percent to 94 percent (73). Given the previously mentioned studies in cognitive research, this is not surprising. The Poynter study found that "only 25 percent of the text is processed" (71). In contrast, caption processing was 29 percent for color and black-and-white photographs, but when a color photo was displayed across three columns (half of the page width), caption processing jumped to 42 percent. These eye-track findings underscore how careful editing of captions and photos can boost journalistic, bimodal storytelling, as Hicks demonstrated decades ago at *Life*. With so much reader attention drawn to this semantic unit of text–image communication, these findings are also red-flag indicators that fake news operators can leverage the contextual misrepresentation of a picture for devious intent.

Even more troubling in this post-truth era are two recent studies revealing that the mere inclusion of a nonprobative photograph (one that does not afford proof or evidence) with a statement or claim can "inflate truthiness," even if the contextual premise is false. The 2012 study by Eryn J. Newman, Maryanne Garry, Daniel M. Bernstein, Justin Kantner, and D. Stephen Lindsay led them to speculate

> that nonprobative photos and verbal information help people generate pseudoevidence. People may selectively interpret information gleaned from a photo or description as consistent with their hypothesis and/or they may use such information to cue the mental generation of thoughts and images consistent with their hypothesis. It is also possible that the ease or fluency with which people bring related information to mind contributes to a feeling of truthiness. (Newman et al. 2012).

The 2015 "truthiness" effect study by Eryn J. Newman, Maryanne Garry, Daniel M. Bernstein, Christian Unkelbach, D. Stephen Lindsay, and Robert A. Nash revealed several replications of the 2012 research as well as additional findings. In relation to the earlier study, "people more often judged the claim 'Macadamia nuts are in the same evolutionary family as peaches' to be true when the claim appeared with a photo of a bowl of macadamia nuts than when it appeared alone," with one participant saying, "I'm going to go with yes because they kind of look like peaches, so that would make sense" (Newman et al. 2015).

The suggestions of these findings and the authors' explanations about the "truthiness" effect have a disturbing likeness to variants of contextual misrepresentation. It is no wonder that fake news online postings get an unwarranted credibility boost simply because of the presence of pictures lifted from the Associated Press, *New York Times*, Getty Images, and similar news sources.

Earlier in this chapter, the examination of the racist troll campaign revealed how legitimate images from news outlets can be trafficked to boost false assault claims.

Readers without a metaliteracy learning foundation are vulnerable to these deceptions. These findings are worthy of more study in terms of psychological cognition—especially in relation to journalistic content. "We trust our eyes in a way that we trust almost no other sense," cautions Apkon (2013), "even if we remain unaware of the reasons for this" (76).

CASE STUDIES OF CONTEXTUAL MISREPRESENTATION

As discussed earlier in the chapter, the metaliteracy learning goals and objectives provide readers with the ability to detect contextual misrepresentation. Readers apply the behavioral domain when they detect or directly identify the conditions for contextual misrepresentation. Readers apply the cognitive domain when they evaluate and determine the credibility of the news organization and its worthiness—and whether or not the contextual misrepresentation is systemic in the organization's publishing characteristics. Readers also gain a level of discernment through the affective domain that enables them to disregard malformed journalistic content, alert others to the corrupt practices, and counter the deceptions. As metaliterate learners, readers apply the metacognitive domain to comprehend how contextual misrepresentation is a deviant form of multimodal communication through social semiotic systems. Metacognition also prepares learners to understand how surreptitious propaganda campaigns employing this type of content misuse can lead to irreversible consequences from governmental policy decisions. Further, reflective thinking prepares learners to understand how such misuse may disparage individuals, communities, and countries—and adversely impact the lives of many people.

The following examples, excerpted from cases presented in the *Picture Prosecutor* blog (http://blog.timesunion.com/pictureprosecutor), illustrate the relationship of metaliterate learning to exposing and combatting contextual misrepresentation.

How Identity Reassignment
Is Part of Contextual Misrepresentation

Two Men Misidentified as Prison Escapees by the New York Daily News

This case study is about two neighbors who end up being depicted as prison escapees by a news organization (Palmer 2015e, 2015f). Photographed while checking a neighbor's property near Malone, New York, the two friends were misidentified as Clinton Correctional Facility escapees Richard Matt and David Sweat in a leaked surveillance camera photo published by the *New York Daily News*. The metro newspaper published it on Twitter, its website, and its June 29, 2015, front page with headlines and caption text claiming that these were the convicted killers who had pulled off one of the most audacious prison breaks in New York history (see figure 5.4). But they were not. The author, as the Picture Prosecutor and acting on a tip from *Albany Times Union* newsroom reporter Keshia Clukey, searched the dense backwoods in Franklin County to identify the real men—Eric Couture and Charlie Coutu—and exposed this case of contextual misrepresentation by the *New York Daily News* (Palmer 2015f).

A surveillance camera mounted on a spruce tree had captured the two friends on June 24, 2015, walking through the Bellmont woods. Within twenty minutes, attack helicopters entered the airspace above the men with machine

FIGURE 5.4
Franklin County Residents Misidentified as Fugitives on
New York Daily News Front Page

guns trained on them. New York State Police officers moved in, accompanied by FBI (Federal Bureau of Investigation) agents—only to determine that these two were not the escapees. They were simply checking a neighbor's property when the camera recorded them. Thus, the FBI and state police were first to verify that Matt and Sweat were not the ones depicted in this image. But the *New York Daily News*, in possession of this leaked image, never authenticated the photo before publication. A tweet posted by a *New York Daily News* reporter on June 28 claimed an "exclusive" picture of the Dannemora fugitives on the lam. After Clukey heard from a law enforcement source that the image did not depict the fugitives, she tweeted that information to the public (Palmer 2015f). (See figure 5.5.)

By eventually identifying and interviewing Couture and Coutu, the author was able to locate the spruce tree and take a picture of the scene juxtaposed with a print of the camera image to replicate the original vantage point, including the white shed in the background (see figure 5.6). The author notified *New York Daily News* editors about the error, first, and then wrote a commentary (Palmer 2015a) for the *Albany Times Union* about this contextual misuse. But editors from the *New York Daily News* were not responsive. Two weeks later, they removed the image from the website following exposure by *New York Post* columnist Keith Kelly (2015) in his story "*New York Daily News* Refuses to Correct Story Misidentifying 'Escapees.'" The *New York Daily News*

Courtesy of Thomas Palmer/Picture Prosecutor

FIGURE 5.5

Evidence Exposing the *New York Daily News*'s Error

FIGURE 5.6

Clukey's Tweet Refuting the *New York Daily News*'s "Exclusive:
Photo of the Escapees" Tweet

has not apologized to Couture and Coutu, despite their call for some acknowledgment of the error, and it hasn't published a correction online or in print.

By ignoring the opportunity to publish a correction, the *New York Daily News* exposes itself to ethics questions at a time when news organizations are struggling to distinguish themselves in a media market filled with fake news operators. "In a story of national interest every journalist is looking to outscoop the pack," the author wrote in his commentary (Palmer 2015a). "Competition has always been a reality in the news business. But the handling of this not-so-explosive photo is an example of the perils news organizations face today in the wilder frontier of digital-first publishing, where scoops are measured sometimes in minutes, even seconds" (Palmer 2015a). Even unintentionally, this newspaper had reassigned, in effect, the identity of the two men to depict an assumptive narrative of Matt and Sweat on the run.

Metaliteracy Domains Analyses

At the *observational level*, metaliteracy learners apply the behavioral domain by understanding that the body language of the men moving across the camera's view does not suggest they are hunted fugitives. Couture, in the foreground, shows a lightness to his step. He also wears sunglasses casually propped on his head. Clukey, as an experienced journalist, pondered these details in the picture: "I can't believe that they would be so calmly walking by. . . . They are too clean. Why are they in new clothing if they have been on the run for more than two weeks?" (quoted in Palmer 2015e). Given these initial signs, readers can be skeptical about the image. Law enforcement, however, has the responsibility to believe this may be an image of the escapees because of the slight resemblance of Couture's physique with that of fugitive Matt. Thus, the FBI and police must prove these men are not the escapees. According to the metaliteracy learning principles, the *New York Daily News*, perhaps unintentionally, fails this level of the metaliteracy analysis by not authenticating with officers the identities of the men in the photo and the camera's location.

Initially, at the *engagement level*, the learner has no option but to believe that the newspaper got it right. Even if he or she uses reverse image search websites such as Google Images, Bing, and TinEye, no online record exists of the surveillance camera photo. This is the situation with any image that appears for the first time from a private collection, is first released by a law enforcement official, or is an unpublished photograph from an archive. But social media users following #Dannemora and related hashtags would be the earliest to know that the authenticity of this image was in question. According to Clukey, law enforcement officials preferred to see inaccurate information spread by news outlets or social media being discredited during this manhunt (in-person conversation with the author; Palmer 2015e).

Metaliterate learners apply the cognitive domain by understanding the fiercely competitive nature of New York City's two major tabloids, the *New York Daily News* and the *New York Post*. They would anticipate risk taking by these outlets to be first in news coverage. Metaliterate learners would evaluate stories in this context. Given both newspapers' award-winning histories and sensational presentation styles, learners would be aware that an error in one story does not necessarily indicate a systemic abrogation of journalistic principles for other content. However, for citing news events for scholarly work or other forms of research, metaliteracy learners should consider verifying reports with other news organizations to judge the trustworthiness of the content.

If metaliterate learners were aware of questionable, unverified claims and questioned the trustworthiness of this newspaper through the affective domain, they could select another news source for stories related to the fugitives. They could also take action through social media to publicize an apparent error by a news organization. For instance, learners could retweet Clukey's Twitter message citing a law enforcement official who claimed the camera image showed local residents—not the fugitives. Members of the Bellmont and Malone communities could also use social media to expose the *New York Daily News*'s error by identifying Couture and Coutu, with their permission. Furthermore, residents in these communities could share evidence with a reporter at the *Malone Telegram* or other news outlets.

Learners must apply metacognition and think reflectively to introduce some level of skepticism to the encounter with a surveillance or handout photo, regardless of the credibility of the source. Misinformation or disinformation can occur as the result of a reference error or due to malicious intent as content changes hands. Metaliterate learners would know that images can become separated from their original context, captioning, or metadata. They understand that the accurate denotation of any handout photo or historical picture is subject to the meaning generated through an author's care in presenting the text–image relationship, elements of which may be lost along the path to publication. Metaliterate learners also understand that newsrooms compete to publish first in our digital era, a race that can be fraught with error. These types of mistakes are consequential. The *New York Daily News's* misidentification was embarrassing and disparaging to Couture and Coutu, who had faced a harrowing experience earlier with law enforcement officials who had assumed they were the fugitives. Metaliterate learners would also be empathetic to how residents in this region may feel that news organizations use different standards when reporting about rural communities compared to urban ones. Furthermore, the *New York Daily News's* apparent indifference toward Couture and Coutu, in this instance, is not consistent with the standards of news organizations that strive for accountability and transparency through their corrections policies.

How Contextual Misrepresentation Can Produce Fake News Narratives

Contextual Misuse of a New York Times *Photo*

This case study describes how a trafficked *New York Times* photo created fake news narratives during the 2016 election period. Cara Cliffe, one of the author's journalism students in his Digital Media I course, researched a fake news site story (Palmer 2017) carrying the headline "Obama Signs Executive Order Banning the Pledge of Allegiance in Schools Nationwide" (see figure 5.7). Notable fact-checking organizations such as FactCheck.org (Wallace 2016) and Snopes (2016) had debunked the story but did not examine the contextual misrepresentation of the photo. Cliffe chose this case for her assignment because some members in her family had believed the story was true (Palmer 2017). Through careful vetting, Cliffe and the author's investigation led to a *New York Times* photo taken by Stephen Crowley to depict President Barack Obama's signing of an ethics bill, the Stop Trading on Congressional Knowledge (STOCK) Act, on April 4, 2012, in Washington, DC (Pear 2012). Crowley was unaware that his photo had been trafficked for one of the most notorious examples of fake news during the 2016 election period (Garcia 2018). The author, as Picture Prosecutor, continued monitoring the contextual misuse of Crowley's photo on various news sites and blogs—where it still remains accessible for deception nearly two years later. Alexa Erickson's (2017) story

Obama Signs Executive Order Banning The Pledge Of Allegiance In Schools Nationwide

By Jimmy Rustling, ABC News - *November 11, 2016*   👁 *47813*   💬 *718*

SHARE

President Obama, seen here signing an Executive Order today which bans the Pledge of Allegiance in all public schools around the country. (AP Photo / Dennis System)

POSTED BY: JIMMY RUSTLING, ABC NEWS   DECEMBER 11, 2016

WASHINGTON, D.C. **(AP)** — Early this morning, **President Obama** made what could very well prove to be the most controversial move of his presidency with the signing of **Executive Order** 13738, which revokes the federal government's official recognition of **the Pledge of Allegiance**. Under the new order, it is now illegal for any federally funded agency to display the pledge or for any federal employee to recite, or encourage others to recite, the pledge while on duty. This law also applies to federal contractors and other institutions that receive federal funding such as public schools. Individuals who violate this order can face fines of up to $10,000 and up to one year in federal prison.

FIGURE 5.7
New York Times Photo Trafficked for a Fake News Story

on the Collective Evolution website calls out President Obama for signing an antipropaganda bill, claiming it "harms" press freedom. But her January 10, 2017, post misappropriates Crowley's photo to depict the signing. The real "harm" to journalism is this contextual misrepresentation of this *New York Times* photo. How ironic.

The key takeaway from this example is that this photograph establishes a historical, visual record of the 2012 signing ceremony, even down to the details of Vice President Joe Biden's tie and recognizable congressional leaders who were present. The use of this photograph for any other story—without its context clarified in a caption—leads to a false narrative. When the photographer credit and caption are absent, the headline and story, in this case, become the de facto caption in support of the false narrative. The mere inclusion of this photo with this bogus story may even boost the story's believability, given the "truthiness" studies mentioned earlier in this chapter (Newman et al. 2012, 2015).

The author has observed how news fact-checkers tend to focus on the falsity of a whole story package instead of examining separate modal content elements, such as photographs, which propel the lie through their visual dominance effect. This suggests a continuing bias oriented toward the importance of the written word over the image, as Garcia explains earlier in this chapter in regard to the nature of journalism. This systemic abuse of one photo also calls into question how the *New York Times* should respond to the misappropriation of its content. Do the *New York Times* and other leading news organizations care about their photographers' works being trafficked for fake news? How much more is being misrepresented or published without permission or media client subscription? Is it possible for the *New York Times* and other news outlets to police other sites in a whack-a-mole online publishing culture? As content stakeholders, must these organizations carry the burden of this responsibility? And if not, who will protect the public from these deceptions?

Metaliteracy Domains Analyses

At the *observational level* or behavioral domain, learners can detect several giveaways in the story presentation to determine that it is bogus. The caption credit line claims that "Dennis System" was the Associated Press photographer, but readers familiar with the TV sitcom *It's Always Sunny in Philadelphia* would know that this is a reference to a systematic method for seducing women. The website URL is *abcnews.com.co* to mimic that of the mainstream ABC News media company. The "co" at the end of the URL is a tipoff. The byline for reporter Jimmy Rustling has a link to a biography page that claims he "has won many awards for excellence in writing including fourteen Peabody awards and a handful of Pulitzer Prizes." No reporter has ever won a "handful" of Pulitzer Prizes. The conflicting posted-by dates of November 11 and December 11 are another indicator. At the *engagement level*, learners may initiate research by making a screenshot of the photograph and uploading it to reverse image search websites such as Google Images, Bing, and TinEye; this will likely lead to the *New York Times*'s online site. However, these reverse image search programs did not reveal this source for the author and his student in spring 2017; identification of the photo required further deduction to narrow the possibilities to the *New York Times* and then a search on its website.

After learners discover one or two bogus details in the story, by applying the cognitive domain, a brief perusal of another article may be sufficient to conclude that contextual misrepresentation and editorial dereliction under the guise of parody are systemic in this organization's publishing mission. By discerning this website's collection of deceptive content and applying the affective domain, the metaliterate learner makes the choice not to share it so as not to spread poisonous disinformation. Depending on the severity of the malicious content, the learner may combat this propaganda through social media tools. The learner may also contact an online news outlet to inform journalists who, in turn, may become allies in the joint mission to debunk the fakery. If the story topic features a shared interest among friends and family, the learner may decide to alert these others about its falsehood. Finally, the learner may notify the affected individuals who have been disparaged by the contextual misrepresentation.

On a *metacognitive level*, metaliterate learners understand how this legitimate photo of Obama from a reputable news source can be misappropriated to prop up a false narrative through the deception of contextual misrepresentation. They carefully reflect on their own thinking and are aware that the combination of modalities—image and text—may fuse to create the false narrative of an event that never occurred. Metaliterate learners also understand how social and political propaganda campaigns leverage these modal manipulations to exacerbate the causes of social division, including bigotry, racism, and ethnocentrism. Regarding the people depicted in these misappropriated photos, metaliterate learners comprehend how contextual misrepresentation strips away an individual's dignity for the purpose of identity reassignment. Such inaccurate portrayals may adversely impact an individual's personal and professional images, depending on the severity of the abuse. In this case, the misuse takes a libelous stab at Obama and a host of administrative and legislative supporters. Finally, metaliterate learners may reflect on their initial reactions to this content, the deconstruction of this corrupt report, and the concern about members of the public who fall prey to these manipulations.

Contextual Misuse of an Associated Press Photo

In this next case study, the Ukraine Investigation news site, now offline, posted what they purported to be photographic evidence of Russian forces entering Luhansk, Ukraine, in July 2014 (see figure 5.8). However, this image is actually an Associated Press photo of Russian forces in 2008 from a series taken by Mikhail Metzel (2008) when forces moved toward the Georgian border and South Ossetia (Palmer 2015c). Several months later in 2015, a US senator, seeking lethal military aid for the Ukrainian government, was duped by the misuse of the same photo (Weinstein 2015). Close vetting of the image revealed that this 2008 archive photo from the Associated Press is a prime example of contextual misrepresentation by the Ukraine Investigation site.

FIGURE 5.8
Unrelated Associated Press Archive Photo
in False "Investigation" Report

The text on the site claimed that the "information" presented was provided by Iryna Veryhina, former head of the Luhansk regional administration, who was dismissed by Ukrainian President Petro Poroshenko in September 2014 (Palmer 2015c). The original caption for the 2008 photo states:

> Russian heavy armoured vehicles in the Ardon Valley, Russia, heading towards the Georgian border and South Ossetia on Saturday, Aug. 9, 2008. Russia sent hundreds of tanks and troops into the separatist province of South Ossetia and bombed Georgian towns Saturday in a major escalation of the conflict that has left scores of civilians dead and wounded. Georgia, a staunch U.S. ally,

had launched an offensive Friday to retake control of breakaway South Ossetia. Russia, which has close ties to the province and posts peacekeepers there, responded by sending in armed convoys and combat aircraft. (Metzel 2008)

As an official in the Luhansk region, Veryhina would know that the rugged, steep terrain behind the Russian forces is not characteristic of eastern Ukraine's steppe landscape. Moreover, anyone familiar with this region would associate the picture's scene with the Russia-Georgia border.

The deconstruction of this false report leads to questions about the purpose of the Ukraine Investigation site, operated from Rochester, New York, which is now offline. Patrick Tucker (2014), technology editor for *Defense One*, described the site as an anti-Russian grassroots organization that gathers content through crowdsourcing, including user-uploaded photos. Whether authentication was attempted or not in this case, user-contributed content from Ukraine and other areas of civil unrest presents verification challenges for any reputable news organization.

This same Associated Press archive photo became problematic for Senator James Inhofe (R-OK) when he attempted to introduce a bill on February 11, 2015, in the US Senate to "arm Ukraine with lethal military aid." His presentation consisted of this photo and others that a Ukrainian delegation claimed were fresh evidence of Russian aggression in Ukraine (see figure 5.9; Inhofe 2015). However, Inhofe's staff did not authenticate the pictures. Adam

FIGURE 5.9

U.S. Senator Inhofe "Duped" by Archive News Photo

Weinstein (2015) debunked many of the images in a comedic smackdown in his *Gawker* story "Senator 'Duped' into Using Old Photos to Promote New War with Russia." This debacle calls into question the responsibility of the Associated Press when its content is misappropriated to create fake news on different publishing platforms. This case demonstrates how irreversible consequences from governmental policy decisions may occur if this malpractice is ignored.

Metaliteracy Domains Analyses

Considering the behavioral domain of metaliteracy, learners would need a sufficient understanding of the geography in the eastern Ukraine region and a practical understanding of clandestine military engagement to make observational assessments. At this level, learners would know that this is a steppe instead of a mountain region, as can be clearly observed behind the column of tanks. Contrary to news report claims that Russia had sent military equipment over the border in secrecy, these tanks are proceeding casually in daylight. This is contrary to the style of warfare noted in the caption text that describes the tanks as "waiting in the ambush." Furthermore, the image is well composed: The photographer is in plain view of the tank crews. The photo was not taken from a distance to avoid confrontation or threat of death. This framing and vantage point would not be typical of a stealthy invasion. Readers at this moment may be suspicious that this image has no relation to the story. At the engagement level, learners may test for authenticity by copying and uploading the photo to reverse image search websites such as Google Images, Bing, and TinEye. These will reveal that this Associated Press photo was created several years earlier and offers no relevancy to this story.

Through a brief scan of the articles on the Ukraine Investigation site, readers apply the cognitive domain by observing that the stories are thematically pro-Ukrainian/anti-Russian. Credible news organizations typically offer a range of stories—not one-sided coverage. Learners encountering an unfamiliar site may also search for information by visiting other sites that comment about the site. They may conclude, at this point, that the site is a propaganda outlet. From an affective domain perspective, readers become aware that the lead photo has been misrepresented and may discern that this site is not worthy of sharing on social platforms because that would only propagate its propaganda mission. Furthermore, learners may identify the misuse of this image in Inhofe's (2015) Senate presentation and use social media platforms to begin debunking it.

Learners apply the metacognitive domain by comprehending through reflective thinking that the likely contextual misrepresentation in this case is a deviant form of multimodal communication in an intersemiotic framework labeled "Investigation." The readers realize that photographs can be misappropriated to falsify claims made by US officials and thus must be authenticated.

If readers cannot do this, then it is appropriate to resist the conclusion until another source can authenticate the claim. In some instances, this is not possible and the claim must be left categorically open for further verification. A position of skepticism requires great discipline by citizens to avoid going with the flow of public opinion. In this case, when the claim about an invasion is not true, readers gain the awareness through metacognition to recognize that their passivity may lead to elected officials implementing unchecked policy decisions that may adversely affect citizens in other nations—and in the United States.

A CONCLUSION WITH A MISSION
IN THE POST-TRUTH ERA

The intersemiotic contextual misrepresentation of photojournalism in online story narratives has been proliferating since long before *fake news* became a term. Such a practice reduces the credibility of news organizations just as surely as unverified stories and images manipulated in Photoshop do. Social media users, empowered with mobile devices, can exacerbate contextual misuse exponentially. Yet, little effort has been expended at recognizing and preventing these malpractices, especially in journalistic education during recent decades. Metaliterate learners, however, have expanding resources for detecting these phenomena. The affective domain even empowers learners to counter false content through degrees of activism. Learners also become aware of their responsibilities as creators to publish rich, accurate multimodal content themselves.

As Facebook, Google, and other online companies hit and miss with attempts to battle online disinformation through detection programs, individuals can take control immediately through metaliterate learning. These efforts are increasingly bolstered by cognitive psychology research, findings in the neurosciences, and the expansion of social semiotics relevant to creating multimodal journalistic content, as deftly demonstrated by Caple's (2013) scholarship. State lawmakers are beginning to introduce initiatives throughout the United States to support teaching media literacy in public schools (Foley 2017). Furthermore, a metaliterate citizenry will likely set higher expectations for news organizations, challenging the Fourth Estate to regain the public's confidence and the media market share that comes with it.

Life executive editor Wilson Hicks (1952) demonstrated through his X factor how the fusion of text and image could propel narrative meaning and, consequently, impact to bring about social change. Behind his concept was an abiding care about the accuracy of these modal relationships—unlike today's morass of contextual misrepresentation across the media spectrum. But intrepid scholarship inspired by Hicks's insights fell short while the online frontier expanded in complexity. With such need for storytelling modes to be woven faithfully to serve the public trust, the time is long overdue to bring journalism back to *Life* in the post-truth era.

REFERENCES

Apkon, Stephen. 2013. *The Age of the Image: Redefining Literacy in a World of Screens*. New York: Farrar, Straus, and Giroux.

Bateman, John A. 2014. *Text and Image: A Critical Introduction to the Visual/Verbal Divide*. New York: Routledge.

Briggs, Mark. (2010, 2013) 2015. *Journalism Next: A Practical Guide to Digital Reporting and Publishing*. Washington, DC: Sage.

Caple, Helen. 2013. *Photojournalism: A Social Semiotic Approach*. New York: Palgrave Macmillan.

Christina, Tyra. 2017. "Gender Inequality in Hollywood and Mass Media." *Odyssey Online*, November 14. www.theodysseyonline.com/gender-inequality-hollywood -mass-media.

Couric, Katie. 2016. "A Message from Katie Couric." UndertheGunMovie.com. Posted May 30. http://underthegunmovie.com/message-from-katie.

Darkwave22. 2009. "Immortal vs. Yakety Sax." YouTube. Posted November 26. www.youtube.com/watch?v=7D7czIg__hA&feature=youtu.be.

Dharapak, Charles. 2012. "Romney 2012." AP Images. Submitted September 12. www.apimages.com/metadata/Index/Romney-2012/5cb623c12ce44ac6936006 669774cb28/37/0.

Drudge Report. 2012. DrudgeReportArchives.com. Originally posted September 21. www.drudgereportarchives.com/data/2012/09/21/20120921_213717.htm.

Edom, Clifton C. (1976) 1980. *Photojournalism: Principles and Practices*. Dubuque, IA: William C. Brown.

Elson, Robert T., and Curtis Prendergast. 1968. *Time Inc.: The Intimate History of a Publishing Enterprise*. New York: Atheneum.

Erickson, Alexa. 2017. "Media Remains Silent as Obama Signs Anti-propaganda Bill That Harms Press Freedom." *Collective Evolution*, January 10. www.collective -evolution.com/2017/01/10/media-remains-silent-as-obama-signs-anti -propaganda-bill-that-harms-press-freedom.

Foley, Ryan J. 2017. "Efforts Grow to Help Students Evaluate What They See Online." *AP News*, December 31. https://apnews.com/64b5ce49f58940eda 86608f3eac79158.

Folkenflik, David. 2016. "Manipulative Editing Reflects Poorly on Katie Couric, Gun Documentary." National Public Radio, "Opinion." Posted May 26. www.npr. org/2016/05/26/479655743/manipulative-editing-reflects-poorly-on-couric -and-her-gun-documentary.

Garcia, Mario R. 2018. "A Picture Can Also Tell a Thousand Lies!" *The Mario Blog*, February 28. www.garciamedia.com/blog/a-picture-can-also-tell-a -thousand-lies.

Garcia, Mario R., and Pegie Stark. 1991. *Eyes on the News*. St. Petersburg, FL: The Poynter Institute for Media Studies.

Gordon, A. David, John M. Kittross, and Carol Reuss. 1996. *Controversies in Media Ethics*. White Plains, NY: Longman.

Hicks, Wilson. 1952. *Words and Pictures: An Introduction to Photojournalism*. New York: Arno Press.

Hurley, Gerald D., and Angus McDougall. (1971) 1975. *Visual Impact in Print*. Chicago: Visual Impact.

Inhofe, James. 2015. Presentation in "Senate Session," February 11. C-SPAN video. 4:56:30. www.c-span.org/video/?324312–1/us-senate-legislative-business.

Irby, Ken. 2003. "A Photojournalistic Confession." *Poynter News*, August 20. www.poynter.org/news/photojournalistic-confession.

Jacobson, Trudi, Tom Mackey, Kelsey O'Brien, Michele Forte, and Emer O'Keeffe. 2018. "Goals and Learning Objectives." Metaliteracy.org. Accessed August 27. https://metaliteracy.org/learning-objectives.

Kelly, Keith. 2015. "Daily News Refuses to Correct Story Misidentifying 'Escapees.'" *New York Post*, August 13. https://nypost.com/2015/08/13/daily-news-refuses -to-correct-story-misidentifying-escapees.

Kobré, Kenneth. (1980, 1983, 1995, 2000, 2004, 2008) 2017. *Photojournalism: The Professionals' Approach*. Woburn, MA. Butterworth-Heinemann.

Kress, Gunther. 2010. *Multimodality: A Social Semiotic Approach to Contemporary Communication*. London/New York: Routledge.

Kress, Gunther, and Theo van Leeuwen. 1996. *Reading Images: The Grammar of Visual Design*. London/New York: Routledge.

Kroll, John. 2014. "How to Build a Better Journalism School: Part 2, Breaking Silos." *John Kroll Digital*, June 19. http://johnkrolldigital.com/2014/06/build-better -journalism-school-part-2-breaking-silos.

Langer, Susanne K. 1942. *Philosophy in a New Key*. Cambridge, MA: Harvard University Press.

Lester, Paul Martin. 1989. "The Ethics of Photojournalism: Toward a Professional Philosophy for Photographers, Editors, and Educators." PhD diss., Indiana University.

Mackey, Thomas P., and Trudi E. Jacobson. 2014. *Metaliteracy: Reinventing Information Literacy to Empower Learners*. Chicago: ALA Neal-Schuman.

Martinec, Radan, and Andrew Salway. 2005. "A System for Image-Text Relations in New (and Old) Media." *Visual Communication* 4 (3): 337–71. https://doi .org/10.1177/1470357205055928.

Medina, John J. 2018. "Rule #10: Vision Trumps All Other Senses." *Brain Rules,* "Vision." Accessed August 28. http://brainrules.net/vision.

Metzel, Mikhail. 2008. "APTOPIX Russia Georgia South Ossetia." AP Images. Submitted August 9. www.apimages.com/metadata/Index/APTOPIX-Russia -Georgia-South-Ossetia/a6a64fb312974d2bb0d8de46c6bff4d9/250/0.

Newman, Eryn J., Maryanne Garry, Daniel M. Bernstein, Justin Kantner, and D. Stephen Lindsay. 2012. "Nonprobative Photographs (or Words) Inflate Truthiness." *Psychonomic Bulletin and Review* 19 (5): 969–74. http://dx.doi .org/10.3758/s13423-012-0292-0.

Newman, Eryn J., Maryanne Garry, Daniel M. Bernstein, Christian Unkelbach, D. Stephen Lindsay, and Robert A. Nash. 2015. "Truthiness and Falsiness of Trivia Claims Depend on Judgmental Contexts." *Journal of Experimental Psychology: Learning, Memory, and Cognition* 41 (5): 1337–48. http://dx.doi .org/10.1037/xlm0000099.

Odyssey. 2018. "This Is Odyssey." *Odyssey Online.* Accessed August 28. www.theodys seyonline.com/this-is-odyssey.

Palmer, Thomas. 2015a. "Amidst Prison Breakout, a Sham-Cam 'Exclusive.'" *Albany Times Union,* "Perspective," August 2, 2.

———. 2015b. "Case 9 [Update]: Reuters Pistol Pic Is a Misfire in the Daily Beast's Ukrainian Conflict Story." *Picture Prosecutor,* May 28. http://blog.timesunion. com/pictureprosecutor/case-9-pistol-pic-is-a-misfire-for-the-daily-beasts-story -about-a-pro-ukrainian-female/669.

———. 2015c. "Case 11: AP Photo Is Off by 6 Years and 550 Miles in Contextual Misuse by Ukraine Investigation Site." *Picture Prosecutor,* June 5. http://blog. timesunion.com/pictureprosecutor/case-11-ap-photo-is-off-by-6-years-and-550 -miles-in-contextual-misuse-by-ukraine-investigation-site/822.

———. 2015d. "Case 12: Documentary Photojournalism Misused as 'Cannibal' Pictures for Faux News Stories." *Picture Prosecutor,* June 29. https://blog. timesunion.com/pictureprosecutor/case-12-cannibal-picture-misuse-causes -indigestion-for-careless-news-sites/886.

———. 2015e. "Case 15: *N.Y. Daily News* Misidentifies Two Landowners as Dannemora Prison Escapees Richard Matt and David Sweat." *Picture Prosecutor,* June 29. https://blog.timesunion.com/pictureprosecutor/case-15-n-y-daily -news-misidentifies-two-camp-owners-as-n-y-prison-escapees-richard-matt -and-david-sweat/1219.

———. 2015f. "Case 15 Update: Mystery Solved in *New York Daily News'* Misidentification of Two Men as Dannemora Escapees Matt and Sweat." *Picture Prosecutor,* August 4. http://blog.timesunion.com/pictureprosecutor/case -15-update-mystery-solved-in-daily-news-misidentification-of-two-men-as -dannemora-escapees-matt-and-sweat/1285.

———. 2015g. "Mission Statement by Thomas Palmer—the Picture Prosecutor." *Picture Prosecutor*, February 5. http://blog.timesunion.com/pictureprosecutor/ mission-statement-by-thomas-palmer-the-picture-prosecutor/67.

———. 2015h. "Q&A: What Is Contextual Misrepresentation in Photojournalism?" *Picture Prosecutor*, February 6. http://blog.timesunion.com/pictureprosecutor/ qa-what-is-contextual-misrepresentation-in-photojournalism/155.

———. 2017. "Case 19: *NYT* Photo Imperiled as Click Bait for Fake News Sites." *Picture Prosecutor*, October 5. http://blog.timesunion.com/pictureprosecutor/ case-17-nyt-photo-imperiled-as-click-bait-for-fake-news-sites/1399.

———. 2018. "Commentary: A *New York Times* Picture Worth a Thousand Lies." *Times Union*, February 25. www.timesunion.com/opinion/article/Commentary-A-New -York-Times-picture-worth-a-12706740.php.

Pear, Robert. 2012. "Obama Signs Bill Banning Insider Trading by Federal Lawmakers." *New York Times*, April 4. https://thecaucus.blogs.nytimes.com/ 2012/04/04/obama-signs-bill-banning-insider-trading-by-federal-lawmakers/ ?_r=0.

Remley, Dirk. 2015. *How the Brain Processes Multimodal Technical Instructions*. Amityville, NY: Baywood.

Silverman, Craig. 2018. "Beware of False Claims of Assaults at 'Black Panther' Screenings." *BuzzFeed News*, February 16. www.buzzfeednews.com/article/ craigsilverman/trolls-are-posting-fake-claims-of-being-assaulted-at.

Silverman, Jonathan, and Dean Rader. 2012. *The World Is a Text: Writing, Reading, and Thinking about Visual and Popular Culture*. Upper Saddle River, NJ: Prentice Hall.

Sklar, Marc. 2018. "How Celebrities Deal with Infertility." Marc Sklar, the Fertility Expert. Accessed August 28. https://marcsklar.com/how-celebrities-deal-with -infertility.

Snopes. 2016. "Obama Signs Executive Order Banning the Pledge of Allegiance in Schools Nationwide." Snopes.com. Posted August 16. www.snopes.com/pledge -of-allegiance-ban.

SPJ (Society of Professional Journalists). 2014. "SPJ Code of Ethics." Revised September 6. www.spj.org/ethicscode.asp.

Stokols, Eli. 2012. "Ann Romney's Plane Makes Emergency Landing in Denver." FOX31 Denver KDVR-TV. Posted September 21. http://kdvr.com/2012/09/21/ ann-romneys-plane-makes-emergency-landing-in-denver.

Trafton, Anne. 2014. "In the Blink of an Eye." *MIT News*, January 16. http://news .mit.edu/2014/in-the-blink-of-an-eye-0116.

Tucker, Patrick. 2014. "The Science of Unmasking Russian Forces in Ukraine." *Defense One*, April 16. www.defenseone.com/technology/2014/04/science-unmasking -russian-forces-ukraine/82693.

Vierig, Christian. 2017. "Street Style: Day 3—LFW September 2017." Getty Images. Created September 17. www.gettyimages.com/license/848614328. Wallace, Caroline. 2016. "Obama Did Not Ban the Pledge." FactCheck.org, "Ask FactCheck." Posted September 2. www.factcheck.org/2016/09/obama-did-not -ban-the-pledge.

Washington Free Beacon. 2016. "Raw Audio of Katie Couric Interview with VCDL Members." SoundCloud. Posted May 24. https://soundcloud.com/washington -free-beacon/raw-audio-of-katie-couric-interview-with-vcdl-members.

Weinstein, Adam. 2015. "Senator 'Duped' into Using Old Photos to Promote New War with Russia." *Gawker*, February 21. http://fortressamerica.gawker.com/senator -duped-into-using-old-photos-to-promote-new-wa-1685511541.

Wilson, Meagan. 2016. "Patricia Manfield: Founder, the Atelier; Musician. Milan." *Coveteur*, June 2. http://coveteur.com/2016/06/21/patricia-manfield-street -style-star-closet.

NICOLE A. COOKE and
RACHEL M. MAGEE

6

Teaching and Learning with Metaliterate LIS Professionals

In a 2012 commencement speech, astrophysicist Neil deGrasse Tyson discussed the perils of fuzzy thinking. He described two camps of people: those who know *how* to think and those who know *what* to think. The distinction here is that people who know what to think view information and knowledge as a product, and those who know how to think realize that building knowledge out of information is a process. Tyson notes that "knowing how to think empowers you far beyond those who know only what to think" (Western New England University 2012). Tyson believes that (science) literacy is a lens that can be used to make sense of the world around us; it is an outlook that enables us to turn the what into the how. In this climate of fake news and inordinate amounts of information, thinking and decision making cannot be performative; rather, we need to be able to think critically and use all of the literacy skills at our disposal. We also need to acquire and use such skills in context, and we need to be reflective in our information consumption, evaluation, and usage. We need to be metaliterate. Mackey and Jacobson (2014) describe metaliteracy as follows:

> Metaliteracy expands the scope of traditional information skills (determine, access, locate, understand, produce, and use

> information) to include the collaborative production and sharing of information in participatory digital environments (collaborate, produce, and share). This approach requires an ongoing adaptation to emerging technologies and an understanding of the critical thinking and reflection required to engage in these spaces as producers, collaborators, and distributors. (1)

In our work as library and information science (LIS) educators, we, the authors, believe that promoting metaliteracy can and should be embraced and supported by dynamic and thoughtful information professionals. In the course of our work to support our students' development into the kind of librarians, educators, and information professionals who know how to think, we have recognized the need for reframing our understanding of their skills, perspectives, and needs as well as our approach to serving our communities and the ways in which we encourage inclusive and multilevel conversations around literacies.

In this chapter, we detail our attempts to augment the ways in which we discuss and teach our students how to be metaliterate. LIS curricula traditionally focus on information literacy, media literacy, and other types of literacy, all of which tend to be siloed in the ways they are understood and applied by information professionals; however, given the current information landscape and cultural climate, we need our students to be more than just information literate, media literate, and literate in other distinct areas. Aspiring information professionals need to be metaliterate, and they need to have a solid ability and willingness to impart this critical thinking lens and skill set to their own students and patrons. In an attempt to transform our curriculum to better serve our students, we are incorporating the concepts of metaliteracy and the ACRL's (2016) *Framework for Information Literacy for Higher Education* into our instructional practices. As a specific example of our recent efforts and approach, we held a Fake News workshop at our institution for students, faculty, staff, and community members where we discussed ways to further extend elements of these frameworks into LIS pedagogy. Students' observations and experiences with the metaliteracy framework provide practical ways for others in LIS education programs to incorporate these ideas. By increasing new LIS professionals' abilities to engage in metaliterate approaches to information, we enhanced their capacity to support communities in developing these same competencies.

A REALIZATION

Prompted in part by the recent interest in and discourse around fake news, none of which is new or surprising to information professionals, we developed a workshop that drew a large audience of students, librarians, educators, and journalists (almost 100 attendees in person and online). This event put into sharp relief the realization that our audience was actively seeking ways to encourage literate practices (in this case the ability to refute fake news) while simultaneously understanding that they lacked the tools necessary to do so. From the questions and conversations that arose in the workshop, along with the questions asked in our graduate LIS classes that semester, it became evident that our assumptions about our students' metaliteracy abilities (as well as their own assumptions) needed to be challenged and their perceptions about teaching and learning needed to be expanded. Questions that arose revealed a disconnect between what they think they know about information literacy, media literacy, and other related literacies and how that knowledge can or should be applied to the current conundrum of fake news. The existing knowledge held by workshop attendees and course participants leaned more toward the *what* described by Tyson. These intelligent people knew specific facts and techniques but were unsure if they applied to the current problem. They were looking for a specific outcome and solution (what can be done to identify and eliminate fake news), instead of stepping back and recognizing that they already possessed the right information and just needed to apply it appropriately and in a new way. They were missing the *how*, not understanding the process of applying their previously acquired skills to a newly named dilemma. They were able to evaluate websites, pick out the photoshopped images, and select a peer-reviewed article, but these skills had been mentally cordoned off and were not being applied to the admittedly complicated fake news phenomenon. Is this indicative of compartmentalization, a disconnect in terminology, or something more?

To address this need, we build on Jacobson and Mackey's (2016) metaliteracy framework and ACRL's (2016) information literacy framework to present key considerations for LIS educators and pedagogy. These center on four main elements drawn from the frameworks and propose detailed methods for enhancing intellectual humility; emphasizing the importance of continued evaluation and assessment of the role of librarians; extending conversations about scholarship beyond our students and scholarly fields to include communities at large; and contrasting actions that we think of as "literate" with abilities and dispositions that remain flexible to new literacy challenges.

FOUNDATIONAL FRAMEWORKS

When considering LIS pedagogy as a whole and specifically regarding acute topics such as fake news, two literacy approaches can be applied as frameworks: metaliteracy (Jacobson and Mackey 2016; Mackey and Jacobson 2011, 2014) and the *Framework for Information Literacy for Higher Education* (ACRL 2016). These frameworks allow for a holistic examination of information as both a topic and a tool.

Metaliteracy

The literature concerning the various kinds of discrete literacies (e.g., information, digital, media, visual, etc.) is extensive but does not always link one to another, and as previously mentioned, this can unintentionally lead to the understanding and practice of literacy in isolation, as opposed to examining literacy in the broadest possible context. To that end, the concept of metaliteracy provides learners and educators an opportunity to consider literacy in a holistic fashion.

Metaliteracy is most often seen in the literature as a way to reframe and expand information literacy practices, particularly in academic libraries (Dunaway 2011; Lux 2013; Witek and Grettano 2014; Appleton 2017); to discuss the teaching of disciplinary content in higher education settings, in cooperation with libraries (Gersch, Lampner, and Turner 2016); and to understand the need to teach technology and social media skills in new ways (Kimmel, Dickinson, and Doll 2014). After a brief examination of the metaliteracy literature, we made several observations. Metaliteracy has become visible in the literature and has been documented as having made a difference in how librarians teach to and learn with their students. However, what is missing from this growing body of articles and chapters are the implications for students and patrons who are taught metaliteracy concepts. How are these concepts being applied in "real life," or not, after an instruction session and outside of a library or research environment? Another omission involves the discussion of metaliteracy in public and school libraries and its potential for use in nonacademic or noncollegiate settings. Also missing from the literature is the use of metaliteracy in graduate LIS programs. Education at this level is equally important, and introducing the concepts of metaliteracy to aspiring information professionals can help transform and improve the field from the inside out.

With this in mind, we argue that there is a gap in the literature, and in LIS practice, in regard to metaliteracy, and education about fake news falls squarely within this gap. Perhaps this gap can begin to explain why people's "library skills" are not being applied to the nonlibrary problem of fake news. It is certainly important to impart metaliteracy approaches in library classrooms; however, if we are to address fake news in a lasting and effective manner, we must also be teaching students (K–12 and graduate LIS students) and members of the community. This is a larger conversation involving a repertoire of concepts, skills, critical thinking, and abilities that extends beyond our colleges and universities and impacts teaching, learning, and professional development at multiple levels.

We believe that metaliteracy is the most appropriate lens through which to examine fake news, precisely because of its applicability to community and its focus on the *creation* of content, not just the distribution and consumption of content. Fake news is as rampant and pernicious as it is because there are so many people and platforms involved in its creation on a variety of levels. Fake news is a multifaceted issue that requires the multidimensional abilities, multiple ways of thinking, and multiple literacies generated in twenty-first-century learning environments. Appleton (2017) describes such environments as "social, multimodal, interactive and open," requiring "an integration of visual, textual, aural, media, digital and collaborative competencies" (171).

The ACRL Framework for Information Literacy for Higher Education

In addition to building on the concept of metaliteracy, we apply the ACRL's (2016) *Framework for Information Literacy for Higher Education*. Specifically, we are working toward the following: reframing LIS educators' assumptions about the skills and experiences of students with regard to literacies; recognizing the educational needs of LIS students; encouraging LIS as a field to reevaluate the role of librarians as a part of the conversation around fake news and literacy in our communities; extending the "scholarship as conversation" element of the framework not just to professionals but to communities at large; and contrasting different definitions of being "literate" based on specific ideas about how to evaluate and reevaluate information on a conceptual level as a metaliterate learner.

This framework, formally adopted by ACRL on January 11, 2016, after being accepted and filed by the ACRL Board on February 2, 2015, builds in part on Wiggins and McTighe's (2005) work that prompts attention to concepts and questions within disciplines, or threshold concepts (Meyer, Land, and Baillie 2010), which "can be thought of as portals through which the learner must pass in order to develop new perspectives and wider understanding" (as cited in ACRL 2016, 3). The framework also builds on the metaliteracy concepts described earlier.

The framework presents six frames that center around interrelated central concepts, which are each presented with accompanying *knowledge practices* and *dispositions*. Knowledge practices are "demonstrations of ways in which learners can increase their understanding" of these central concepts, and dispositions "describe ways in which to address the affective, attitudinal, or valuing dimension of learning" (ACRL 2016, 2). The framework is intended to prompt flexible implementation rather than prescribe specific standards or outcomes and "opens the way for librarians, faculty, and other institutional partners to redesign instruction sessions, assignments, courses, and even curricula" (ACRL 2016, 3). We find this approach particularly relevant to our work in reorienting to and reenvisioning our students, pedagogical techniques, and curricula.

For the work described in this chapter, we relied heavily on two of the central concepts and their associated knowledge practices and dispositions: "Research as Inquiry" and "Scholarship as Conversation." Each of these concepts highlights the importance of engaging beyond the academy with communities, framing research as extending to the "community at large," with the process potentially focusing on "personal, professional, and societal needs" (ACRL 2016, 7). Thinking of scholarship as a conversation recognizes the authority structures and power relationships that inform these discussions and frames scholarship as a discursive, "ongoing conversation in which information users and creators come together and negotiate meaning" (ACRL 2016, 8).

We apply this expanded perspective to our engagement with our community, which we conceptualize as including not just our fellow LIS faculty but also our students and their service communities. By taking this approach, we are able to extend our understanding of the impacts of and current difficulties surrounding literacy practices. Though there are many contexts in which these ideas are relevant, they came to the fore in our recent work addressing fake news, which in turn prompted the reflections and recommendations shared in this chapter.

UNDERSTANDING THE FAKE NEWS CONTEXT

Subsequent to the 2016 presidential election, fake news became a hot topic, a *cause du jour*, and a moral crisis that needed to be addressed immediately. Citizens became justifiably concerned about false information being rapidly spread on social media and through broadcast outlets and about the implications of this misleading information. Fake news was being blamed for any number of political and societal ills, and the discussion and impact of this new ethical dilemma escalated so quickly that keeping up with it and addressing it succinctly and efficiently became difficult. And then the questions of whose problem fake news was and who should address it entered into the conversation. The confusion and finger-pointing around the issue were intense, further confounding an already complicated issue. However, what was missing from the initial conversations was the idea that fake news is not a new phenomenon; it just had a new name and intensity.

Librarians, in particular, know that false and misleading information have always been an issue and thus have always worked to impart skills to members of their communities to help them combat misinformation and disinformation (Cooke 2017, 2018). Misinformation (which can range from blatant lies, to hoaxes, to satire, to missing facts) and disinformation (when misinformation is purposeful and meant to deceive) are age-old information problems (think about propaganda and yellow journalism)—problems that concern multiple disciplines and professions, including information professionals, journalists, educators, and more. All of us are now faced with a new dimension to an old problem: How do we educate, and reeducate, our constituents to critically evaluate all information and information sources, not just the ones conveniently, and sometimes erroneously, labeled fake news?

THE FAKE NEWS WORKSHOP

On February 1, 2017, we set out to address growing conversation and concern around the concept of fake news with a workshop held at the iSchool at the University of Illinois Urbana–Champaign (U of I; Cooke et al. 2017). This work explicitly aligned with the concepts of community described in the ACRL *Framework*, with current LIS students; undergrads and grad students from U of I at large; practicing librarians in school, public, and community college contexts; journalism students and faculty; and members of the general public all joining in the conversation. In addition to reaching in-person attendees, the workshop was also streamed live to a virtual audience, and a recording of the event is available online (http://media.ischool.illinois.edu/dl/events/FakeNews_Feb1_17.mp4).

The workshop brought together multiple scholars, including the authors of this chapter as well as Dr. Stephanie Craft, a full professor of journalism in the College of Media at U of I, whose research focuses on news literacy, trust practices, and performance and journalism ethics. The concluding panelist was Dr. Barbara Jones, an affiliate faculty member at the U of I School of Information Sciences and former director of the American Library Association's (ALA) Office of Intellectual Freedom.

> Craft addressed the "threat" of fake news from a journalistic perspective, calling for news literacy initiatives that teach people how to identify visual markers of fake news and assess source credibility as well as addressing the social, commercial, and political contexts of news production.
>
> Magee focused on social network sites and their connection to fake news, with discussion of how teens assess information credibility in these contexts. She also discussed how literature from communication and media literacy scholarship has identified a "skills-based approach" to media literacy as "necessary but not sufficient" (Livingstone 2004), indicating a need for more complex ways to conceptualize and address information and the information and communication technology (ICT) contexts where it is shared.
>
> Cooke brought important historical context to the presentation, highlighting that post-truth, truthiness, and alternative facts, framed as misinformation and disinformation, have long been a part of information literacy conversations. She shared techniques to identify and move past these kinds of information, including developing an awareness of one's own biases and using fact-checking sources, as well as critically assessing the source, angle, and credibility of individual sources.
>
> Jones detailed multiple examples of misleading news and discussed the ALA's News Know-How project (Office for Intellectual Freedom

2014), which focuses on engaging youth in developing information literacy skills, including methods for identifying facts and opinions and checking facts and sources.

Taken together, the themes of these presentations concurred with the idea that current approaches to literacy, credibility assessment, and engagement with news and other information are not supporting a fully engaged evaluation of information, content creators, and sources. This can be compounded by current discourse around fake news and information. Though false and low-quality information have always been a part of the landscape, the currency of these topics and the way they are discussed by the media, politicians, and the public at large prompted our audience to increase their attention and concern.

We were surprised that the audience expressed such a desire for guidance in ways to address this information climate. Attendees made it clear that they felt at a loss and described needing help not just for their professional work but for their own personal information practices and surrounding social interactions. This experience prompted us to examine ways to address gaps in experience and understanding on the part of our students, as well as our own conceptions and approaches to LIS pedagogy. In the following section we share ideas and techniques that we are using to refine our school's curriculum, discussing not just the conceptual underpinnings but also some of the practical methods we are employing in this work.

APPLICATIONS TO LIS EDUCATION AND CURRICULA

As we begin to rethink our classes and curricula at large, we focus our attention on four main areas that have implications for course design, in-class interaction, and cross-course planning. These areas arise from the concept of metaliteracy and its intersections with the *Framework for Information Literacy for Higher Education* (ACRL 2016). They include reframing assumptions, recognizing educational needs, extending scholarship as conversation, and contrasting literate actions with metaliterate abilities/dispositions. In the same spirit that the ACRL *Framework* builds on the concept of metaliteracy, we consider these ideas part of "a renewed vision of information literacy as an overarching set of abilities in which students [and we would add communities and LIS educators and faculty] are consumers and creators of information who can participate successfully in collaborative spaces" (ACRL 2016, 2, citing Mackey and Jacobson 2011).

Reframing Assumptions

Though we have long been aware that our LIS students need scaffolding to understand the literacy skills and needs of their service populations, the experience of the Fake News Workshop highlighted existing gaps in our LIS students' ideas, techniques, and confidence levels for addressing the, at times, contentious climate around information literacy. We see that these gaps are related to assumptions that occur in several areas, including the skills and abilities of service populations, the literacy skills of our own students, and, most important, LIS educators' understandings of their students and their courses.

It can be easy to take for granted that LIS students have a strong understanding of metaliteracy concepts; after all, they are committed to the information professions, they are often taking classes that build their technical skills, and they are engaging in this work during the digital information age. However, the metacognitive and collaborative elements of metaliteracy can be complex for students, who may have less previous instruction and experience with thinking about their own thinking and working with others to build their abilities. It can also be easy to assume that graduate LIS courses are addressing the needs of our students, or that if we could just get all library service providers to share the right set of criteria for assessing the credibility of information, our communities would be able to effectively navigate misinformation and disinformation. Assumptions about our students and communities inform each other and can compound to decrease the impact and effectiveness of library services and programs as well as LIS education.

To fully address the potential impact of these assumptions, consider the concept of intellectual humility. Scholars frame intellectual humility as a core competency or trait of individuals capable of critical thinking, with the key ability of "being aware of one's biases and prejudices as well as the limitations of one's viewpoint and the extent of one's ignorance" (Elder and Paul 2012). The ACRL (2016) *Framework* describes intellectual humility as a disposition characterized by the ability of learners to "recognize their own intellectual or experiential limitations" (7). Individuals who demonstrate intellectual humility consistently examine their own perspectives and motivations. We see a need to develop the disposition of intellectual humility, not only in our students, but also in LIS faculty and educators. Intellectual humility requires us to step beyond our own experiences and understandings of literacy and learning. This is key for assessing our own perspectives, but also for better understanding what our students do not know. In an effort to encourage ourselves, our colleagues, and our students to embrace this disposition, we offer a series of questions to prompt engagement with intellectual humility:

- How did you learn about literacy? How do you assess information?
- What gaps do you see in your students' understanding of literacy?
- What gaps do you see in your students' understanding of service populations?
- What gaps do your students see (and fail to see) in their own approaches to literacy and library service?

- What elements of metaliteracy, such as metacognition and collaboration, do you promote in your instruction?
- Do you (or your students) think of literacy skills as static or dynamic?
- Are you still developing your own literacy skills?
- How do you model intellectual humility to your students?
- How can you explicitly promote intellectual humility to your students?

These questions are intended as a starting point for engaging with new perspectives on our, our students', and our communities' understandings of literacy. However we engage with the disposition of intellectual humility, having this open approach enables us to better recognize and address the educational needs of our students.

Recognizing Educational Needs

Embracing intellectual humility in our work with LIS students goes hand in hand with reorienting our understandings of the needs of our students and our communities. Within the case study of our Fake News Workshop, we saw that students had bigger gaps in skills and confidence than we had suspected. These would not have been as evident without our community-centered approach to discussion, which recognized students as valued in the conversation and key for the development of metaliterate communities. Because we embraced the students' perspectives, they felt comfortable sharing their concerns and needs for their own learning and development. This community emphasis is key for the approach to pedagogy we describe here. We identify two areas where we can approach our work differently: reassessing the roles of information professionals in the conversations around fake news and information literacy, more broadly construed, and taking steps to reevaluate and then address the needs of LIS students to be better equipped for these roles. In the discussions that arose during the Fake News Workshop, one comment highlighted tensions around the ways literacy can operate:

> The goal of news literacy is to make skeptical news consumers, but what can happen is that you can make cynical news consumers. . . . Journalists alone just doing better journalism isn't going to help us, if people are unwilling to kind of take those facts and process them in a kind of rational way.

In the conversation around fake news, this line between content, content producers, and other people is precisely where librarians and information professionals have an opportunity to step in and engage differently than we have before. If traditional approaches to developing and supporting literacy have not worked in the ways we hoped, then a reassessment (in addition to a disposition of intellectual humility) is in order. From our perspective, this calls for proactive engagement in community conversation and practice around information literacy. By incorporating metaliteracy concepts into the way we approached our workshop design and subsequent curricular adjustments, it was clear how crucial it is to engage in continued evaluation of our students' skills and abilities, as was the importance of understanding the needs, skills, and interests of our service populations. We found that embedding this expanded LIS approach to literacy education within community-oriented concepts enabled more responsive and relevant librarianship as well as scholarship.

Effective engagement with our communities requires librarians and information professionals to develop and employ skills in a variety of areas, moving beyond customary approaches to literacy instruction. This has direct implications for the design of curricula and instruction practices. For LIS educators and faculty, there are several key elements in this area of work, including assessing the skills and abilities of LIS students, determining their needs, restructuring pedagogy and course content, and continually reassessing each of these key components. Potential techniques that could prove effective in moving through these stages include using preassessments in literacy- and instruction-oriented courses to understand students' conceptions of literacy skills priorities; prioritizing in-class discussions on metaliteracy and the ACRL *Framework* (e.g., how do students respond to the concept of knowledge practices and dispositions?); examining ways to connect literacy to other concepts central to the work of library and information professionals; and employing postassessments with students to understand the effectiveness of these approaches. Instructors might also consider going beyond course evaluations to facilitate explicit discussions about pedagogy with students during class.

In our own work responding to the educational needs of LIS students, we have placed an emphasis on developing specific courses and orienting our instruction across courses to highlight the concepts of cultural competence and engagement via community inquiry. Cultural competence within the context of LIS speaks to the idea that diverse and otherwise marginalized populations "require libraries to get to know them personally, and they deserve quality programming, services, and resources that are tailored to their information needs" (Cooke 2016, 2). Similarly, we have built upon the concept of community inquiry, which supports "collaborative activity and . . . creating knowledge connected to people's values, history, and lived experiences" (Bruce, Bishop, and Budhathoki 2014, 1).

Transforming Theory into Practice

A specific example of how these conversations and frameworks have immediately influenced the curricula at our school occurred during the fall 2017 semester in a class titled Use and Users of Information (taught by Cooke).

A class centered on information behavior (the individual, community, and sociopolitical processes by which people need, seek, and use information) was co-created by twenty-five students who embarked on content and projects (book reviews and group projects) related to the class theme of "fake news." Explicitly focusing on the affective dimension of information behaviors and practices, students discovered the wide range of emotions that come with information consumption and then applied that understanding to the phenomenon of fake news. Why do ordinarily smart people fall prey to fake news, misinformation, disinformation, hoaxes, lies, satire, parodies, and propaganda? A big part of this is emotion: people identify with the information that corresponds with their existing beliefs (whether the information is true or false) and gravitate toward ideas that do not make them uncomfortable, fearful, frustrated, or confused (Cooke 2018). People also engage with information that is easy and gets the job done without extra work on their part (e.g., information that flows freely to their social media feeds). This focus on the affective domain of information consumption, as opposed to the cognitive domain (i.e., the mental processing and application of information), was new for students. Certainly, they had all experienced emotional reactions to information, but they had not given those reactions conscious intellectual thought. The subsequent application of this new knowledge to the problem of fake news was unquestionably an enlightening process, one that will enable them to better teach critical thinking skills to *their* students and patrons once they become librarians and information professionals.

An example of a theoretical discussion that proved particularly challenging for the entire class, both instructor and students, was information poverty (Chatman 1996; Britz 2004). As the phrase suggests, some people and communities lack information and/or access to information for a wide variety of reasons, and this can be considered a deficit. However, information poverty cannot be thought of exclusively as a deficit. Information consumption can be a purposeful choice—information consumers can willfully ignore news, media, and other sources that are not convenient or that upset them—and sometimes information is out of reach because it is financially inaccessible (e.g., articles and journals that exist behind paywalls). As such, "poverty" is not always a function of socioeconomic or class status, and one group's perception of what constitutes poverty could be another group's notion of wealth. Students learned not to make assumptions about people's understanding or situations and were able to apply this principle back to fake news. An easy solution to fake news might be to flood information consumers with "good" information, but if they reject said information because they do not think they are experiencing any deficits and do not consider themselves to be information poor, they will not gain additional insights or perspectives in their learning. If they consistently gravitate toward their preferred sources of information because they are easy, they comfort them, they do not disagree with them, and so on, such an approach will not be successful. So, what is the best way to help people combat fake news? As information professionals, we are still trying to figure this out. We can definitely address cognitive practices of information seeking and use and critical thinking skills, but addressing people's emotional responses and actions is a more difficult task.

This particular conversation on information poverty was an exercise in intellectual humility, which enabled the class to consider cultural competence and community inquiry and to examine literacy and critical thinking skills within a larger real-life context. Contextualizing literacy within the development of applicable skills in interacting with diverse communities and building understanding of the populations we serve helps our students support their patrons and students and step into new, more proactive roles in addressing metaliteracy development and application. At the conclusion of the sixteen-week semester, students left with a better understanding of their own thinking and assumptions about information consumption and fake news, and as a result, they had a more nuanced understanding of the information consumption habits of the people they will be serving in practice.

CONCLUDING THOUGHTS

Our work has been designed to align with the metaliteracy and ACRL frameworks through our mutual investments in community. Collaborating with our students to understand their needs, to learn ways to understand and support our diverse communities, and to extend our conversations in ways that include these stakeholders has helped us to make progress in addressing gaps in our students' skills and confidence. We have endeavored to approach this work by exercising our own intellectual humility and by valuing the input of our students and communities. We have been able to extend a conversation that reframed our understanding of student experiences to identify student and community needs. We have built on this discussion by developing pedagogical strategies that connect theory and practice, in our classrooms and in our approaches to educational leadership. This work, which encourages our students to be metaliterate rather than simply applying literacy heuristics and skills, enables them to think through and capably address information issues, whether it be fake news or the next "new" difficulty or crisis.

Recent conversations about fake news have highlighted gaps in graduate-level pedagogy, particularly in professional and service-oriented academic programs. We have seen our students actively seeking ways to address issues of misinformation, disinformation, lies, satire, omitted information, and other problematic forms of information. Applying the metaliteracy framework and elements of the ACRL *Framework* to these conversations has opened ways for us, as LIS educators, to adjust our approaches to our courses and instruction, with the goal of encouraging our students to learn how to think rather than what to think. This work is an important part of educating information professionals but is also relevant to students and educators in many fields. Metaliteracy abilities are key for all students and all communities. Our work to support and engage our students has centered on the ideas of reframing our assumptions about our students, taking new steps to recognize their educational needs, extending conversations about our scholarship into our communities at large, and prompting our students to develop metaliteracy thought processes rather than taking heuristic or specific action-based approaches to assessing information. By explicitly teaching and encouraging LIS students to adopt the practices and dispositions of metaliteracy within community-centered practice, we can directly address the not-new phenomenon of fake news.

REFERENCES

ACRL (Association for College and Research Libraries). 2016. *Framework for Information Literacy for Higher Education*. Chicago: American Library Association. www.ala.org/acrl/sites/ala.org.acrl/files/content/issues/infolit/Framework _ILHE.pdf.

Appleton, Leo. 2017. "Metaliteracy in Art and Design Education: Implications for Library Instruction." In *The Handbook of Art and Design Librarianship*, edited by Paul Glassman and Judy Dyki, 169–78. London: Facet.

Britz, Johannes J. 2004. "To Know or Not to Know: A Moral Reflection on Information Poverty." *Journal of Information Science* 30 (3): 192–204.

Bruce, Bertram C., Ann P. Bishop, and Nama R. Budhathoki, eds. 2014. *Youth Community Inquiry: New Media for Community and Personal Growth*. New York: Peter Lang.

Chatman, Elfreda A. 1996. "The Impoverished Life-World of Outsiders." *Journal of the American Society for Information Science* 47 (3): 193–206.

Cooke, Nicole A. 2016. *Information Services to Diverse Populations: Developing Culturally Competent Library Professionals*. Santa Barbara, CA: ABC-CLIO.

———. 2017. "Post-truth, Truthiness, and Alternative Facts: Information Behavior and Critical Information Consumption for a New Age." *The Library Quarterly: Information, Community, Policy* 87 (3): 211–21.

———. 2018. *Fake News and Alternative Facts: Information Literacy in a Post-Truth Era*. Chicago: ALA Editions.

Cooke, Nicole, Rachel M. Magee, Stephanie Craft, and Barbara Jones. 2017. "Fake News: A Workshop Presented by the iSchool." Workshop held at the University of Illinois Urbana–Champaign, February 1. http://media.ischool.illinois.edu/dl/ events/FakeNews_Feb1_17.mp4.

Dunaway, Michelle K. 2011. "Connectivism: Learning Theory and Pedagogical Practice for Networked Information Landscapes." *Reference Services Review* 39 (4): 675–85.

Elder, Linda, and Richard Paul. 2012. "Critical Thinking: Competency Standards Essential to the Cultivation of Intellectual Skills, Part 4." *Journal of Developmental Education* 35 (3): 30–31.

Gersch, Beate, Wendy Lampner, and Dudley Turner. 2016. "Collaborative Metaliteracy: Putting the New Information Literacy Framework into (Digital) Practice." *Journal of Library and Information Services in Distance Learning* 10 (3–4): 199–214.

Jacobson, Trudi E., and Thomas P. Mackey, eds. 2016. *Metaliteracy in Practice*. Chicago: ALA Neal-Schuman.

Kimmel, Sue C., Gail K. Dickinson, and Carol A. Doll. 2014. "The Cultural Commons of Teen Literacy." In *Educational Media and Technology Yearbook*, edited by Michael Orey, Stephanie A. Jones, and Robert Maribe Branch, vol. 38, 139–151. Cham: Springer International.

Livingstone, Sonia. 2004. "Media Literacy and the Challenge of New Information and Communication Technologies." *The Communication Review* 7 (1): 3–14.

Lux, Vera J. 2013. "Reimaging Information Literacy as Metaliteracy in a Credit Library Course." *University Libraries Faculty Publications*, no. 44. https://scholarworks.bgsu.edu/ul_pub/44.

Mackey, Thomas P., and Trudi E. Jacobson. 2011. "Reframing Information Literacy as a Metaliteracy." *College and Research Libraries* 72 (1): 62–78.

———. 2014. *Metaliteracy: Reinventing Information Literacy to Empower Learners*. Chicago: ALA Neal-Schuman.

Meyer, Jan H. F., Ray Land, and Caroline Baillie, eds. 2010. *Threshold Concepts and Transformational Learning*. Rotterdam, the Netherlands: Sense.

Office for Intellectual Freedom. 2014. *News Know-How Initiative*. Chicago: American Library Association. http://digital.americanlibrariesmagazine.org/html5/reader/production/default.aspx?pubname=&edid=96e78987-507f-4e7c-bcb2-7a50419016ff.

Western New England University. 2012. "Dr. Neil deGrasse Tyson's Commencement Address at Western New England University." YouTube. Posted May 23. www.youtube.com/watch?v=EsZYLhYYplU.

Wiggins, Grant P., and Jay McTighe. 2005. *Understanding by Design*. Alexandria, VA: Association for Supervision and Curriculum Development.

Witek, Donna, and Teresa Grettano. 2014. "Teaching Metaliteracy: A New Paradigm in Action." *Reference Services Review* 42 (2): 188–208.

ALLISON HOSIER

7

First, Teach Students to Be Wrong

In 2011, Mackey and Jacobson proposed metaliteracy as a framework for integrating the impact of emerging technologies, online communities, and related literacies into our understanding of information literacy. A key way in which metaliteracy expands on traditional notions about information literacy is in its tenet that a learner is not just a user of information but also a creator of information through dynamic, participatory environments such as those encountered via social media. As Mackey and Jacobson (2011) state, "While information literacy prepares individuals to access, evaluate, and analyze information, metaliteracy prepares individuals to actively produce and share content through social media and online communities" (76). This shift in thinking infused goals and concepts that had previously been associated with information literacy with new relevance in the changing information environment.

The advent of the current post-truth climate following the 2016 presidential election has made the profound influence that social media can have on how we perceive the world and act within it clearer than ever. Mackey and Jacobson could not have foreseen the current political climate in which we find ourselves, but their metaliteracy model did anticipate the need to teach students not only to be ethical users of information but also responsible creators and sharers of information. As McGarrity (2016) states in her discussion on using metaliteracy to cultivate agency in learners, "Agency is about empowerment, but it's also about responsibility" (167). Wallis and Batista (2016) take this idea further by suggesting that "students who are growing as metaliterate learners should develop awareness of how information affects their lives and influences society as a whole" (29). As active participants in social information environments, students have the ability to impact the world around them in ever-changing ways. Because of this, it is important to teach them to be not only ethical users of information but also empowered and ethical creators of information.

The ACRL (2016) *Framework for Information Literacy for Higher Education* introduced an expanded definition of information literacy that connects to the metacognitive, information creation, and participation elements of the metaliteracy learning goals and objectives (Jacobson and Mackey 2013; Mackey and Jacobson 2014). This new definition of information literacy provides practitioners with more freedom than ever before to expand beyond instruction that portrays the student primarily as a user of information. Faculty and librarians now have the flexibility to teach students about their role as creators of information and the responsibilities that come with that role.

Teaching students about these expanded roles was the purpose of a freshman seminar titled Empowering Yourself as a User and Creator of Information, which was first taught by the author in fall 2017 at the University at Albany, SUNY. This chapter first introduces the context in which this course was designed and taught as well as explores its connections to metaliteracy. The author then considers a specific lesson from the course on the topic of being wrong as an illustration of the importance of the course's themes in the current post-truth climate.

CONTEXT AND BACKGROUND

Freshman seminars at the University at Albany are offered through the Office of Student Engagement and are a chance for first-year students to meet in a small classroom setting where they can get to know their peers and have more direct contact with their instructor than they might in a large lecture hall. The title, focus, design, and content of these one-credit courses is largely up to the discretion of the instructors as long as the students have the opportunity to interact with one another as part of the course. Topics about navigating university life must also be integrated with the course's main content. This gives the instructors who volunteer to teach these courses tremendous leeway to teach about topics and themes that are of interest to them in ways that will be meaningful to first-year students.

Empowering Yourself as a User and Creator of Information was based on an information literacy course the author had taught previously but with a renewed focus on real-world issues rather than library-based research skills. This was intended in part to reflect developments in the field brought on by metaliteracy and the ACRL (2016) *Framework*. Additionally, reframing the course in this way allowed the author to delve further into connections between metaliteracy and the post-truth world by exploring issues related to fake news and misinformation. Students would learn not only how to evaluate information and use it ethically but also how to create and share information responsibly.

According to the learning goals created for the course, the students would learn to do the following:

- Critically evaluate information using recommended criteria.
- Identify internal and external factors that complicate the process of evaluating information.
- Apply recommended practices for responsible information creation and sharing.
- Apply recommended strategies for being a successful first-year college student to a variety of educational and social activities.

It is worth noting that even students who are aware of their role as information creators may have difficulty seeing themselves as having the potential to influence others through social media in any meaningful way, especially considering that their audiences tend to be limited to relatively small groups of followers. However, the ways in which students from Marjory Stoneman Douglas High School in Parkland, Florida, used social media in the days following a shooting at their school in 2018 to rally others around gun control issues proves the reach even those with previously small audiences can have (Witt 2018). In a less positive example, Eric Tucker had only a handful of followers when he posted a tweet claiming that paid protesters had been transported by bus to a Trump campaign rally in Texas in 2016. The tweet went viral and continued to influence others even after it had been debunked and Tucker had posted a retraction (Maheshwari 2016). While the Parkland students were able to anticipate the impact they could have through social media, Tucker had no reason to suspect that his own post would have such reach. This shows that being aware of one's role and responsibilities as an information creator can make a difference.

Research also shows other ways in which it is important for students to learn about their responsibilities when it comes to creating and interacting with information online. Anderson and colleagues (2014), for example, found that uncivil blog comments can contribute to a perception of polarization even when the content of the blog post itself is neutral. Berger and Milkman's (2012) findings suggest that people tend to share information based on how it makes them feel with little regard for how accurate it is, which can contribute to the spread of misinformation. Craker and March (2016) show that while certain personality types can predispose someone to becoming an "Internet troll," the social reward that comes with having a negative power influence over others is also an important factor. These selected examples make it clear that one does not need to be a celebrity with thousands of followers (or even want to be one) to influence others online and be influenced by them in turn.

RELATIONSHIP TO METALITERACY

Metaliterate learning is concerned not just with cognitive and behavioral objectives but also with objectives that fall into the affective and metacognitive domains (Forte et al. 2014). The first three learning goals for the Empowering Yourself as a User and Creator of Information course have a direct relationship to all four metaliteracy domains. There is also a clear relationship between these goals and some of the knowledge practices found in the *Framework* (ACRL 2016). Table 7.1 shows the relationship between the course goals and a selected set of metaliteracy learning objectives and knowledge practices from the *Framework*.

TABLE 7.1

Learning Goals for Empowering Yourself as a User and Creator of Information and Related Metaliteracy Learning Objectives and ACRL *Framework* Knowledge Practices

COURSE LEARNING GOAL	METALITERACY LEARNING OBJECTIVES (2014, SELECTED)	METALITERACY LEARNING OBJECTIVES (2018, SELECTED)	FRAMEWORK KNOWLEDGE PRACTICES (SELECTED)	RELATED TOPICS FROM COURSE SYLLABUS
Critically evaluate information using recommended criteria.	Place an information source in its context (e.g., author's purpose, format of information, and delivery mode) in order to ascertain the value of the material for that particular situation. (Goal 1, Objective 1) Appreciate the importance of assessing content from different sources, including dynamic content from social media, critically. (G1, O5) Compare the unique attributes of different information formats (e.g., scholarly	Critically assess information from all sources, including dynamic content that circulates online. (Goal 1, Objective 9) Critically evaluate and verify user-generated content and appropriately apply in new knowledge creation. (G3, O7)	Use research tools and indicators of authority to determine the credibility of sources, understanding the elements that might temper this credibility. Assess the fit between an information product's creation process and a particular information need.	Evaluating information Searching for information Complications of searching for information Fake news

COURSE LEARNING GOAL	METALITERACY LEARNING OBJECTIVES (2014, SELECTED)	METALITERACY LEARNING OBJECTIVES (2018, SELECTED)	FRAMEWORK KNOWLEDGE PRACTICES (SELECTED)	RELATED TOPICS FROM COURSE SYLLABUS
	article, blog, wiki, online community), and have the ability to use effectively and to cite information for the development of original content. (G3, O3)			
Identify internal and external factors that complicate the process of evaluating information.	Distinguish between editorial commentary and information presented from a more research-based perspective, recognizing that values and beliefs are embedded in all information. (G1, O2) Value user-generated content and critically evaluate contributions made by others: see self as a producer as well as consumer of information. (G3, O8)	Acknowledge that content is not always produced for legitimate reasons, and that biases exist, both subtle and overt. (G1, O2) Distinguish between editorial commentary and a research-based perspective, recognizing that values and beliefs are embedded in all information. (G1, O6) Examine how you feel about the information presented and how this impacts your response. (G1, O10)	Understand that many disciplines have acknowledged authorities in the sense of well-known scholars and publications that are widely considered "standard," and yet, even in those situations, some scholars would challenge the authority of those sources. Monitor the value that is placed upon different types of information products in varying contexts.	Being wrong Complications of searching for information Dealing with disagreement Fake news
Apply recommended practices for responsible information creation and sharing.	Distinguish the kinds of information appropriate to reproduce and share publicly, and private information disseminated in more restricted/discreet environments. (G2, O2) Apply copyright and Creative Commons licensing as appropriate to the creation of original or repurposed information. (G2, O4) Recognize the ethical considerations of sharing information. (G2, O5)	Identify and follow the specific intellectual property attribution expectations in the setting in which you are working. (G2, O5) Participate conscientiously and ethically in collaborative environments. (G3, O2)	Acknowledge they are developing their own authoritative voices in a particular area and recognize the responsibilities this entails, including seeking accuracy and reliability, respecting intellectual property, and participating in communities of practice. Develop, in their own creation processes, an understanding that their choices impact the purposes for which the information product will be used and the message it conveys.	Being wrong Dealing with disagreement Fake news Creating information

The first learning goal for the course states that as a result of what they learn in the course, students will be able to "critically evaluate information using recommended criteria." This learning goal and the associated lessons on evaluating information, searching for information, complications of searching for information, and fake news (listed in the fifth column) have applications related to metaliteracy learning objectives describing how a metaliterate learner assesses context when evaluating and comparing sources of information, including nontraditional sources found through social media. Learning objectives from both the 2014 version (Forte et al. 2014), which was active at the time the course was being planned and implemented, and the revised 2018 version (Jacobson et al. 2018) are included. The knowledge practices from the *Framework* (shown in the fourth column) further speak to ways in which a learner might assess the credibility of a source and its value in a particular context. The same mapping has been done for two more of the course's stated learning goals. (The fourth learning goal for the course is not included as part of the table because it was created to fulfill a common freshman seminar requirement and does not relate to the more metaliterate learning goals and content of the course.)

As seen in table 7.1, specific topics for the course included the basics of evaluating information, dealing with disagreement, fake news, creating information, and more. However, before teaching students these abilities and concepts, the author decided to begin with a lesson on an important related topic: being wrong.

TEACHING STUDENTS ABOUT BEING WRONG

The short lesson the author taught on being wrong occurred at the beginning of the Empowering Yourself freshman seminar course. The structure of the lesson is described in more detail later in the chapter. The goals for the lesson included the following:

- To address common issues related to students' overconfidence with regard to the course's overall themes
- To introduce students to factors such as confirmation bias that complicate the process of deciding what we believe
- To help students recognize the value of an optimistic model of wrongness

This section explores these three goals in detail. The author outlines relevant research related to each goal as well as explores the relation of each goal to metaliteracy in addressing misinformation.

Overconfidence and Reflective Thinking

Research has shown that students' confidence in their information-seeking abilities does not always match their proficiency with the skills related to those abilities (Molteni and Chan 2015). In teaching information literacy courses, the author has observed in particular that students have difficulty not only with recognizing misinformation such as fake news when they encounter it but also with recognizing how they have the potential to be misled by misinformation. They seem to believe they are savvy enough not to be fooled by "alternative facts."

In establishing their Reflective Judgment Model, King and Kitchener (1994a) provide some insight into developmental factors that may inform some of this overconfident thinking. In their book *Developing Reflective Judgment: Understanding and Promoting Intellectual Growth and Critical Thinking in Adolescents and Adults*, the authors share the findings of the first few decades of research that led to this model, which represents a developmental progression in the ways people understand the process of knowing and justifying their beliefs in the face of problems with no clear-cut answers. A comprehensive secondary analysis of this model was later conducted by Wood (1997), and in 2002 and 2004, King and Kitchener provided updated literature reviews and reflections on the research supporting the model, which continues to be used in current research studies on development and education.

The Reflective Judgment Model is divided into seven stages (King and Kitchener 1994b). At one end of the spectrum, prereflective thinkers in stage 1 and stage 2 tend to view knowledge as absolute and predetermined; alternative beliefs are unacknowledged or outright denied. On the other end of the spectrum, reflective thinkers in stage 7 recognize how evidence and opinion can be pieced together to support a particular conclusion while acknowledging that such a conclusion is subject to critique and may be changed at any time in the face of new evidence.

King, Kitchener, and Wood (1994) suggest that most traditional-age undergraduate students qualify as quasi-reflective thinkers who function somewhere in the middle of the spectrum at stage 3 or stage 4. These quasi-reflective stages are ones in which thinkers tend to believe that there is a right answer to a given problem but that the answer may not have been identified yet. When experts disagree about a problem, thinkers in these stages may assume that one of the experts is simply wrong rather than attempting to negotiate meaning from varying perspectives. Such thinkers fail to recognize the importance of evidence when reasoning toward a conclusion. They also tend not to differentiate between the value of lay opinions, including their own, and the opinions of experts. A few students may start to develop toward stage 5 thinking by the time they are seniors. Stage 5 thinkers allow for a little more interpretation but have not yet entered a stage of reflective thinking where the importance of context is adequately understood (King and Kitchener 1994b).

Typical undergraduate students are confident that they can distinguish between "right" and "wrong" information because they are at a developmental stage where personal feelings rather than evidence take precedence when it comes to deciding what to believe. The author's experience in having students search for information on Google seems to support this, indicating that students are often chiefly concerned with first identifying the "right" answer and then only retroactively justifying the credibility of the source if asked to do so. When one relies more heavily on a "feeling" that something is right than on evidence of its credibility, it is easy to be confident in one's ability to avoid being misled in the process of seeking information. The assumption is that if something is wrong, it will be easy to perceive it as wrong.

Though there is at least one example of a study that connects King and Kitchener's model to information literacy via the ACRL (2000) *Information Literacy Competency Standards for Higher Education* (Jackson 2008), there does not yet appear to be any work that directly connects metaliteracy or the *Framework* (ACRL 2016) to this model. However, the potential for making these connections is clearly there, particularly with regard to the emphasis metaliteracy and the *Framework* both place on the importance of context, which is a hallmark of reflective thinking. Critical thinking is also a key component of metaliteracy, the *Framework*, and the Reflective Judgment Model.

Confirmation Bias and Complicating Factors

Students who are still developing as metaliterate learners and reflective thinkers may fail to recognize that their feelings about whether or not information is accurate or truthful are often affected by factors that are beyond their control. Two such factors are confirmation bias and filter bubbles.

Ever since the advent of "alternative facts," think pieces about issues surrounding confirmation bias and filter bubbles have abounded, especially in popular left-leaning media, including examples by Beck (2017), Kolbert (2017), Oremus (2017), and Spinney (2017). The suggested solution for these issues is often to teach students (and ourselves) to make a point of seeking out information from credible or unbiased sources that represent a diversity of views on an issue, including views with which the students may disagree. This would certainly help students expand beyond their respective echo chambers and would enable them to use their more well-rounded knowledge to make more informed decisions about what to believe. However, while such a solution may address issues related to the filter bubble, it may be less effective at resolving issues related to confirmation bias.

In a widely cited literature review of key research on confirmation bias, Nickerson (1998) shows that the tendency to favor evidence in support of our existing beliefs is one for which proof can be found in a variety of populations, regardless of demographic factors such as education level. This would seem to run counter to the solution suggested earlier, in which overcoming the effects of confirmation bias is treated as a matter of proper training. In fact, Nickerson argues that common models of education that require college students to pick and defend a position on a particular issue actually reinforce confirmation bias rather than combat it. In her book the *Influential Mind: What the Brain Reveals about Our Power to Change Others*, Sharot (2017a) cites similar findings that show that people with stronger analytic abilities are more likely to twist data to suit their preferred conclusions than are those with lower reasoning abilities.

It is important to teach students that confidence (earned or unearned) in one's ability to properly evaluate information is not enough to overcome confirmation bias in order to avoid a perception of immunity that may interfere with any potential inclination toward metacognition and critical thinking. To do this, we must make clear to learners and to ourselves where confirmation bias comes from and why it is so pervasive.

Thomas Gilovich documents the various failures of reasoning that all humans suffer from in his widely cited 1991 book *How We Know What Isn't So: The Fallibility of Human Reason in Everyday Life*. These failures include our tendency to misperceive or misinterpret random data (Gilovich 1991f), incomplete data (Gilovich 1991g), and ambiguous data (Gilovich 1991d), often in ways that cause us to see patterns where there are none. Gilovich discusses these in a section of his book titled "Cognitive Determinants of Questionable Beliefs." These tendencies can lead to failures of reasoning such as confirmation bias.

"Why have we evolved a brain that discards perfectly valid information when that information does not fit with its current view of the world?" asks Sharot (2017a, 24). She suggests several theories, including that the ability to reason is intended to enable us to persuade others rather than uncover the truth. She also argues that this may be our default setting since much of the information that contradicts what we know about the world is, in fact, generally wrong. Nickerson (1998) and Gilovich (1991c) also explore a number of theories for why the human brain works this way. While there does not appear to be one accepted theory to understand how we think about information in these contexts, these authors at least generally agree that if confirmation bias and other failures of human reasoning did not serve some evolutionary purpose, these behaviors would have been selected against a long time ago.

So there are cognitive factors involved in confirmation bias that we can become aware of but which Gilovich (1991a) suggests we cannot entirely resolve in part because they are a product of how our brains have evolved over time. In addition to these cognitive factors, Gilovich also identifies motivational (1991e) and social determinants (1991b) of questionable belief that are also discussed by Schulz (2010b) and Sharot (2017c). Our motivation to continue believing something we want to be true despite contraindicative evidence stems mainly from our desire for consistency. Schulz (2010a) points out that we all have mental models of the world, whether we are aware of them or not. When it comes to deciding what we believe, we prefer to believe things that are consistent with that mental model. According to Gilovich (1991d), our preference is so strong that we often go to great lengths to massage the evidence we are presented with until it matches our expectations of how the world should work. We believe information that is inconsistent with such models only if we have absolutely no other choice.

There are also powerful cultural and social forces at work that make it difficult for us to change our beliefs. As Schulz (2010b) points out, "We do not just hold a belief; we hold a membership in a community of believers" (143). Nickerson (1998) notes that the question of whether we choose the people we associate with based on what they believe or whether we choose what we believe based on the people we associate with has never been adequately settled by research. Lewandowsky, Ecker, and Cook (2017) comment on the false consensus effect, which leads people to persist in beliefs they believe are widely shared regardless of whether or not this is actually the case. Meanwhile, Sloman and Fernbach (2017) show that although we need others to fill in the gaps in our understanding of the world, this can lead to an echo chamber effect. What we believe is reinforced by those around us in such a way that to believe differently on any given issue would be to lose membership in our community of believers and thus a part of our identity.

Adding to the problem is that when we do encounter disagreement, our first reaction is not to present a rational, well-reasoned, evidence-based argument to persuade the other person to our point of view or to let him or her do the same (Sharot 2017a). Instead, according to Schulz (2010a), we tend to make one of three assumptions about people with whom we disagree. The first is what Schulz calls the "Ignorance Assumption," meaning we believe the other person is simply not in possession of enough evidence to realize that he or she is wrong. The second is what Schulz refers to as the "Idiocy Assumption," meaning we believe the other person has adequate evidence but is not smart enough to interpret the evidence correctly. The third is the "Evil Assumption," meaning we believe the other person has adequate evidence and knows what the evidence means but that he or she is willing to distort or ignore it for malevolent purposes. In other words, we always believe ourselves to be in the right, and in most social situations, the proper etiquette is simply to keep our disagreement to ourselves (Schulz 2010b). To express disagreement, as Gilovich (1991b) puts it, is to risk being disliked. It is also to risk being wrong.

Teaching students about being wrong empowers them as consumers and creators of information in two key ways. First, this approach awakens students to the idea that while the skills they have developed as information seekers are valuable when it comes to evaluating sources, there is still more to learn than finding and analyzing these materials, as in traditional information literacy instruction. Lessons that include a discussion of confirmation bias and other factors are more metaliterate in nature and illustrate that relying on a personal feeling about whether information is "right" or "wrong" simply is not enough. Second, it also helps them begin to move toward a more optimistic model of wrongness that allows for more flexibility in their worldview and encourages the intellectual risks that are necessary for learning.

Metaliteracy and Models of Wrongness

In her book *Being Wrong: Adventures in the Margin of Error*, Kathryn Schulz (2010c) explores two "models of wrongness." The first is what she refers to as a pessimistic view of error in which making mistakes is considered abnormal and therefore unacceptable and deeply embarrassing. In this model, error must be avoided at all costs. Another is the optimistic model, in which error is thought of not as an obstacle on the path to truth but as the path itself. This requires accepting, at least to some degree, that absolute certainty when it comes to deciding what qualifies as "the truth" is not achievable and that the best we can hope for, based on known and accepted facts and evidence, is "truth for now." As an example of this more optimistic approach, Schulz cites the scientific method itself, which uses facts and evidence to establish theories with the understanding that the theories may change if new information comes to light.

Metaliteracy is a natural fit for the optimistic model of wrongness. Among the goals and learning objectives that describe a metaliterate learner, this can perhaps most clearly be seen in goal 4, objective 1, which states that a metaliterate learner is someone who is able to "recognize that learning is a process and that reflecting on errors or mistakes leads to new insights and discoveries" (Jacobson et al. 2018). This objective, which relates to the meta-cognitive domain of metaliterate learning, shows that a metaliterate learner is someone who does not necessarily avoid error but instead treats the experience of being wrong as a natural and important part of the learning process, a learning opportunity rather than a sign of failure.

Unlike the pessimistic model of wrongness, being wrong actually supports learning in senses both large and small. Accepting that the conclusions drawn from available facts and evidence may change if new evidence comes to light is what makes progress possible. The ability to reflect on errors and mistakes in ways that lead to new insights and discoveries is what allows change and growth to happen.

Adopting an optimistic model of wrongness is not an easy task. Being wrong is an intellectually and emotionally uncomfortable experience, as Schulz (2010d) thoroughly documents. However, due in part to factors such as confirmation bias and other failures of reasoning discussed earlier in this chapter, being wrong is also a universal experience, which is why teaching students how to avoid being wrong by itself is of limited use at best. It is especially important to acknowledge the inevitability of being wrong in the current post-truth climate where, as Lewandowsky, Ecker, and Cook (2017) put it, "a large share of the populace is living in an epistemic space that has abandoned conventional criteria of evidence, internal consistency, and fact-seeking" (359). In fact, these authors go so far as to suggest that the problem of misinformation is not that it leads to people being misinformed but that it has led people to stop believing facts altogether and has created uncertainty about whether facts are knowable at all. Sharot (2017b) further acknowledges that "we've become accustomed to finding support for anything we want to believe" (7).

An optimistic model of wrongness that promotes the idea of "truth for now" is different from the alternative epistemic reality described earlier by Lewandowsky, Ecker, and Cook (2017). An alternative epistemic reality is one that rejects facts and evidence in order to maintain a preferred worldview. By contrast, "truth for now" relies heavily on available facts and evidence, drawing reasonable conclusions from this information while acknowledging that the accepted truth about something may change if new facts and evidence come to light. This way of thinking is a key characteristic of both metaliteracy and the more reflective stages of the Reflective Judgment Model.

Teaching students to adopt a more optimistic model of wrongness will enable them to take more intellectual risks and perhaps to be more adaptive when facts and evidence go against what they want to believe rather than falling victim to the alternative epistemic realities that characterize the current post-truth climate. It is not a replacement for teaching students how to evaluate information but rather an improvement of these lessons. Such an enhancement is necessary since research shows that even when people try to evaluate information, they are generally unable to recognize that something is incorrect until they receive an explicit correction or a retraction (Lewandowsky et al. 2012). As a further complication, such corrections and retractions work only under very specific conditions (Ecker, Lewandowsky, and Tang 2010; Guillory and Geraci 2013). Otherwise, misinformation can continue to have a significant influence on one's thinking even if the individual understands that it is not reliable. In some cases, belief in false information actually increases when a correction is given (Ecker, Hogan, and Lewandowsky 2017). As Lewandowsky and colleagues (2012) point out, judging a source's credibility is itself a function of belief and "correcting misinformation is cognitively indistinguishable from misinforming people to replace their preexisting correct beliefs" (124). It is necessary, therefore, for us not only to teach students and ourselves how to properly evaluate information but to take into account the psychological processes through which we interpret information and form perceptions (Garrett, Weeks, and Neo 2016).

All of this means that models of instruction that focus on helping students learn to "debunk" misinformation may not be enough on their own. Instead, giving students insight into how beliefs are formed and reinforced is a necessary step toward helping them to develop a more metacognitive and reflective approach to the information they encounter and create. Teaching students that it is sometimes necessary and even desirable, though often difficult, to admit error and perhaps change one's beliefs is also key to the learning process.

STRUCTURE OF THE LESSON

The short lesson on being wrong taught by the author included elements that challenged common beliefs and illustrated the universal nature of being wrong. Though this lesson was intended for a freshman seminar on empowering oneself as a user and creator of information, it follows a simple structure that can easily be adapted to any instructional situation or subject. This section describes each stage of the lesson.

PART 1

Five Common Beliefs

The lesson began with a slide showing five common beliefs related to science and medicine, taken from an article by Megan Scudellari (2015) that had been featured in *Nature*. The article was chosen for several reasons. The instructor felt it was safe to assume that the five myths discussed by the article's author would likely already be familiar to students and thus need little introduction. The article is provocative without being overly political and includes arguments that seem to be well supported by quotes and citations from experienced scientists and researchers rather than a pop piece created as clickbait to sell advertisements.

The beliefs outlined in the article are as follows:

- Screening saves lives for all types of cancer.
- Antioxidants are good and free radicals are bad.
- Humans have exceptionally large brains.
- Individuals learn best when taught in their preferred learning style.
- The human population is growing exponentially.

The students were told that at least one of the beliefs being shown was a myth that was not supported by scientific or medical research. Once they had been given a few minutes to think, the students were asked to indicate their answer by holding up a piece of paper whose color corresponded with the choice they felt was likely to be a myth (e.g., A was red, B was blue, etc.). Having students respond simultaneously in this way exposed some of the differences in their thinking; they could immediately see that not everyone had picked the same answer. The author–instructor took advantage of this variation by calling on students with different answers and asking them to explain their reasoning.

It is interesting to note that in defending their answers, most students had an easier time making a case for why the other choices were likely to be based on fact than they did explaining why their choice was likely to be a myth, which is in line with what research says about human reasoning (Nickerson 1998). When pressed, students generally supported their answers by describing personal experience or vaguely recalled sources found on the Internet to which they felt they could attribute adequate authority on the topic. It seemed that they believed these ideas were true simply because they had never encountered information that would indicate otherwise. The choices they suspected to be false were the ones with which they tended to be least familiar.

The trick, of course, was that according to Scudellari's (2015) article, none of these common beliefs are supported by scientific research. The evidence suggests that they are all myths. Therefore, everyone in the class was wrong. At this point, students might have revolted, resentful at being tricked by their instructor. However, the fact that everyone had been tricked meant everyone shared the same experience of being wrong. There was no reason to be embarrassed or uncomfortable because all were on equal ground.

Students may also have been somewhat mollified by the next part of the lesson, in which the instructor shared her own personal experience with being wrong. This experience was given in the form of a story about the lyrics of a popular song by the Canadian rock band Barenaked Ladies. This story modeled the experience of being wrong in a way that was relatable to students and made it clear that being wrong is something that happens to everyone, even their professors.

PART 2

Personal Narrative

In the TED Talk that accompanies her book on being wrong (discussed earlier), Schulz (2011) begins by telling the audience a story of a time when she took a road trip with a friend and remarked on an unusual symbol she kept seeing alongside the highway. To her, the symbol appeared to be a Chinese character. She asked her friend what the character might mean and why it showed up so frequently in roadside signs in the United States. At this point in the video, she reveals the symbol to the viewer: it is a common sign to indicate a nearby picnic area, which she had mistaken for a Chinese character. As intended, the reveal gets a laugh from the audience.

When we talk about issues like confirmation bias or being wrong, we tend to frame the conversation as though they are something that happens only to other people, ones who are less smart or less diligent than ourselves. However, the research discussed earlier in this chapter shows that this is not the case. Having seen Schulz's video, the author decided that an important component of a lesson on this topic would be to show students that no one is immune to being wrong by acknowledging her own personal experience with error.

The author chose to tell a story about a time when she made a mistake about the lyrics of a popular song by the Barenaked Ladies called "If I Had $1,000,000." In the song, which was originally released in 1992, Ed Robertson, one of the band's lead singers, describes the romantic gifts he would buy if, as the song title suggests, he had a million dollars. Meanwhile, Steven Page, the second lead singer, responds to Robertson's lines with humorous, increasingly ridiculous commentary. In one such line, Robertson offers to buy his romantic interest an exotic pet, an idea that Page builds on by giving examples of the type of exotic pets that might be on offer—specifically, a llama or an emu.

At one time, this line in the song had been the subject of discussion between the author and a group of colleagues at a former job. The author insisted to these colleagues that the reason the line was funny was because llamas and emus are technically the same thing, citing personal experience growing up near an emu farm in western New York as proof of her authority on the topic. Her colleagues expressed skepticism that this was correct, but the author continued to believe that she was right.

The author was not right. A simple search for images on the Internet will reveal that this is the case. The author's mistake was likely the result of confusion caused by the knowledge that llamas and emus are both related to other animals with which she was familiar (llamas are related to alpacas; emus are related to ostriches). As for the emu farm, the author first thought she may have been confusing this with several alpaca farms that still exist in her hometown but a *Weekly World News* article from 1991 seems to confirm that such a farm did exist in the area during the time she was growing up there (Jimison 1991).

Why share this story with students? Some instructors may be resistant to the idea of revealing their own stories of error to students in this way, even if the error in question was nothing more than a silly mistake. After all, in a classroom, status matters. An instructor must establish himself or herself as an authority not only on the topic being taught but on how the classroom itself works. For some, that authority is hard-won and is not worth risking for the sake of telling a humorous story that at best might win a few laughs.

This is a valid fear. It is also valid to feel uncomfortable telling an embarrassing personal story about oneself to a group of strangers. It may be one thing to do this as Schulz did in front of an audience of peers as part of a short presentation. To do it in front of students at the start of a semester-long course may be another matter entirely.

The author decided to take the risk and confront her own story about being wrong to help students understand that being wrong in ways big and small truly is something that happens to everyone, even professors and others in positions of authority. The hope was also to get students to start thinking a little differently about their own experiences of being wrong and to feel more comfortable with taking intellectual risks rather than always relying on the instructor to give them the right answer. This goal is similar to one discussed by Wallis and Battista (2016), who describe a lesson in which sharing power in the classroom is meant to make it clear to students that their ideas and experiences are as valid as those of the instructor.

That said, the story to be told had to be chosen carefully. The author selected the story in question for several reasons. First, it was one in which the case was clearly defined: a llama and an emu are obviously not the same thing. It was also a case where a possible explanation for the error could be provided: the false authority the author claimed based on the vague memory of having grown up near an emu farm. More important, it was a case where being wrong should not have mattered. One's professional and personal reputations do not generally suffer due to benign errors regarding the lyrics of popular songs. An error like this one is not likely to have a lasting impact on one's life.

But the error did matter. It must have mattered, considering that the realization of this discovery based on documented facts, rather than anecdote or memory, was a significant life lesson that continues to affect the author to this day. Perhaps the reason the error mattered was because it happened in front of peers and colleagues, people whom the author respected and whose respect she sought. Disagreeing with peers or colleagues on an intellectual level is one thing. Making a dumb mistake in front of them was another.

Students in a freshman seminar course may not yet be able to relate to the types of intellectual debates that can arise between colleagues in a field of study. However, they can certainly relate to the embarrassment one often feels when making a silly or obvious mistake in front of peers or colleagues.

While this lesson could have been taught without telling a personal story to illustrate the point, the same lesson would be much less effective at conveying that being wrong is something that happens to everyone. The tension between an optimistic and a pessimistic model of wrongness is in whether error is seen as "basically aberrant or basically normal" (Schulz 2010c, 29). Modeling for students the inevitability and universality of being wrong helps move them toward understanding error as "basically normal," even for those they might regard as authority figures. This is an important step in adopting a more optimistic view of wrongness where, as metaliteracy shows us, errors are a valuable learning opportunity rather than something to be treated as "basically aberrant."

PART 3

Reflection

The personal narrative portion of the lesson was followed by a lecture on the cognitive, motivational, and social factors that affect how we form beliefs and continue to hold on to them even when they are proven to be erroneous. These same ideas, taken from Gilovich (1991a–g), Nickerson (1998), and Schulz (2010a–d), in particular, were discussed earlier in this chapter.

At the end of the lecture, students were asked to reflect on a time when they had been wrong about something, large or small. Students were not asked to make these reflections public in any way. They did not have to share them with the instructor or with anyone else in the class. They were not graded on this task. The only goal was to prompt them to think about their personal experience with the topic at hand in the hope that they would start to see that experience in a new light.

Later in the semester, students were given another assignment that was similar in nature. This one was graded. This time, instead of reflecting on a time when they had been wrong about something, students were asked to describe a time when they had disagreed with someone. This assignment followed a lesson inspired by Robb Willer's (2016) research and accompanying TED Talk "How to Have Better Political Conversations." In this lesson, students learned to think about the role people's values play in their views on controversial issues and how an appeal to those values when dealing with disagreement rather than rehearsing one's own positions can lead to more impactful conversations. In some cases, students described stories in which, in retrospect, they may have been the ones in the wrong and had learned something from that experience. That they were willing to admit this in a graded assignment seemed like progress on the path toward shifting to a more optimistic model of wrongness.

FUTURE DIRECTIONS

While this lesson on being wrong worked well in the setting in which it was implemented, there are clear opportunities for changes. One change, which will be part of future iterations of the course, is a more formal assessment for the lesson. In the original version of the lesson, students were allowed to keep their reflections on being wrong private to avoid the potential for embarrassment. This obviously limited the value the exercise might have had for measuring student learning. In the new version of the lesson, students will be asked to define in their own words the two models of wrongness and reflect on the potential limitations and value they might find in both models with a particular focus on their role as new college students. These reflections will not need to include potentially private information and will better show both students' understanding of the two models and any shift in thinking they might be starting to experience as a result of the lesson.

CONCLUSION

The course created by the author was intended to help students empower themselves in a post-truth world by cultivating an awareness of the potential impact that the information they use, create, and share can have on how others perceive and interact with the world. The ability to impact others in this way means that one must practice certain responsibilities that come with using and creating information. A lesson on being wrong is a necessary part of learning about these responsibilities in order to move students toward a more optimistic model of wrongness supported by metaliteracy. This optimistic model of wrongness can help students avoid falling victim to alternative epistemic realities where facts are determined by strict adherence to personal ideology and instead learn the value of evidence in creating and sometimes changing one's beliefs.

REFERENCES

ACRL (Association of College & Research Libraries). 2000. *Information Literacy Competency Standards for Higher Education.* Chicago: American Library Association. www.ala.org/acrl/standards/informationliteracycompetency.

———. 2016. *Framework for Information Literacy for Higher Education.* Chicago: American Library Association. www.ala.org/acrl/standards/ilframework.

Anderson, Ashley A., Dominique Brossard, Dietram A. Scheufele, Michael A. Xenos, and Peter Ladwig. 2014. "The 'Nasty Effect:' Online Incivility and Risk Perceptions of Emerging Technologies." *Journal of Computer-Mediated Communication* 19 (3): 373–87.

Barenaked Ladies. 1992. "If I Had $1,000,000." In *Gordon,* produced by Michael Phillip Wojewoda. Reprise Records.

Beck, Julie. 2017. "This Article Won't Change Your Mind: The Facts on Why Facts Alone Can't Fight False Beliefs." *The Atlantic,* March 13. www.theatlantic.com/science/archive/2017/03/this-article-wont-change-your-mind/519093.

Berger, Jonah, and Katherine L. Milkman. 2012. "What Makes Online Content Viral?" *Journal of Marketing Research* 49 (2): 192–205.

Craker, Naomi, and Evita March. 2016. "The Dark Side of Facebook: The Dark Tetrad, Negative Social Potency, and Trolling Behaviours." *Personality and Individual Differences* 102 (November): 79–84.

Ecker, Ullrich K. H., Joshua L. Hogan, and Stephan Lewandowsky. 2017. "Reminders and Repetition of Misinformation: Helping or Hindering Its Retraction?" *Journal of Applied Research in Memory and Cognition* 6 (2): 185–92.

Ecker, Ullrich K. H., Stephan Lewandowsky, and David T. W. Tang. 2010. "Explicit Warnings Reduce but Do Not Eliminate the Continued Influence of Misinformation." *Memory and Cognition* 38 (8): 1087–1100.

Forte, Michele, Trudi Jacobson, Tom Mackey, Emer O'Keeffe, and Kathleen Stone. 2014. "2014 Goals and Learning Objectives." Metaliteracy.org. Updated September 11. https://metaliteracy.org/learning-objectives.

Garrett, R. Kelly, Brian E. Weeks, and Rachel L. Neo. 2016. "Driving a Wedge between Evidence and Beliefs: How Online Ideological News Exposure Promotes Political Misperceptions." *Journal of Computer-Mediated Communication* 21 (5): 331–48.

Gilovich, Thomas. 1991a. "Challenging Dubious Beliefs: The Role of Social Science." In *How We Know What Isn't So: The Fallibility of Human Reason in Everyday Life*, 185–94. New York: The Free Press.

———. 1991b. "The Imagined Agreement of Others: Exaggerated Impressions of Social Support." In *How We Know What Isn't So: The Fallibility of Human Reason in Everyday Life*, 112–24. New York: The Free Press.

———. 1991c. "Introduction." In *How We Know What Isn't So: The Fallibility of Human Reason in Everyday Life*, 1–8. New York: The Free Press.

———. 1991d. "Seeing What We Expect to See: The Biased Evaluation of Ambiguous and Inconsistent Data." In *How We Know What Isn't So: The Fallibility of Human Reason in Everyday Life*, 49–74. New York: The Free Press.

———. 1991e. "Seeing What We Want to See: Motivational Determinants of Belief." In *How We Know What Isn't So: The Fallibility of Human Reason in Everyday Life*, 75–87. New York: The Free Press.

———. 1991f. "Something Out of Nothing: The Misperception and Misinterpretation of Random Data." In *How We Know What Isn't So: The Fallibility of Human Reason in Everyday Life*, 9–28. New York: The Free Press.

———. 1991g. "Too Much from Too Little: The Misinterpretation of Incomplete and Unrepresentative Data." In *How We Know What Isn't So: The Fallibility of Human Reason in Everyday Life*, 29–48. New York: The Free Press.

Guillory, Jimmeka J., and Lisa Geraci. 2013. "Correcting Erroneous Inferences in Memory: The Role of Source Credibility." *Journal of Applied Research in Memory and Cognition* 2 (4): 201–9.

Jackson, Rebecca. 2008. "Information Literacy and Its Relationship to Cognitive Development and Reflective Judgment." *New Directions for Teaching and Learning*, no. 114: 47–61.

Jacobson, Trudi E., and Thomas P. Mackey. 2013. "Proposing a Metaliteracy Model to Redefine Information Literacy." *Communications in Information Literacy* 7 (2): 84–91.

Jacobson, Trudi, Tom Mackey, Kelsey O'Brien, Michele Forte, and Emer O'Keeffe. 2018. "Goals and Learning Objectives: Draft Revision (April 11, 2018)." Metaliteracy.org. https://metaliteracy.org/learning-objectives.

Jimison, Susan. 1991. "Grandmom Hatches Bird Eggs with Her Own Body!" *Weekly World News*, May 14: 37.

King, Patricia M., and Karen Strohm Kitchener. 1994a. "Creating a New Theoretical Model of Reflective Judgment." In *Developing Reflective Judgment: Understanding and Promoting Intellectual Growth and Critical Thinking in Adolescents and Adults*, 20–43. San Francisco: Josey-Bass.

———. 1994b. "The Seven Stages of Reflective Judgment." In *Developing Reflective Judgment: Understanding and Promoting Intellectual Growth and Critical Thinking in Adolescents and Adults*, 44–74. San Francisco: Josey-Bass.

———. 2002. "The Reflective Judgment Model: Twenty Years of Epistemic Cognition." In *Personal Epistemology: The Psychology of Beliefs about Knowledge and Knowing*, edited by Barbara K. Hofer and Paul R. Pintrich, 37–61. Mahwah, NJ: Lawrence Erlbaum.

———. 2004. "Reflective Judgment: Theory and Research on the Development of Epistemic Assumptions through Adulthood." *Educational Psychologist* 39 (1): 5–18.

King, Patricia M., Karen Strohm Kitchener, and Phillip K. Wood. 1994. "Research on the Reflective Judgment Model." In *Developing Reflective Judgment: Understanding and Promoting Intellectual Growth and Critical Thinking in Adolescents and Adults*, 124–88. San Francisco: Josey-Bass.

Kolbert, Elizabeth. 2017. "Why Facts Don't Change Our Minds." *The New Yorker*, February 27. www.newyorker.com/magazine/2017/02/27/why-facts-dont -change-our-minds.

Lewandowsky, Stephan R., Ullrich K. H. Ecker, and John Cook. 2017. "Beyond Misinformation: Understanding and Coping with the 'Post-Truth' Era." *Journal of Applied Research in Memory and Cognition* 6 (4): 353–69.

Lewandowsky, Stephan, Ullrich K. H. Ecker, Colleen M. Seifert, Norbert Schwarz, and John Cook. 2012. "Misinformation and Its Correction: Continued Influence and Successful Debiasing." *Psychological Science in the Public Interest* 13 (3): 106–31.

Mackey, Thomas P., and Trudi E. Jacobson. 2011. "Reframing Information Literacy as a Metaliteracy." *College and Research Libraries* 72 (1): 62–78.

———. 2014. "Developing the Metaliterate Learner by Integrating Competencies and Expanding Learning Objectives." In *Metaliteracy: Reinventing Information Literacy to Empower Learners*, 65–96. Chicago: ALA Neal-Schuman.

Maheshwari, Sapna. 2016. "How Fake News Goes Viral: A Case Study." *New York Times*, November 20. www.nytimes.com/2016/11/20/business/media/how-fake -news-spreads.html?_r=0.

McGarrity, Irene. 2016. "Developing Agency in Metaliterate Learners." In *Metaliteracy in Practice*, edited by Trudi E. Jacobson and Thomas P. Mackey, 159–82. Chicago: ALA Neal-Schuman.

Molteni, Valeria E., and Emily K. Chan. 2015. "Student Confidence/Overconfidence in the Research Process." *The Journal of Academic Librarianship* 41 (1): 2–8.

Nickerson, Raymond S. 1998. "Confirmation Bias: A Ubiquitous Phenomenon in Many Guises." *Review of General Psychology* 2 (2): 175–220.

Oremus, Will. 2017. "The Filter Bubble Revisited." *Slate*, April 5. www.slate.com/articles/technology/technology/2017/04/filter_bubbles_revisited_the_internet_may_not_be_driving_political_polarization.html.

Schulz, Kathryn. 2010a. "Our Minds, Part Two: Belief." In *Being Wrong: Adventures in the Margin of Error*, 87–111. New York: Ecco.

———. 2010b. "Our Society." In *Being Wrong: Adventures in the Margin of Error*, 133–58. New York: Ecco.

———. 2010c. "Two Models of Wrongness." In *Being Wrong: Adventures in the Margin of Error*, 25–46. New York: Ecco.

———. 2010d. "Wrongology." In *Being Wrong: Adventures in the Margin of Error*, 3–24. New York: Ecco.

———. 2011. "On Being Wrong." Presentation at TED2011, March. TED.com. www.ted.com/talks/kathryn_schulz_on_being_wrong.

Scudellari, Megan. 2015. "The Science Myths That Will Not Die." *Nature*, December 16. www.nature.com/news/the-science-myths-that-will-not-die-1.19022.

Sharot, Tali. 2017a. "Does Evidence Change Beliefs? (Priors)." In *The Influential Mind: What the Brain Reveals about Our Power to Change Others*, 11–34. New York: Henry Holt.

———. 2017b. "Prologue: A Horse-Sized Syringe." In *The Influential Mind: What the Brain Reveals about Our Power to Change Others*, 1–10. New York: Henry Holt.

———. 2017c. "Why Do Babies Love iPhones? (Others, Part 1)." In *The Influential Mind: What the Brain Reveals about Our Power to Change Others*, 149–73. New York: Henry Holt.

Sloman, Steven, and Philip Fernbach. 2017. "Introduction: Ignorance and the Community of Knowledge." In *The Knowledge Illusion: Why We Never Think Alone*, 1–18. New York: Riverhead Books.

Spinney, Laura. 2017. "How Facebook, Fake News, and Friends Are Warping Your Memory." *Nature*, March 7 (corrected March 8). www.nature.com/news/how-facebook-fake-news-and-friends-are-warping-your-memory-1.21596?WT.mc_id=TWT_NatureNews.

Wallis, Lauren, and Andrew Battista. 2016. "The Politics of Information." In *Metaliteracy in Practice*, edited by Trudi E. Jacobson and Thomas P. Mackey, 23–46. Chicago: ALA Neal-Schuman.

Willer, Robb. 2016. "How to Have Better Political Conversations." Presentation at TEDxMarin, September. TED.com. www.ted.com/talks/robb_willer_how_to _have_better_political_conversations.

Witt, Emily. 2018. "How the Survivors of Parkland Began the Never Again Movement." *The New Yorker*, February 19. www.newyorker.com/news/news -desk/how-the-survivors-of-parkland-began-the-never-again-movement.

Wood, Phillip K. 1997. "A Secondary Analysis of Claims Regarding the Reflective Judgment Interview: Internal Consistency, Sequentiality and Intra-individual Differences in Ill-Structured Problem Solving." In *Higher Education: Handbook of Theory and Research*, edited by John C. Smart, 243–312. Edison, NY: Agathon Press.

JACLYN PARTYKA

8
Fictional Affect and Metaliterate Learning through Genre

The advent of what a number of commentators and critics are calling the "post-truth era" has special implications for the first-year writing classroom because it is often the first introduction undergraduate students have to college-level academic research and writing. Within the context of the 2016 election and its surprising aftermath, I found it especially important, as a first-year writing and literature instructor, to address how the rhetoric of post-truth presents new challenges to how first-year students conceive of and approach academic research and writing.

For instance, where it was once typical for nonscholarly sources like online journalism and government documents to be considered authoritative, the continued denigration of the professional press's veracity and the lack of government transparency by the current presidential administration has given these familiar information genres new meaning. The rhetoric of post-truth essentially brings to the fore how many of the expectations we have about undergraduate research rests on a number of assumptions we now take for granted. Originally added to the *Oxford English Dictionary* in 1985, "post-truth" was named 2016's word of the year for denoting the "circumstances in which objective facts are less influential in shaping political debate or public opinion than appeals to emotion and personal belief" (*OED Online* 2018). Likewise, the rise of new information genres circulated through online platforms—such as memes, infographics, and social media and message board posts—has further muddied the already brackish waters. While there is an assumption that first-year students, as so-called digital natives, will be more attuned and adept at deciphering the nuances related to these new online information genres, a more accurate assessment would be that the undergraduate student's familiarity with and use of these genres and platforms often lacks true metacognitive reflection. Thus, in a moment when traditional measures of authority are called into question and modes of digital literacy are increasingly important, I suggest that genre analysis alongside a contemporary approach to fictionality is a significant factor in how students develop affective metaliteracy in the first-year writing classroom.

This chapter argues that an emphasis on genre can help students parse the nuanced rhetorical differences between opinion-editorials, mainstream journalism, personal blogs, social media platforms, corporate websites, primary source historical documents, academic articles, and fictional novels in a way that acknowledges how contemporary research practices are often a slippery negotiation among these different information sources. Furthermore, including literary texts within this network allows students to develop emotional connections and affective response in regard to important contemporary issues like racism, feminism, and nationality. This mode of thinking critically about how information shifts to accommodate different genres, modes, and rhetorical functions is especially important at a historical moment when misreading or misinterpreting modes of fictionality, from satire, untruths, and exaggerations, threatens to undermine the norms of not only higher education but also the nation.

POST-TRUTH AND FICTIONALITY

While discussions of post-truth have touched on a number of important contemporary subjects, such as the use of malicious content on social media and the systematic erosion of the public's trust in not only political but also journalistic institutions, the role of fictionality has often been absent from these ruminations. At its root, fictionality is "the intentional use of invented stories and scenarios" (Nielsen, Phelan, and Walsh 2015, 62). However, while this definition was once restricted to the study of literary texts, some significant epistemological shifts in contemporary culture have led to the widening of this definition. In many ways, our current climate of fake news and alternative facts is an aftershock of postmodernism, a literary and cultural movement of the 1970s and 1980s when texts, genres, and information were no longer governed by preestablished rules and conventions. For example, the conflation of history with fiction in some postmodernist writing, what Linda Hutcheon refers to as "historiographic metafiction," calls attention to itself as a construction and in the process undermines the constructed nature of other generic categories (Hutcheon 1989, 105). Thus, when "the postmodernists fictionalize history . . . they imply that history itself may be a form of fiction" (McHale 1987, 96). In sum, according to Dan Punday (2010), "we have lost confidence in our ability to grasp facts and history objectively because of the pernicious influence of [postmodernist] deconstruction" (20). Likewise, in their theorization of metaliteracy, Mackey and Jacobson frame postmodernism as a catalyst for the need to develop new literacy frameworks. Invoking Jean-François Lyotard's claim that a postmodern condition fragmented by technological change has redefined the mythic power of knowledge institutions like science, politics, and philosophy, they argue that there is a need to contend with a decentered model of information literacy (Mackey and Jacobson 2014). Essentially, as institutions of information, such as journalism, libraries, and universities, have accommodated generic innovation, new media, and permeable disciplinary boundaries, the borders of fictionality must expand beyond the literary.

Fortunately, some scholars have recognized a break with the literary through fictionality as a means to analyze nonfictional and communicative genres. For example, Richard Walsh (2007) views fictionality as a "rhetorical resource integral to the direct and serious use of language within a real-world communicative framework" (15–16). This emphasis on fictionality and communication is supported by a group of narratologists who claim that "fictionality is, among other things, a vehicle for negotiating values, weighing options, and informing beliefs and opinions" (Nielsen, Phelan, and Walsh 2015, 62). Beyond the literary, fictionality becomes a rhetorical framework that can be wielded strategically across multiple disciplines. To wit, the mission statement of the Centre for Fictionality Studies (2018) hosted by Aarhus University is rooted in this sort of interdisciplinary perspective:

> Examining why and how persons and media use fictionality as a means to achieve specific ends is crucial to understand our contemporary, medialized society. Since fictionality is a communicational strategy that crosses traditional genres, media and research areas, an interdisciplinary approach to fictionality as quality is more useful than uni-disciplinary approaches to fiction as generic category.

The emphasis on mediation here is key to understanding how the rhetoric of fictionality has moved beyond literary genres to influence other modes of communication. In this way, "the issue of fictionality appears when disciplinary boundaries are in question" (Punday 2010, 21). By widening the concept of fictionality in regard to quality rather than generic category, fictionality models interdisciplinary thinking that emphasizes the rhetorical function of constructed narratives across genres.

Some have described this shift in emphasis as the "narrative turn" in the humanities, where the study of constructing stories has, again, moved beyond the literary to encompass disciplines "ranging from the fine arts, the social and natural sciences, to media and communication studies, to popular therapy, medicine, and managerial studies" (Kreiswirth 2010). For example, Hayden White's (1980) work on narrativity within historical writing emphasizes how the act of interpreting the official historical record is a continual process of reinvention and construction in line with dominant cultural and sociological modes. According to White, the function of narrative is to "translate *knowing* into *telling*" such that the act of constructing a story is united with the rhetorical and communicative purpose of specific disciplines (5). In sum, according to Walsh (2007), "the general point here is that all narrative, fictional and nonfictional, is artifice. Narratives are constructs, and their meanings are internal to the system of narrative" (14). Thus, within the context of the narrative turn, the ability to recognize how storytelling and gestures of fictionality manifest in sometimes unlikely places has become an essential lesson for first-year students who interact with an increasingly multimodal, digital, and interdisciplinary world.

FICTION IN THE WRITING CLASSROOM

Ironically, while the borders of fictionality have widened across disciplines and discourses, the emphasis on interdisciplinarity in the university has resulted in the decline of literary instruction overall. The move away from fiction in the classroom is likely influenced by the shift in K–12 Common Core standards to privilege informational texts over literature (Arata 2015). The 2009 framework of the National Assessment of Educational Progress (NAEP) suggests students gradually, but significantly, increase the proportion of informational texts they read, such that by the time students reach the twelfth grade, they should be reading 70 percent of informational texts compared to only 30 percent of literary works (Common Core State Standards Initiative 2018). Informational texts include historical, scientific, and technical texts and literary nonfiction, a genre that expresses content-based information about a specific subject. The reasoning behind this shift is largely motivated by a desire to expose students to more complex and interdisciplinary texts outside of literary fiction, which is largely seen as aesthetic entertainment rather than vocationally based content.

As a result of these changes in the field of English composition, literature has a stigmatized history in the classroom. In 1993, for instance, Erika Lindemann (1993) notably called for the removal of literary texts in the first-year composition classroom, arguing that literature-based freshmen writing courses focus more on "consuming texts, not producing them" (313). Part of Lindemann's caution relied on the outdated assumption that instructors who teach literature in writing classes wish only to lecture on their niche research interests rather than to provide practical instruction in writing across various discourse communities within the university. She claims that

> literature courses are not humanistic. They present the teacher's or the critic's truths about the poetry, fiction, and drama being studied. They rarely connect literature with life. If students get to write a paper or two, they must assume the disembodied voice of some abstruse journal as they analyze the ingrown toenail motif in *Beowulf*. Such assignments silence students' voices in the conversation literature is intended to promote. In other words, literature teaching offers the writing teacher no model worth emulating. (313–14)

While I concede that the use of literary texts (or, for that matter, all course texts) can sometimes reveal an individual instructor's subjective affinities, Lindemann's model here neglects to consider the merits of using literature to teach larger conceptual thinking. Her claims that there is nothing "humanistic" about literature and that the literary has little connection with real life are wildly disingenuous.

First, the rise of realism and historical fiction within contemporary literature over the past few decades has created imaginative space for students to reflect on important issues within the contemporary world. So, while perhaps the function and form of Beowulf's toenails may not resonate directly with today's interdisciplinary student body, Toni Morrison's fictionalization of America's troubled history of pre–Revolutionary Era slavery has real correlations with contemporary racial ideologies, historical reasoning, and political science today. As discussed later in this chapter, it is *the way* that literature is framed within a larger conceptual apparatus that allows students to recognize fiction's rhetorical effects.

Second, while some believe the humanities have been systematically under siege by a lack of funding, a declining enrollment, and the reframing of the university education as a means toward professional outcomes (Jaschik 2017), James F. English (2012) avers that many academic sectors continue to support a comprehensive liberal arts education in the humanities, recognizing that the teaching of "moral values" continues to be a valuable and desirable goal of the contemporary university. Perhaps the most persuasive evidence for the inclusion of humanities education could be the idea that a conscientious development of soft skills, such as cooperation, problem solving, and communication, results in improved academic and professional performance (Chamorro-Premuzic et al. 2010). Recent findings by Google's Project

Aristotle have supported this premise; project teams that exhibit strong soft skills are the most successful (Strauss 2017). In response to this perceived gap in learning across all disciplines in higher education, Cathy Davidson (2017) has called for a new model of education that transforms learning dynamics to look beyond the classroom to accommodate learning for a new, more connected, and technological world.

However, these anecdotes that feign surprise at the unexpected capitalist advantages of humanities education often miss the mark, failing to recognize the university as anything other than a conduit of professionalization. In contrast, Gary Tate's (1993) original retort to Lindemann attempts to reclaim the "human" in the humanities:

> I refuse to look at my students as primarily history majors, accounting majors, nursing majors. I much prefer to think of them and treat them as people whose most important conversations will take place outside the academy, as they struggle to figure out how to live their lives—that is, how to vote and love and survive, how to respond to change and diversity and death and oppression and freedom. (320)

I share Tate's pronouncements here, adding that much of the value associated with teaching literature and other so-called noninformational texts centers around feelings and abstractions—a sentiment that has special implications for a post-truth era "in which audiences are more likely to believe information that appeals to emotions or existing personal beliefs, as opposed to seeking and readily accepting information regarded as factual or objective" (Cooke 2017, 212). Reading about imaginative characters and events often allows students to understand different living conditions, historical moments, and moral conflicts in a way that resembles the real world but is ultimately detached from much of its political and ideological baggage. This is not to say that fiction cannot be overtly political—of course it can—but the element of fictionality here becomes "an invitation to extrapolate the relevance of the story to our understanding of and engagement with our reality" (Nielsen, Phelan, and Walsh 2015, 71). So, if we are to take this definition of the post-truth era seriously, where emotions are integral to how and why the veracity of information has seemingly lost its rhetorical power, then fiction, in its ability to create affective emotional response, should be part of the solution.

INSTITUTIONAL CONTEXT

The course Inventing Facts: Digital, Historical, Fictional was taught under Temple University's First-Year Writing Program within the standard guidelines for English 0802: Analytical Reading and Writing. Analytical Reading and Writing is a portfolio-based class for which students complete and revise three argument-based papers over the course of the semester. While there is a standard syllabus issued by the department, instructors are welcome to design alternative versions of the course as long as the course adheres to the standards and parameters of the department's syllabus.

I have been teaching a version of Analytical Reading and Writing almost every semester since 2009, so my approach to the course has evolved in kind with the program's various standard syllabi. For instance, in 2010–2014, the program used the essay collection *Cultural Conversations: The Presence of the Past*, edited by Stephen Dilks, Regina Hansen, and Matthew Parfitt (2001), as part of the standard syllabus. My unit and assignment on "Genres of History" using Lin-Manuel Miranda's (2008) Broadway musical *Hamilton: An American Musical* was inspired by a combination of two previous units and readings from this collection on the standard syllabus: "The Frontier—How Do We Imagine the West?" and "Art and the African American Experience."

Additionally, while the program suggests that nonfiction texts be the primary focus of the course, in some instances literary writing has been integrated strategically. For example, from 2010–2012, the program used Octavia Butler's novel *Kindred* as part of the standard syllabus. The science fiction elements of *Kindred*, for instance, allowed students to consider the ethical and moral implications of a modern-day African-American woman being sent back in time to experience slavery firsthand. As I continued to refine the course, I found that Toni Morrison's (2008) *A Mercy* used historical fiction to elicit similar, but more nuanced, effects so I adopted Morrison as a replacement.

Finally, Temple's First-Year Writing Program also works closely with the university library, building two required library sessions into the course to introduce students to research databases supplied by the library and to teach them how to navigate the research process with the help of a librarian, so there is a pointed attention to information literacy strategies by design.[1]

COURSE STRUCTURE AND ASSIGNMENTS

I designed the Inventing Facts syllabus with the goal of creating content units that encourage students to pursue their own interests and curiosities while also defamiliarizing and complicating media and content they encounter in their daily lives. I also wanted to design units that historicize significant civil rights issues around gender, class, and race in an effort to help students synthesize contemporary conflicts around these issues within a larger history. I believe that a sort of "strategic presentism" modeled in this course allows students to think "critically about the past in the present in order to change the present" (Coombs and Coriale 2016, 88). Finally, I wanted to build assignments that allowed students to encounter a variety of different informational genres across different media since I believe that contemporary methods of reading embrace multimodal and lateral reading and research practices.

Exposing students to a variety of genre types foregrounds the constant project of informational assessment and reflection as supported by both the ACRL (2016) *Framework for Information Literacy for Higher Education* and the four domains of metaliterate learning (Jacobson et al. 2018). For example, the ACRL (2016) *Framework* begins with the tenet that "Authority Is Constructed and Contextual," a standard that is often interpreted in relation to the institutional qualifications and authority of the source's author. However, I suggest that expanding this definition to include genre brings more nuance to this framework since a reader's existing knowledge or assumptions about how different types of sources or genres function within an information network also signifies authority. The network of authority and information is important here; while some of the initial theorizations around metaliteracy have emphasized the importance of reading across networked spaces, using Pierre Bourdieu's work as a framework, my approach to metaliteracy in this course was centered on thinking of genre as an intertextual network and the act of academic research as a means of engaging with this network (Webb, Schirato, and Danaher 2002). In information literacy studies, this approach is often understood through threshold concepts that frame scholarship as a conversation, where "information seekers need to find, read (or watch), interpret, and understand more than one piece of information; they need to understand that each is just one voice of many within a larger scholarly conversation" (Bravender, McClure, and Schaub 2015, 12).

This approach manifested in both the variety of course materials and the range of writing assignments and classroom activities. One of the hallmarks of the post-truth turn is the sheer amount of information now available to students on digital and online platforms. In a classroom increasingly beholden to electronic texts, PDFs, and a student research culture defined by Internet searching (both online and through electronic databases), students must often contend with the flattening of information reception caused by the consumption of text on digital platforms. However, by emphasizing genre as a key touchstone throughout the course, students can better familiarize themselves with the nuances of genre and assess how digital platforms create new generic forms and interpretive obstacles. This approach meets Paul Gilster's (1998) original definition of digital literacy as "the ability to understand and use information in multiple formats from a wide range of sources when it is presented via computers" (1). Thus, in addition to excerpts from academic books and articles (often ones they accessed via e-books or scanned PDFs), students also listened to auditory material such as a podcast episode and two musical albums; analyzed visual media such as memes, websites, and blogs; and, finally, read a novel.

UNIT I
Digital Literacy and Fake News

This unit meets an objective of the third goal of metaliterate learning, to "critically evaluate and verify user-generated content," by asking students to perform close readings of the dynamic online and cultural systems behind digital objects like memes and social media posts (Jacobson et al. 2018). The learning goals for this unit are arranged around three major content areas: (1) meme genres and the concept of "spreadable media"; (2) the history of fake news and practicing online information literacy; and (3) the cultural and sociological implications of troll culture (Jenkins, Ford, and Green 2013). During this unit, students demonstrate metaliterate learning by both researching and engaging with participatory digital media environments and performing metacognition on their own methods of consuming and producing digital content on social media.

The first content area on meme genres asks students to reflect on their own use of online platforms and how the digital material they "like" or "share" online functions within existing social communities and networks. By analyzing meme genres and how specific Internet languages and stock images become easily reproducible, this unit models close textual reading alongside sociological analysis and encourages students to meet the first goal of the metaliteracy framework, through the objective to "critically assess information from all sources, including dynamic content that circulates online" (Jacobson et al. 2018). In initial discussions, many students admitted to a lack of reflection in regard to how or why they spread content to their networks online, supporting Nicole Cooke's (2017) assessment that while "Internet users are well versed in the mechanics of playing games, photoshopping, creating memes and mashups, and other skills, . . . this does not equate to discernment of the information being manipulated and presented to them" (215). To counter this tendency, students posted memes they had encountered on various social media feeds to a class discussion board and then analyzed them according to the underlying rhetorical purpose of the posts. By centering their analysis on Jenkins, Ford, and Green's (2013) framework of "sticky" versus "spreadable" digital media, students were able to speculate on how certain digital objects can either accommodate niche audiences or garner widespread viral attention. After reviewing these posts in larger class discussion, students then collaborated in flash minipresentations to explain how memes can also be categorized into different genre forms such as photo fads, stock character images, and strategic photoshops (Shifman 2014). These presentations allowed students to practice essential skills like summarizing the argument and format of an academic article while also applying the analytical method and ideas to their own examples, such that Limor Shifman's explanation of photo fads like "planking" can help explain new YouTube video challenges like "The Cinnamon Challenge" (Shifman 2014). By tracing how meme trends have shifted beyond photo challenges to accommodate video platforms, students practice using the key terms and ideas they encounter in scholarly articles in order to explain their own analyses and examples.

The second content area of this unit attempts to historicize the contemporary post-truth era alongside other key moments in epistemological reading. Widely used in political rhetoric, oxymoronic terms like *alternative facts* are wielded as weapons in an ongoing process to discredit and sow skepticism in political opponents, while similar terms like *fake news* and *post-truth* have slowly invaded the mainstream consciousness of the past few decades. Henrik Skov Nielsen, James Phelan, and Richard Walsh (2015) recognize the risks of this expansion of fictionality into the political sphere:

> The employment of fictionality in political discourse will tend to contribute—again for better or worse—to a logos-immunization of the discourse whereby arguments and counter-arguments have to take place on other levels and with other forms of appeal than those based in facts and documented evidence. (69)

Thus, in order to account for this shift and how it affects pedagogy in the first-year writing classroom, students read essays by Robert Darnton (2017) and David Uberti (2016) who show how the phenomena of fake news and literary hoaxes span centuries. Calling attention to the long history behind these information systems helps students develop their own metacognitive approach to academic and online research. In response to these readings, students posted short metacognitive responses to the problem of fake news and reflected on how their understanding of the concept changes in response to the essays. They also filled out Vanessa Otero's (2017) Media Bias Chart and practiced online research strategies in groups. Finally, after reflecting on the readings, their discussion board posts, and the Media Bias Chart, we used class discussion to build classroom guidelines for both "ethical argumentation" and "digital citizenship," including insights such as these:

- Be responsible for what you post.
- Your followers and the network you follow can be conflated with you as a person; be aware of how you present yourself.
- Be confident and sure in what you post—but do not troll others.
- Who we are online is not who we are.
- Be confident in what you are saying but be open to changing your mind.
- Influence an argument; do not try to win.

These guidelines support Alice Horning's (2013) assumption that "for individuals to function well in a democratic society, to be able to work and play successfully, and to be able to access, use, and contribute to the cornucopia of information on the Web efficiently and effectively, superior literacy skills are simply essential" (4).

The stakes here become especially salient when we move into the final content block of this unit, which focuses on malicious online content and trolling. While material surrounding this topic can be sensitive, I feel that there is value in presenting students with some unsavory elements of the Web, since the nature of anonymity in online spaces can breed unethical digital behaviors. As Nicole Cooke (2017) points out, "an inordinate amount of web-based information is salacious and malicious to the point of being damaging to individuals and groups of people" (211). In this way, the importance of being able to recognize how and when fictionality is used for misleading purposes expands beyond the rhetorical goals of the first-year writing classroom as a means to model good citizenship.

The writing assignment for this unit is essentially a close reading and summary paper; students must perform an analytical genealogy of a digital object, demonstrating how the object reflects a specific issue related to digital literacy found in one of the course readings. By evaluating content across different genres of writing, from academic articles to dynamic digital documents found on social media networks and in online forums, this assignment models the first goal of metaliterate learning in its approach, requiring students to perform an "informed, inquisitive investigation" of the various feedback and social mechanisms characteristic of digital genres (Mackey and Jacobson 2014). The assignment includes the following guided questions to help the students with this sort of evaluation and analysis:

- Who is the creator/author of this object?
- Where was it posted? In what context? For what purpose?
- How reliable is this source given what it is reporting/depicting? Is it biased in any way?
- What was the rhetorical purpose of posting or distributing this object?
- What communities or audiences does it appeal to and why?
- Is the content of the object referential in any way? What kind of knowledge is required to understand this object?

As is common with many first-year writing students, initial reactions to the assignment were wary of both the assignment's open-endedness and the unconventional scope of the analysis. However, once students practiced how to analyze memes around key terms from the readings in the flash minipresentations, the expectations for the paper became clearer. In addition, the "yes-yes-no" format of the *Reply All* podcast episode we listened to as a class focused on closely analyzing a single tweet and modeled how digital objects often have many referential layers that appeal to niche communities (Gimlet Media 2016).

Overall, the resulting papers from this unit provided students with the tools to research and reflect on a variety of online content that confused or interested them. Through the process of recontextualizing media content presumably familiar to them, students practiced adaptive research strategies and metacognitive reflection integral to metaliterate learning (Mackey and Jacobson 2014).

UNIT II

What's the Point of Stories That Aren't Even True?

Drawing from some of the rhetoric around fake news and post-truth from the first unit, the second unit considers the relationship between fiction, history, and contemporary culture as a means to cultivate the affective domain of metaliteracy, where learning activities center on emotional engagement and reflection (Jacobson et al. 2018). These learning goals are achieved through a close study of Toni Morrison's 2008 novel *A Mercy* as a means for students to consider how fictional representations of marginalized groups are both related to and distinct from other kinds of historical representations. Morrison's novel, a neo–slave narrative, dramatizes a pre–Revolutionary Era America through a diverse group of female characters attempting to maintain their community on a remote farm in Virginia. The diverse cast of female characters in this novel range from a young sixteen-year-old Angolan slave to a Native American female servant, a mixed-race orphan, and a British mail-order bride.

Initially, students struggled with the cognitive domain of metaliteracy as they were reluctant to engage with the novel due to its foreign time period and nonlinear narrative style. Just as understanding format and delivery mode is a key feature of metaliteracy's original learning objectives in the face of new media, Morrison's postmodernist approach to narrative required students to acclimate to an unfamiliar narrative mode. However, as the course went on and we outlined strategies for reading literary fiction, they become more acclimated to the novel as we plotted important events, characters, and narrative techniques as a group.

In addition, in light of their analysis during the previous unit, when students explored how digital objects are constructed to have a rhetorical purpose, students read Morrison's historical fiction through the lens of Hayden White's (1980) work on historical narrativity and how narratives of history are constructed in response to dominant moral and social codes. In online responses to White's essay, students related these ideas to *A Mercy*, often emphasizing how the content of the novel pushed them beyond their general knowledge of American history to include the marginalized voices of women, Native Americans, and people of color. Many students, for instance, emphasized how the shifting points of view of the novel allowed them to relate better to the characters, fostering in the process a more nuanced understanding of America's troubled history of slavery and how these tensions still resonate today.

The most significant moments in class discussion often occurred when I asked students to reflect on how certain events and passages in the novel resonated beyond the eighteenth-century setting of the novel. As Sune Auken (2015) points out, "One of the most significant features of works of literature is their ability to transcend their particular situation—the time and situation in which they were written" (170). This effect was best demonstrated in our reading of a scene in the novel when Florens, the young Angolan slave girl, encounters a group of Puritan authorities on her travels and they question and inspect her body due to the suspicious blackness of her skin. As the only I-narrator in the novel, Florens gives an account of this violation that is especially affecting, one that emphasizes the dehumanization in the scene. In response to this passage, many students were able to reflect on a time when they also had been judged or violated due to their outside appearance. At least two students later used this passage to help narrate their own experiences with racial profiling in their research papers on the novel. While these students were able to recognize themselves in Florens's narration, other students used this passage to reflect on the emotional stakes of dehumanization for historically marginalized groups overall as represented by contemporary activist movements like Black Lives Matter.

Thus, while the form and content of Morrison's novel allows students to practice actively reading a literary text, it also invites them to emotionally engage with the characters in productive ways. For example, many students are initially wary of Sorrow, the young mixed-race orphan character in the novel, since the majority of the novel is narrated or focalized by characters unsympathetic to Sorrow due to her difference. However, when students finally encounter a chapter focalized through Sorrow's perspective, they are able to better understand that her difficulties socializing with others stem from loss and trauma. Students recognize how Sorrow's struggle to connect with other characters is often due to her inability to find anyone that looks like her. It is these kinds of affective responses, in both class discussions and research papers, that demonstrate how fiction provides productive space for emotional engagement and positive metacognitive reflection. Fiction offers the metaliterate learner a way to experience the kind of active border crossing, between character, author, and reader, characteristic of fictional storytelling. To identify with a fictional character is akin to actively reframing an understanding of oneself and others.

UNIT III

Genres of History

The final content unit continues the focus on the affective domain of metaliteracy to foreground more adaptive and active research strategies. In this unit, students are tasked to compare historical information and academic research in different generic formats in an effort to trace how our understanding of certain ideas, persons, or events has changed over time and how narratives of these subjects encompass different rhetorical purposes. While I previously taught a version of this unit using readings on the American West from the *Cultural Conversations* anthology, I have since updated this unit to harness the popular success of Lin-Manuel Miranda's *Hamilton* musical. The added resources include the cast soundtrack and Miranda's collaborative *Hamilton Mixtape* album alongside primary source documents, excerpts from Ron Chernow's *Hamilton* biography, and scholarly articles on historiography and hip-hop as a form of political resistance. Through this expanded use of media, students are able to synthesize their understanding of historical moments, figures, and legacies in relation to textual, visual, and auditory genres.

The affective domain of metaliteracy manifests in how students initially react to searching for information using library databases. While the first unit defamiliarized cyberliteracies supposedly common to students, such as using online search engines and participating in social networks, this final unit introduces students to research databases provided by the library and special collections, as a way to foreground new research pathways beyond the simple Internet search. In a research workshop, for instance, students reviewed the difference between primary source and secondary source documents before collaboratively writing synthesis paragraphs around an idea or theme from a particular song from Lin-Manuel Miranda's *Hamilton*. Students first reviewed the songs, using online collaborative annotations from Genius (https://genius.com) to generate research topics and questions before heading to the library's collection of databases to find an academic source to synthesize with the lyrics. Understandably, the open-endedness of the assignment frustrated some students, as they were unsure of how to navigate the databases. Though I modeled how historical databases, such as America's Historical Newspapers (Readex) and ProQuest Historical Newspapers, provide access to digitized primary source documents, students initially struggled to find a relevant source to synthesize their material. Some students strained to come up with workable search terms from the song material. Others found the format and language of historical documents from the eighteenth century to be difficult to read or understand.

However, these initial setbacks became worthwhile, as groups were able to collaborate on synthesis paragraphs that gave historical weight to Miranda's dramatizations in *Hamilton*. One group, for example, synthesized the song "The Room Where It Happens" with a historical account of the founders debating over the location of the nation's capital and the national debt, comparing the political conflict behind closed doors to the kind of public shaming and Twitter wars that characterized the 2016 presidential election. The kind of "strategic presentism" modeled here demonstrates the benefits of framing historical research as a way of contextualizing contemporary events (Coombs

and Coriale 2016). Drawing a comparison between the secret political nego-
tiations of the founding fathers and a contemporary political climate characterized by social media branding and online personal attacks allowed these
students to recognize how online platforms may have created more transparency within politics, while also understanding that they have led to new problems as well.

Finally, since the assignment for this unit is often the most demanding in
regard to research, students scaffold research for their paper using a variety
of in-class visual presentations during which they share their research strategies and process. First, during a group research session in a computer lab, students collaborate to find research that synthesizes a song from the *Hamilton
Mixtape* into a short presentation. As Mackey and Jacobson point out (2014),
this kind of assignment allows metaliterate learners to practice "synthesizing
and adapting information so that it effectively moves from one format . . . to
another" (89). Later, students present their own individual research propos-
als to the class, sharing their research inspirations and strategies, and asking
classmates for feedback on outstanding questions. The ability to share information, question methodologies, and reframe goals as a group allows each
student to reflect "on [his or her] own thinking as a knowledgeable and collaborative participant, [and] the learner becomes a teacher of others" (Mackey
and Jacobson 2014, 89).

CONCLUSION AND REFLECTION

This chapter has shown that fictional texts, alongside more traditional research
from peer-reviewed academic essays, digital sources, and historical texts can
be beneficial to developing deep affective learning related to critical thinking
about ethics, social relationships, and personal reflection. While it is likely
that fiction will continue to have a strained relationship with first-year writing, since informational texts are still preferred by university administrators
and standard curricula, I contend that using fictionality as a frame can help
first-year writing students develop a more nuanced understanding of the rhetorical purposes of texts across various kinds of media. We must continue
challenging traditional assumptions about writing instruction by introducing
dynamic media elements and genres that speak to our learners.

The effectiveness of the specific metaliteracy goals outlined in the course
became evident in end-of-term student reflections. One student remarked
how completing research for this course led to the realization that "sometimes
things on the Internet are not true" and that seeking out multiple perspectives and scholarly sources has helped with the assessment of information
encountered online. Another student reflection focused on the usefulness and

novelty of synthesizing a variety of different materials and sources, such as scholarly articles, photographs, newspapers, novels, and even newsreels from the special collection archives.

Finally, the first-year writing class is by nature metaliterate in its emphasis on writing as an evolving and personal process and on the writing classroom as a community for learners to come together and share at all levels. Currently, Temple University's First-Year Writing Program is structured around a standard syllabus and holistic grading process that requires students to complete three papers of similar academic rigor to be graded by groups of instructors in different sections. As such, there can be little assignment innovation outside of the standard argumentative essay, at least in this course, within this program. This is a common concern in writing programs that requires a rethinking and reframing of our institutional practices to make room for innovation.

For instance, metaliteracy's focus on producing original multimedia content and sharing information empowers learners to expand these strategies beyond a standardized writing curriculum (Jacobson et al. 2018). The emphasis on collaborative and creative participation through various multimodal platforms in this course could easily complement the kind of remix of visual, auditory, and textual genres modeled by Miranda's *Hamilton Mixtape*. Likewise, the "Digital Literacy and Fake News" unit would likely benefit from more direct classroom engagement with social media platforms, such that the students could share the curation of a class Twitter feed that models different frameworks for analyzing various memes and viral content related to course ideas. Regardless, practicing metaliteracy, in whatever assignment format, will help writing students foreground themselves as active participants and creators of discourse both within and beyond the academy. The ability to understand how and why narratives are constructed—across multiple genres and formats—can only benefit students as they begin to develop their own writing strategies in a post-truth world.

NOTE

1. While there is a standard library presentation built around the program's standard syllabus, I was fortunate to work with one of Temple's reference librarians, Rebecca Lloyd, who tailored her presentation to my course material during both the Spring 2017 and Fall 2017 semesters. Additionally, during the Fall 2016 Honors version of this course, I coordinated a visit to Temple's Special Collections Research Center with the assistance of Josué Hurtado and Katy Rawdon, who introduced my students to special collections materials in relation to my "Genres of History" unit. Finally, I am also very thankful to librarians Kristina DeVoe and Caitlin Shanley who helped me theorize the beginnings of my "Digital Literacy and Fake News" unit and for their helpful workshop, Information Literacy in the Era of Alternative Facts, hosted by Temple's General Education department on March 28, 2017.

REFERENCES

ACRL (Association of College & Research Libraries). 2016. *Framework for Information Literacy for Higher Education*. Chicago: American Library Association. www.ala .org/acrl/standards/ilframework.

Arata, Stephen. 2015. "Literature and Information." *PMLA* 130 (3): 673–78. doi:10 .1632/pmla.2015.130.3.673.

Auken, Sune. 2015. "Utterance and Function in Genre Studies: A Literary Perspective." In *Genre Theory in Information Studies*, edited by Jack Andersen, 155–78. Studies in Information. Bingley, UK: Emerald Group.

Bravender, Patricia, Hazel McClure, and Gayle Schaub. 2015. *Teaching Information Literacy Threshold Concepts: Lesson Plans for Librarians*. Chicago: American Library Association.

Centre for Fictionality Studies. 2018. "About." Aarhus University. Accessed September 6. http://ficitionality.au.dk/about.

Chamorro-Premuzic, Tomas, Adriane Arteche, Andrew J. Bremner, Corina Greven, and Adrian Furnham. 2010. "Soft Skills in Higher Education: Importance and Improvement Ratings as a Function of Individual Differences and Academic Performance." *Educational Psychology* 30 (2): 221–41. doi:10.1080/01443410903560278.

Common Core State Standards Initiative. 2018. "English Language Arts Standards: Introduction; Key Design Consideration." Accessed September 6. www.corestandards.org/ELA-Literacy/introduction/key-design-consideration.

Cooke, Nicole A. 2017. "Posttruth, Truthiness, and Alternative Facts: Information Behavior and Critical Information Consumption for a New Age." *The Library Quarterly* 87 (3): 211–21. https://doi.org/10.1086/692298.

Coombs, David Sweeney, and Danielle Coriale. 2016. "V21 Forum on Strategic Presentism." *Victorian Studies* 59 (1): 87–89. https://doi.org/10.2979/ victorianstudies.59.1.04.

Darnton, Robert. 2017. "The True History of Fake News." *NYR Daily*, February 13. www.nybooks.com/daily/2017/02/13/the-true-history-of-fake-news.

Davidson, Cathy N. 2017. *The New Education: How to Revolutionize the University to Prepare Students for a World in Flux*. New York: Basic Books.

English, James F. 2012. *The Global Future of English Studies*. Malden, MA: Wiley-Blackwell.

Gilster, Paul. 1998. *Digital Literacy*. New York: Wiley.

Gimlet Media. 2016. "#83 Voyage into Pizzagate." *Reply All* (podcast), December 8. https://gimletmedia.com/episode/83-voyage-into-pizzagate.

Horning, Alice. 2013. *Reading, Writing, and Digitizing: Understanding Literacy in the Electronic Age*. Newcastle upon Tyne, UK: Cambridge Scholars.

Hutcheon, Linda. 1989. *The Politics of Postmodernism*. New Accents. London; New York: Routledge.

Jacobson, Trudi, Tom Mackey, Kelsey O'Brien, Michele Forte, and Emer O'Keeffe. 2018. "Goals and Learning Objectives." Metaliteracy.org. Accessed September 6. https://metaliteracy.org/learning-objectives.

Jaschik, Scott. 2017. "Humanities Majors Drop." *InsideHigherEd News*, June 5. www.insidehighered.com/news/2017/06/05/analysis-finds-significant-drop -humanities-majors-gains-liberal-arts-degrees.

Jenkins, Henry, Sam Ford, and Joshua Green. 2013. *Spreadable Media: Creating Value and Meaning in a Networked Culture*. New York: New York University Press.

Kreiswirth, Martin. 2010. "Narrative Turn in the Humanities." In *Routledge Encyclopedia of Narrative Theory*, edited by David Herman, Manfred Jahn, and Marie-Laure Ryan, 377–82. London: Routledge.

Lindemann, Erika. 1993. "Freshman Composition: No Place for Literature." *College English* 55 (3): 311–16. https://doi.org/10.2307/378743.

Mackey, Thomas P., and Trudi E. Jacobson. 2014. *Metaliteracy: Reinventing Information Literacy to Empower Learners*. Chicago: ALA Neal-Schuman.

McHale, Brian. 1987. *Postmodernist Fiction*. New York: Methuen.

Miranda, Lin Manuel. 2015. *Hamilton: An American Musical*. Atlantic Records. Accessed via Spotify.

Morrison, Toni. 2008. *A Mercy*. New York: Vintage.

Nielsen, Henrik Skov, James Phelan, and Richard Walsh. 2015. "Ten Theses about Fictionality." *Narrative* 23 (1): 61–73. https://doi.org/10.1353/nar.2015.0005.

OED Online. 2018. "post-truth, adj." Oxford University Press. Accessed January via subscription: www.oed.com.

Otero, Vanessa. 2017. "The Chart, Version 3.0: What, Exactly, Are We Reading?" *All Generalizations Are False* (blog), November 8. www.allgeneralizationsarefalse .com/the-chart-version-3-0-what-exactly-are-we-reading.

Punday, Daniel. 2010. *Five Strands of Fictionality: The Institutional Construction of Contemporary American Fiction*. Columbus: The Ohio State University Press.

Shifman, Limor. 2014. "The Cultural Logic of Photo-Based Meme Genres." *Journal of Visual Culture* 13 (3): 340–58. doi:10.1177/1470412914546577.

Strauss, Valerie. 2017. "Analysis: The Surprising Thing Google Learned about Its Employees—and What It Means for Today's Students." *Washington Post*, December 20. www.washingtonpost.com/news/answer-sheet/wp/2017/12/20/ the-surprising-thing-google-learned-about-its-employees-and-what-it-means -for-todays-students.

Tate, Gary. 1993. "A Place for Literature in Freshman Composition." *College English* 55 (3): 317–21. https://doi.org/10.2307/378744.

Uberti, David. 2016. "The Real History of Fake News." *Columbia Journalism Review*, December 15. www.cjr.org/special_report/fake_news_history.php.

Walsh, Richard. 2007. *The Rhetoric of Fictionality: Narrative Theory and the Idea of Fiction*. Theory and Interpretation of Narrative. Columbus: The Ohio State University Press.

Webb, Jenn, Tony Schirato, and Geoff Danaher. 2002. *Understanding Bourdieu*. London; Thousand Oaks, CA: SAGE.

White, Hayden. 1980. "The Value of Narrativity in the Representation of Reality." *Critical Inquiry* 7 (1): 5–27.

KIMMIKA L. H. WILLIAMS-
WITHERSPOON

9

Poetic Ethnography and Metaliteracy

Empowering Voices in a Hybrid
Theater Arts Course

The Theater Studies curriculum at Temple University's Department of Theater exemplifies the metacognitive domain of metaliteracy to effectively consume and produce information. This program offers a number of community-based learning (CBL), performance, and Theater Studies courses that promote performance ethnography, digital storytelling, and public discourse.

Specifically, the course THTR 2008 Poetic Ethnography operates both as ethnodrama and as a theater hybrid that incorporates several tightly structured field site audio and video digital storytelling projects into its thirteen-week curriculum. These projects encourage students to expand their knowledge base, investigate multiple forms of information-gathering methodologies, and develop performative and distributive content across multiple cultural and social platforms.

In this age of fake news and false truths, students create new forms of knowledge through their research and the development of alternative ethnographies. In courses like these, through the process of research and new knowledge production, students gain lifelong learning skills that help them develop more nuanced, personal narratives that tell more complete and factual stories about communities, individuals, and contemporary events. This chapter, then, looks at how Poetic Ethnography teaches students how to develop ethnographic and personal narratives set to poetry about Philadelphia neighborhoods and their people—giving voice to the sometimes voiceless in our communities, while simultaneously learning metaliteracy and metacognitive learning strategies.

FUSING ETHNOGRAPHY, PERFORMANCE, AND METALITERACY

Metaliteracy is defined as "an overarching, self-referential and comprehensive framework that informs other literacy types" (Mackey and Jacobson 2011, 70). In today's popular culture, with its ever-burgeoning social media environment, undergraduate and graduate students alike need to develop a comprehensive understanding of knowledge production in the age of new media and what is fast becoming a technocentric information disfranchisement, or technocracy. When our ability to exercise rights and privileges in a society becomes inherently linked with access to information and one's ability "to critically evaluate, share and produce content in multiple forms," then teaching metaliteracy across disciplines takes on an even greater importance as we prepare the next generation of democratic citizenry (Mackey and Jacobson 2011, 62).

There are four learning domains associated with metaliteracy: behavioral, cognitive, affective, and metacognitive. Metaliteracy's learning goals include teaching students how to critically evaluate content, apply information technology ethics, share new knowledge across a variety of environments, and build connections between lifelong learning and research methods (Jacobson et al. 2018).

For several years now, the theater department at Temple University has taught students how to create performative content for public consumption. With the rise in popularity of choreopoems like Ntozake Shange's ([1975], 1997) *For Colored Girls Who Have Considered Suicide When the Rainbow Is Enuf* and devised theater developed from first-person narratives of real events like Anna Deavere Smith's (1992) *Fires in the Mirror*, theater practitioners and consumers are encountering innovative ways to process news and alternative news across multiple platforms that contribute to the arts *and* information literacy. For artists and theater practitioners alike (which includes actors, playwrights, and designers along with performance artists and poets), learning to utilize nuanced and layered research methods that lead to the ability to critically evaluate community websites and social media sources as data can be an invaluable tool or knowledge set.

Today's print, broadcast, and social media must grapple with a political climate that romanticizes questionable policies and practices of the past under the guise of "making America great again." From the unconscious bias in the Associated Press's "looting" versus "finding" reporting in the aftermath of Hurricane Katrina in 2005 (Noveck 2005; Shalby 2017; Williams-Witherspoon 2006) to President Trump's reference to the "alt-Left" in his efforts to place blame for the death of Heather Heyer in Charlottesville, Virginia, in 2017 (Lee 2017), so much of contemporary, traditional media generates and reifies news that sensationalizes and "pathologizes" victims, communities of color, the disenfranchised, and minorities. In this atmosphere, some young people are looking for ways to curb their fears and anxieties about an uncertain tomorrow. Many of those students are drawn to performance in popular culture to resist oppression and to contribute to the public discourse. Young people, like my students at Temple University, are finding art-based performance courses that place an emphasis on original work as one such way to resist retro-exclusionary dialogue and to contribute to new knowledge creation.

CONTEXTUALIZING THE DISCOURSE

As a tool to help promote behavioral, cognitive, affective, and metacognitive learning and transformative new media content, metaliteracy encourages critical thinking and thoughtful content creation in a digital age (Jacobson et al. 2018). New knowledge formation takes on many forms, and in performance, content can be created, developed, and reproduced through various modalities. Many young people today employ new media content (blogs, hashtags, tweets, and YouTube videos) to give themselves agency as media producers and to help counter half-truths and fake news.

At Temple University, an innovative brand of socially engaged performance poetry and devised theater is providing a new way to meet some students' needs for radical intellectualism and for contributing to the public discourse as new knowledge producers. This new, hybrid brand of devised theater performance relies heavily on course work that teaches students to appreciate metaliteracy and to use its methods of inquiry and content production.

Of course, I did not know that when I first created the Poetic Ethnography course in 2011; however, in hindsight, by collecting and repurposing information (field notes, research data, interviews, and participant observations), I see that metaliteracy models a method of lifelong learning and encourages student participation in new knowledge production in a digital age that aligns with the goals of this course. The four domains of metaliteracy—behavioral, cognitive, affective, and metacognitive (Jacobson et al. 2018; Mackey and Jacobson 2014, 85–86)—in theater and performance pedagogy translate into doing, understanding, transforming, and reflecting. As a hybrid Theater Studies performance course (part theater studies/part anthropology of performance), the Poetic Ethnography curriculum uses scaffolded research and writing assignments along with nontraditional deliverables, such as poetry, video, and audio podcasts, to teach competencies for each of the four domains.

Theater and performance studies scholars are just beginning to investigate the connection between devised theater and metaliteracy, offering considerable promise for the future. For many of the students who come to the class from myriad disciplines across the university, the majority of the outcomes, assignments, and nontraditional deliverables required in the course encourage students to think critically about metaliteracy as radical activism, socially engaged art production, and alternative social commentary as well as the varied ways in which alternative content can be delivered (Williams-Witherspoon 2013, 169–183; Williams-Witherspoon 2017, 1).

PERFORMANCE POETRY AND DEVISED THEATER

While *performed research* creates a built-in challenge for the student researcher/ performance artist around issues of *authorship*, devised theater performance, has, nevertheless, quickly become a method of exploration that takes data and research findings directly to the people through its performative component:

> As more and more ethnic and urban social research necessitates finding new and creative ways to disseminate data beyond just the usual scholarly community, performance is increasingly becoming one of the new, innovative vehicles of choice through which information is distributed to a wider audience. (Williams-Witherspoon 2015, 39)

Filtered through a multimedia, technocentric lens, as a theater and performance poetry genre, the Poetic Ethnography course pushes the metaliteracy aesthetic into a contemporary iteration of traditional dramaturgy. In much the same way that traditional aesthetics deals with the polar opposites of beauty and ugliness and the full spectrum between its two poles, metaliteracy graphs that notion of *truth* to *beauty* and its counterpart *fake news* to *ugliness*. Students are encouraged to create work based on observations, images, and representations of Philadelphia neighborhoods that purposely address "the good, the bad, and the ugly" and everything in between. To help facilitate that work and that level of critical investigation, at the beginning of each class period, students are given prompts that are often based on news items or current events. Aesthetics also provides a platform for students to talk about emotions and feelings in opposition to pure intellectualism.

Aesthetics can be culturally specific and tied to a recognizable set of principles. According to its dictionary definition, aesthetics can be manifested through tastes, styles, behaviors, appearances, or outward expressions. In this way, *truth* is likened to *beauty* and agreed upon by the dictates of a given society. When its polar opposite *untruth* or *fake news* becomes the norm, *ugliness* holds sway over a nation and the very fabric of society is disrupted.

From design elements to directorial vision, theater relies on research and a full understanding of environment and character in the world of the play. For many of the millennials who are drawn to the genre, performance poetry and devised theater rely heavily on research, observation, and reflection; but what they do best is to give young people voice and agency to constructively respond to the news that they are consuming.

As Jan Cohen-Cruz (2010) writes, "The engaged artist embraces rigorous connection and exchange, becoming involved in the issues and people at the source of [his or her] work, not assuming a need to keep a critical distance" (5). Devised theater is by definition, then, engaged performance. This form of art comes directly out of research in communities. Relying on participant observations, interviews, and personal narratives, the hallmark of devised theater is in the performances—created as original works based on collaboration and ensemble.

To create devised theater, students immerse themselves in research materials and computer resources that they must learn how to access and critically evaluate for viability and usefulness. Relying on the voices and characters of research subjects to tell their own stories, both researcher and researched are given a platform from which to frame their journeys and to reframe the all-too-often negative social narratives that are reified and constantly replayed in popular culture and on the nightly news.

Devised theater productions are growing in popularity. In ¡*Oye! For My Dear Brooklyn*, Modesto Flako Jimenez (2018) looks at gentrification in New York City's ongoing wars over property and residential rights. According to Melena Ryzik (2010), theater critic for the *New York Times*, *The Footprint: The Battle over Atlantic Yards* was a musical that grew out of a devised theater concept, dramatizing the battle over the Brooklyn Yards Project that would lead to the Brooklyn Nets' Barclays Center stadium in the heart of what once was a residential community. Likewise, Temple University's production of my play *SHOT! Requiem for a Bullet* (Williams-Witherspoon 2009) tackled the topic of violence in the black community and was based on research in North Philadelphia's so-called Badlands. Following its run, *SHOT!* was reprised at the University of Indiana in Pennsylvania (2009), the Kennedy Center (2010) and the University of Akron (2011).

Devised theater is incredibly intersectional. Cobbled together from multiple stories, this type of contemporary theater performance is conceptually nonlinear and filtered through diverse cultural lenses. For nontraditional artists, devised theater offers a quick and an efficient way to mount productions that speak to the contemporary cultural moment without the benefit of the great deal of production capital that is needed to produce traditional theater.

Devised theater usually presents journeys of self-discovery, and often-times, the work marries history and memory as it collides with the ever-present now. Because metaliteracy emphasizes critical thinking and self-reflection as a method of inquiry and distillation, it is intuitively integral to devised theater development. Researching varied data sources, interviewing participants, and observing activities and events in community settings allow ensemble theater artists to compare and contrast data sources and to juxtapose diverse perspectives with their own to paint a more objective and inclusive truth.

Metaliteracy also teaches us that in today's digital world *truth* and *memory* can, unfortunately, easily be compromised by the mere repetition of *false truths* or lies. Without the benefit of scrutiny or fact-checking, lies or *false truths*, through the sheer number of times they are repeated in the public discourse (either through word of mouth or "likes" and "shares" in social media), become transformed in the public transcript to *possibilities* that then become morphed into *alternative facts*.

In this nihilistic political climate, to combat the morphing of lies into alternative facts, performance arts such as devised theater, performance poetry, and spoken word and immersive performance have emerged as new brands of radical protest art tasked with chronicling current events and keeping the truth. This brand of protest art is an art of resistance that harkens back to the resistant art production of earlier periods, such as the Harlem Renaissance and the Black Arts Movement (BAM) of the 1960s, and dares to "speak truth to power." Whether for risk or for recompense, more and more young artists are embracing metaliteracy as a model of inquiry and using it to create poetry, performance, and devised theater, not just to chronicle the issues and events of the day, but also to reaffirm their own humanity.

THTR 2008 POETIC ETHNOGRAPHY

Temple University's Department of Theater offers the course Poetic Ethnography each spring as a lower-level performance course. This class teaches an introduction to performance studies literature, performance poetry-writing technique, and how individuals, like Temple students, can exercise their own agency as information consumers *and* producers. This metacognitive approach to ethnographic learning and performance relies heavily on fieldwork, personal narrative and descriptive writing, digital storytelling, and devised performance. As a community-based learning course, students choose a neighborhood or community site outside of their usual field of experience on which to conduct observation and research. Over the several weeks of the semester, students create nontraditional poetic ethnography in and around those sites.

In the second half of the semester, in addition to creating aural and video digital storytelling pieces for wider distribution on the Internet through spaces like Facebook, YouTube, and Thick Descriptions (http://thickdescriptions .blogspot.com), students (many of whom have had limited to no theater or performance training) learn how to take their written words as arts producers and infuse it with theatricality, a process culminating in a final performance of devised theater offered free for the university and surrounding community.

The truth about poverty and police violence in and around communities of color, the Black Lives Matter marches, and the kidnapping and trafficking of young girls along with other current events of 2016–2017 went from the page to the stage in the spring 2017 devised theater production of *And If They Come for Me*, produced in Temple University's Randall Theater. Black, brown, yellow, and white students, like those in the spring 2017 production of *And If They Come for Me*, used elements of urban culture to tell their own stories across ethnicities. Their work was anchored to influences from urban culture, hip-hop, BAM rhetoric, and a commitment to social activist engagement.

Some of the student work used escapism and fantasy, but the majority of the work came straight from the nontraditional poetic ethnographies students had conducted while doing field research in Philadelphia neighborhoods. Many of the pieces in the show, like the ensemble piece for the missing black girls in Washington, DC (Jarrett, Reyes, and Shortell 2017), are ripped from the heart and sinew of young people, who are far removed from Jim Crow/Jane Crow ideologies and overt forms of oppression and who seemingly now feel blindsided by our current political climate.[1] As seen in the spring 2018 class performance *This Is Habitual*, with pieces like "Momma Can't look at Parks and Has Been Robbed by Land" about the high school shooting in Florida, "Die Like a Girl" about the challenges young women must surmount in urban communities, and "If My Tongue Were a Weapon" offering thoughts on gun control and social protest, each year student work becomes more and more socially engaged. The students' work and subsequent devised theater performances try to make sense of the news—its irony, its shock and awe.

Sample Assignments

To prepare students for a semester of ethnographic field research, one of the assignments given to them at the beginning of the semester involves partnered interviews. After a series of introductory writing exercises and the reading of cross-curricular text to help students develop a lexicon for fieldwork and research methods, students are paired in groups of two and they conduct their first practice partnered interviews in the classroom. The students work with a set of sample questions developed by the instructor to elicit rich interview material using a very quick and easy format. Students are encouraged to record these interviews with their cellphones and/or other electronic devices, and then as homework, over the next several weeks, they learn how to transcribe the interviews and then turn that interview material into poetic ethnography.

This collaborative part of the course illustrates the "learner as teacher" aspect of metaliteracy because students share their knowledge with their learning partners who will hear the outcome of those pieces during the following scheduled classes (Jacobson et al. 2018). In doing so, students learn from one another very quickly about personal privacy, informed consent, and information ethics. Through this assignment, students learn by doing to be precise and authentic as they frame their partners' narratives poetically.

This exercise quickly establishes the importance of truth, authenticity, and accountability. By midsemester, and several drafts later, in a follow-up component to that earlier exercise, students turn those same "partner pieces" into a digital storytelling format and incorporate the subject's voice or line of dialogue at some point in the body of an audio podcast. Incorporating the interviewee's voice somewhere within the body of the poem contrasts narration and character, further nuancing the story being told and the perspective through which listeners access the work. These podcasts are eventually distributed to a wider audience through various online platforms.

By the third week in the class, students choose a field site approved by the instructor. Based on their personal interests and their research questions, field sites can differ greatly from student to student—from a neighborhood church near a residence hall or apartment to a senior-living facility as a volunteer reading weekly to the elderly, to a self-help support service group like Alcoholics Anonymous that might meet once or twice a month, and everything in between.[2]

Over the course of the semester, students spend several weeks visiting their field sites, mapping the areas, and researching the field sites or participants and their digital footprints in other media. In addition, they develop literature reviews, observe participants, participate in events in or around their field sites, and, eventually, interview participants from their sites. In keeping with the name of the class, each assignment includes field site reports that have to be turned in, along with students' field site notes written in a nontraditional poetic format—what I have labeled poetic ethnographies.

To facilitate a more dynamic field research experience, students are required to attend at least three community events in their field sites. Following community site visits, students submit response papers critiquing the social events as theater, along with poetic critiques and interpretations of the events at the very next scheduled class period. After their interviews with individuals from their field sites, students prepare audio interview excerpts and poetic responses. These scaffolded assignments culminate in the development of two poetry videos that are usually shot by their class partners (from their earlier "partner piece" assignments) in each of the students' field sites and then edited. Akin to a music video, these poetry videos are eventually distributed to a larger online population through the use of Facebook, Twitter, the Theater Department's e-mail discussion list, blogs, and YouTube.

Throughout the semester, in addition to fieldwork, at the beginning of each class, students receive *lines* of text based on a variety of topics and current events and then take seven to fifteen minutes per class for free writing. The goal is to promote critical thinking by asking students to quickly evaluate new information, determine its value, and assign its meaning in relation to their own lives and then use that line of information in the body of an ethnographic text to communicate and share its meaning to a larger audience.

Students are encouraged to think about themselves and their field sites juxtaposed with the world around them. In a further example of listener as learner, following the in-class prompts, another ten to fifteen minutes are spent allowing some of the students to share their work and receive feedback and criticism from their peers using, as a rubric, my ritual call after each piece for "comments, criticisms, suggestions, questions." Sometimes, based on those initial moments of sharing work aloud in the classroom, students are told to mark individual pieces as "performance worthy" for consideration for the final show.

As a result of prompts, homework assignments, field research, and the variety of deliverables required for the course, by the end of the semester, students have amassed anywhere from thirty to forty ethnographies set to poetry that speak to their personal journeys of self-discovery and their field site research.

In preparation for the devised theater component of our final performance project, students choose from their list of poetic ethnographies that have previously been marked "performance worthy" (either during midterms, when their journals are turned in for review, or during the weekly sharing opportunities in class). Each student gets to narrow down his or her work to four or five stories for possible incorporation into the final production. By the end of the semester, as a final component, students memorize, rehearse, and perform a devised theater performance (or choreopoem), conceived and directed by the instructor, for the university community.

The students' poetic ethnographies are developed into an original devised theater performance that is then mounted, with limited production values (i.e., minimal set design, lighting, soundscape, and projections), for three or four free shows that are open to the community in our black box theater. As part of our commitment to community engagement, students are encouraged to invite field site participants and members of the community to those performances, where they are then recognized and publically thanked for their contributions. Coming full circle by the semester's end, community participants are given voice when they recognize their own stories on stage and hear their own words performed back to them as part of a larger narrative.

Community-Based Learning

Poetic Ethnography is a dedicated community-based learning (CBL) course, and as such, our primary course objective for the class is to promote metro engagement. As part of that metro engagement, in CBL courses, students are encouraged to experience the city of Philadelphia and beyond. During the course of the semester, students not only have to get out and interact with a community broadly defined as outside of their own field of experience; but beyond that, students have to really dive in and learn all about that community using multiple methodologies.

In CBL courses, students are responsible for researching their field sites, learning the history of those communities and then reviewing articles and news reports written about the areas to contextualize the various (or singular) narratives about the people in those communities that can become reified in the public discourse. This method of inquiry promotes a robust examination of the news generated in traditional media (print and television) to restrict inaccuracies and biases in policies and representation. In certain communities under scrutiny, investigating multiple news stories and news sources broadens one's perspective. As novelist Chimamanda Adachie (2009) warns in her TED Talk, there is a danger in relying on "the single story" as a way of *pretending to know*, while, in actuality, codifying individuals and stereotyping whole communities.

Outcomes

Somewhere between the beginning of the semester and the final performances, students are transformed into critical knowledge *learners* and new knowledge *producers*. Using a series of cross-curricular readings, students are introduced to some of the key issues in performance studies and the anthropology of performance discourse.

Course readings on conducting research by scholars like Victor and Edith Turner (2007); using theater to promote community activism and community engagement by artists/activists like Jan Cohen-Cruz (2010, 134–64); and writing rich ethnographies that contain "thick description" by anthropologists like Clifford Geertz (1988) give students an overview of the importance of the work. However, it is through the process of research, development, rehearsal, and performance of the original poetic ethnographies that students also learn the foundation skills in theater, including techniques in theatricality, collaboration, ensemble performance, and the creation of devised theater.

A fundamental goal in the metaliteracy framework in arts and humanities courses is finding ways to engage students while translating academic knowledge or discipline-specific knowledge into applied experience. THTR 2008 Poetic Ethnography fits that model because it teaches students how to make meaningful connections between the field research they conduct, the ethnographies in poetic form that they develop, and the multiple modes of distributing alternative content through a diverse series of deliverables.

Metaliteracy objectives encourage students to learn how to evaluate research materials from various environments and to distill useful data to create and share new knowledge production as active participants and knowledge creators. The audio podcasts, poetry videos, and devised theater performances each represent yet another method of nontraditional distribution of news and research data.

Poetic Ethnography aligns nicely with the metaliteracy goals of developing students into new knowledge producers who create and share news content across multiple platforms. What makes this course so special is precisely that the assignments and deliverables, including the audio interview excerpts, digital storytelling projects, poetry videos, and devised theater performances, are so diverse and have such a broad and wide-reaching audience appeal.

My department and the university at large embrace the CBL courses like Poetic Ethnography because their wide-reaching audience appeal has the potential to translate into audience development for nontraditional theater productions and an ever-growing digital footprint. Through this course and program, we are developing critically conscious, new knowledge producers who are creating original and repurposed information ready to share as alternative content gleaned from multiple personal, community, and literary sources.

Poetic Ethnography assignments are structured in such a way so as to encourage students who may not have been intuitively and socially engaged before coming into the classroom. In this course, the students begin to pay attention to media consumption and the oftentimes singular narratives that are associated with particular communities and marginalized groups. Requiring students to research areas contextualized against their digital footprints, as evidenced by news stories written about those communities in various news outlets, helps to improve metaliterate learning through mindful media consumption. When students encounter fake news items that directly contradict their experiences on the ground conducting field research in those various sites, they have now developed strategies to help "write that wrong."

Community Engagement

In Poetic Ethnography, students are encouraged to think critically about sociopolitical issues in municipalities related to people living/working/commuting in their various neighborhoods. Because we know that art has the power to transform lives, students enrolled in Poetic Ethnography create work in and around social change by crafting poetic ethnographies and personal narratives about Philadelphia neighborhoods and the people in those local communities. As Shannon Jackson (2011) suggests, "Sometimes theatre is about spectacle, a discourse that supports fragile delineation between a consumptive society of the spectacle and presumably anti-consumptive forms of image-making" (20). By researching, creating, performing, and distributing poetic ethnographies using several online and performance modalities, Poetic Ethnography students are, in fact, becoming metaliterate learners—learning to be critical consumers of new media and conscientious producers of new knowledge. This student-driven new knowledge formation, as ethnographies in poetic form, works to give voice to the sometimes voiceless in our communities.

As a way to give back and to encourage accountability, field site participants are always invited to attend our performances. Because of the commitment to community engagement, Temple University, the Center for the Performance and Cinematic Arts, and the Theater Department always offer performances, like the Poetic Ethnography final projects, free and open to the public. The content created in the course—the digital storytelling items, podcasts, videos, and performances—in accordance with metaliteracy objectives that encourage the creation and sharing of new knowledge, is always made available online in multiple modalities as a ready repository of alternative news. Relying on incredible creativity and innovation, as Mackey and Jacobson (2014) suggest, these digital storytelling components continue to evolve as new, emerging technologies and platforms evolve; they engage learners "in diverse media, writing, and inventive narrative structures" (190).

Reframing the Narrative

Part theater studies/part anthropology of performance, Poetic Ethnography encourages students to reframe the narratives they encounter and create understandings. It combines theater competencies, the anthropology of performance canon, and now, thanks to a better understanding of the metaliteracy model (Mackey and Jacobson 2014, 22–26), a more purposeful synthesis of how performance poetry can be produced, used, and shared, in performance, as new media. By recasting and reinventing traditional conceptions of information literacy, this course has evolved as a method of reframing traditional narrative structures and formats to literally give voice to empowered learners.

The accoutrements of youth culture—rap, hip-hop, R&B (rhythm and blues), comic books, graphic novels, and the like (along with multiple racial signifiers and gender identities)—are tied to this new wave of spoken word, performance poetry, and devised theater. Using this kind of immersive, community-based theater, through the rigor of the work, the performer-ethnographers' lived creative experiences push an agenda of inclusiveness. As their new mode of expression with online technologies and social media, this kind of performance art encourages an innovative cadre of artists and activists to tease apart notions of intersectionality.

In her critique of *12 Years a Slave*, bell hooks (2013) suggests, "we have this fatigue of suffering" from only seeing "people slaughter each other." Contemporary devised theater performers imagine possibilities and increased "life chances" (Gandy 1998, 3). This seems to be one mechanism that young artists and activists are using to gain momentum and reframe the discourse in the public transcript.

Combating the proliferation of untruths, half-truths, and alternative truths made popular during Donald Trump's presidential campaign and his subsequent conservative, Republican administration, millennial artists and performers are creating alternative histories of empires and civilizations of the past, alongside technologically advanced images of futures where people have to, and continue to, fight back, refusing to perish (Gonzales 2013). This kind of theater performance uses radical protest art to help the audiences see past their present circumstances and to understand the value of social activism. Applying these new forms of performance art through theater allows young people the opportunity to quickly hold up a mirror to society. Using the influences of the past to project themselves into and predict a conceptual new future helps encourage audiences to contemplate our sometimes inimical lived experiences side by side with our unlimited possibilities.

As metacognitive thinkers, students in arts and humanities courses that make learning by doing a priority, like Poetic Ethnography, are redefining knowledge creation, knowledge distribution, and knowledge consumption. In a political climate where *truth* as a concept is continually contested, twisted, and turned inside out by anyone with the power and the means to do so, young people are finding ways to add their voices to the public discourse. It is imperative, then, that we in the academy infuse our curricula with discussions about metaliteracy and how it can be used to enhance any area of study and develop course work and assignments to teach these competencies so that our students learn how to be exemplary knowledge producers.

There is no exclusive way to conduct field research, just as there is more than one way to write ethnography. Encouraging students to conduct field research in local communities or neighborhoods demystifies fieldwork. I have found that by encouraging students to create field notes in poetic form, Poetic Ethnography reframes the narrative and makes ethnography—as stories about people—more viable.

Poetic Ethnography encourages creativity, critical thinking, and the production of new knowledge, all key aspects of metaliteracy (Jacobson et al. 2018). That new knowledge is distributed through various modalities—live performance, audio podcasts, and video content—that anyone can access online. This form of knowledge production and distribution decenters media *space* and promotes knowledge sharing. The Poetic Ethnography curriculum significantly impacts student behavioral competencies and affect. For this reason, I have found metaliteracy to be a perfect complement to my pedagogy.

As Donna Witek and Teresa Grettano (2014) suggest, metaliteracy promotes student empowerment, metacognitive awareness and social engagement, all of which are objectives in my course. I firmly believe that for those of us teaching in the arts and humanities, incorporating metaliteracy learning goals and objectives into our curricula creates a win-win scenario for our students.

Poetic Ethnography offers a ready example of the curricular benefits that metaliteracy provides Temple University students, even in performance courses like mine. This course incorporated several of the competencies that make up metaliteracy, including the ability to critically evaluate content (both print-based and online); the development of an understanding of information technology ethics, including issues of privacy, consent, intellectual property, and communication ethics; the ability to share information across a number of environments; and the development of research strategies that help promote lifelong learning outcomes (Jacobson et al. 2018). Through the frame of metaliterate learning, Poetic Ethnography students are better prepared to be conscientious news consumers and new knowledge producers.

CONCLUSION

Poetic Ethnography teaches students to access, analyze, evaluate, create, and participate in new knowledge formation by creating content in and about community that is then distributed in different forms. Researching and developing performance poetry and devised theater operates in tandem with teaching metaliteracy learning objectives. As a learning modality, "metaliteracy promotes critical thinking and collaboration in a digital age" (Mackey and Jacobson 2011, 62).

By teaching metaliteracy in arts and humanities courses like Poetic Ethnography, students not only learn to think critically about sociopolitical issues in municipalities through stories set to poetry about people living, working, and commuting in their various neighborhoods; they also learn the value of investigating and interrogating various online data sites and sources and to combat fake news by creating alternative forms of new knowledge for public consumption. Clearly, there is value in course work that teaches metaliteracy through art and performance curricula. Temple University's Theater Studies course THTR 2008 Poetic Ethnography relies heavily on metaliteracy pedagogy to teach students how to build thoughtful social content to combat and reframe fake news, contribute new layers of truth to the ongoing public discourse, and become more cautious and conscientious new media consumers combating a post-truth world.

NOTES

1. *Jim Crow/Jane Crow* is a term coined by writer/publisher Haki Madhubuti and used in a lecture presented at the Charles L. Blockson Collection, Sullivan Hall, Temple University, in March 2015.
2. In line with Institutional Review Board exemptions for class work, vulnerable populations are never used in our field research, and in the beginning of the semester, we spend several class periods talking about research protocols, consent/assent, and the protection of research participants and their personal information.

REFERENCES

Adichie, Chimamanda Ngozi. 2009. "The Danger of a Single Story." TED Talk. Published October 7. https://www.youtube.com/watch?v=D9Ihs241zeg.

Cohen-Cruz, Jan. 2010. *Engaging Performance: Theatre as Call and Response*. Abingdon, Oxon, UK: Routledge.

Deavere Smith, Anna. 1992. *Fires in the Mirror*. New York: Anchor Books.

Gandy, Oscar. 1998. *Communication and Race: A Structural Perspective*. London: Arnold.

Geertz, Clifford. 1988. "Thick Description: Toward an Interpretive Theory of Culture." In *High Points in Anthropology*, 2nd ed., edited by Paul Bohannan and Mark Glazer, 531–52. New York: McGraw-Hill.

Gonzales, Michael A. 2013. "What Is Afrofuturism?" *Ebony*, October 1. www.ebony .com/entertainment-culture/black-alt-enter-afrofuturism-999#axzz4vn7up6dg.

hooks, bell. 2013. "Black Female Voices: bell hooks and Melissa Harris-Perry on Black Womanhood, Politics, Media, Love." *Melissa Harris-Perry* (MSNBC), November 8.

Jackson, Shannon. 2011. *Social Works: Performing Arts, Supporting Publics*. New York: Routledge.

Jacobson, Trudi, Tom Mackey, Kelsey O'Brien, Michele Forte, and Emer O'Keeffe. 2018. "Goals and Learning Objectives." Metaliteracy.org. Accessed September 10. https://metaliteracy.org/learning-objectives.

Jarrett, Laura, Samantha Reyes, and David Shortell. 2017. "Missing Black Girls in DC Spark Outrage, Prompt Calls for Federal Help." CNN.com. Posted March 26. www.cnn.com/2017/03/24/us/missing-black-girls-washington-dc/index.html.

Jimenez, Modesto Flako. "Incoming: ¡Oye! For My Dear Brooklyn." The Public Theater, New York, January 6–13. https://publictheater.org/Tickets/Calendar/ PlayDetailsCollection/UTR-2018/Oye-For-My-Dear-Brooklyn.

Lee, Kurtis. 2017. "President Trump Says the 'Alt-left' Was Partly to Blame for the Violence at Charlottesville. Wait. What's the Alt-left?" *LA Times*, August 16. www.latimes.com/nation/la-na-pol-alt-left-20170816-story.html.

Mackey, Thomas P., and Trudi E. Jacobson. 2011. "Reframing Information Literacy as a Metaliteracy." *College and Research Libraries* 72 (1): 62–78.

———. 2014. *Metaliteracy: Reinventing Information Literacy to Empower Learners*. Chicago: ALA Neal-Schuman.

Noveck, Jocelyn. 2005. "'Looting' versus 'Finding': How to distinguish." *Seattle Times*, September 4. www.seattletimes.com/nation-world/looting-vs-finding-how-to-distinguish.

Ryzik, Melena. 2010. "In Brooklyn: Dramatizing Real Discord." *New York Times*, November 9. www.nytimes.com/2010/11/10/theater/10footprint.html.

Shalby, Colleen. 2017. "What's the Difference between 'Looting' and 'Finding'? 12 Years after Katrina, Harvey Sparks a New Debate." *LA Times*, August 29. www.latimes.com/nation/la-na-harvey-20170829-story.html.

Shange, Ntozake. (1975) 1997. *For Colored Girls Who Have Considered Suicide When the Rainbow Is Enuf*. New York: Scribner.

Turner, Victor, and Edith Turner. 2007. "Performing Ethnography." In *The Performance Studies Reader*, 2nd ed., edited by Henry Bial, 323–36. London: Routledge.

Williams-Witherspoon, Kimmika L. H. 2006. "Clear View from Under Water." In *The Lion Speaks: An Anthology for Hurricane Katrina*, edited by Stephanie Rose, 75–83. Chicago: Interstices.

———. 2009. *SHOT! Requiem for a Bullet*. Performed at Tomlinson Theater. Philadelphia: Temple University.

———. 2013. "On *SHOT!*: A Rationale for Research and Dramas Depicting Violence in the 'Hood.'" *Theater Topics* 23 (2): 169–83.

———. 2015. "Performing *SHOT!*: Personalizing North Philly, Poverty and Performance Poetry." In *Ethnographies in Pan Pacific Research: Tensions and Positionings*, edited by Robert E. Rinehart, Elke Emerald, and Rangi Matamua, 36–55. New York: Routledge.

———. 2017. "Performance Poetry: Auto-ethnography and *Engagement* as Social Activist Theater." *Consciousness, Literature and the Arts* 18 (1): 1–20. www.dmd27.org/kimmika.html.

Witek, Donna, and Teresa Grettano. 2014. "Teaching Metaliteracy: A New Paradigm in Action." *Reference Service Review* 42 (2): 188–208.

About the Editors and Contributors

THOMAS P. MACKEY, PhD, is Professor in the Department of Arts and Media, Division of Arts and Humanities, at SUNY Empire State College. His research examines metaliteracy as an empowering pedagogical framework for innovative teaching and learning. He has collaborated extensively with Trudi Jacobson to develop metaliteracy and to publish and present on this model nationally and internationally. Tom has published numerous books, conference proceedings, and peer-reviewed journal articles. He is a member of the editorial team for *Open Praxis*, the open-access, peer-reviewed academic journal about open, distance, and flexible education that is published by the International Council for Open and Distance Education (ICDE). Tom served as an administrator at SUNY Empire State College for ten years as Associate Dean and Dean of the Center for Distance Learning (CDL) and in senior management roles as Vice Provost for Academic Programs and Interim Provost. Previously, he was a faculty member in the Department of Information Studies, at the University at Albany. Tom serves on the Board of Directors for the Mohawk Hudson Humane Society in the Capital Region of New York. He can be reached at Tom.Mackey@esc.edu.

TRUDI E. JACOBSON, MLS, MA, is the Head of the Information Literacy Department at the University at Albany and holds the rank of Distinguished Librarian. She has been deeply involved with information literacy throughout her career and thrives on finding new and engaging ways to teach students, both within courses and through less formal means. Tom Mackey and she originated the metaliteracy framework to emphasize the metacognitive learner as producer and participant in dynamic information environments, which was first proposed in "Reframing Information Literacy as a Metaliteracy" (*C&RL*, 2011). She co-chaired the Association of College & Research Libraries Task Force that created the *Framework for Information Literacy for Higher Education*, is a member of the Editorial Board of *Communications in Information Literacy*, and is the series editor for Rowman & Littlefield's Innovations in Information Literacy series. Trudi, who has published extensively, was the 2009 recipient of the national ACRL Instruction Section Miriam Dudley Instruction Librarian Award. Trudi can be reached at tjacobson@albany.edu. Her website is trudijacobson.com.

■ ■ ■ ■ ■

ALLISON B. BRUNGARD, MLIS, is the STEM librarian at Slippery Rock University of Pennsylvania. She has more than seventeen years of academic library experience. She serves as the liaison to biology, chemistry, engineering, environmental science, geology, mathematics, and physics students and faculty. Allison teaches information literacy courses and was recently appointed to the ACRL Science and Technology Section's Information Literacy Taskforce. She co-authored "Information Literacy in Science Writing: How Students Find, Identify, and Use Scientific Literature" in the *International Journal of Science Teaching* (2016). Allison earned her MLIS from the University of Pittsburgh. Allison's e-mail address is allison.brungard@sru.edu.

JOSH COMPTON, PhD, is Associate Professor in the Institute for Writing and Rhetoric at Dartmouth College. His research explores the theory and application of inoculation theory, with special attention to the contexts of health, sport, and education. He has been named Distinguished Lecturer by Dartmouth College, has won the Outstanding Professor Award from the National Speakers Association, and has twice won the L. E. Norton Award for Outstanding Scholarship. Josh can be contacted via his e-mail address at joshua.compton@dartmouth.edu.

NICOLE A. COOKE, PhD, MEd, MLS, is Associate Professor and Program Director at the School of Information Sciences, University of Illinois Urbana–Champaign, where she is also Program Director for the MS in Library and Information Science program. Her research and teaching interests include human information behavior (particularly in the online context), critical cultural information studies, and diversity and social justice in librarianship (with an emphasis on infusing them into LIS education and pedagogy). Cooke was awarded the 2017 ALA Achievement in Library Diversity Research Award, presented by the Office for Diversity and Literacy Outreach Services, and the 2016 ALA Equality Award. She has also been honored as the University of Illinois YWCA's 2015 Leadership Award in Education winner in recognition of her work in social justice and higher education, and she was selected as the University of Illinois's 2016 Larine Y. Cowan Make a Difference Award for Teaching and Mentoring in Diversity. She was also named a Mover & Shaker by *Library Journal* in 2007. Cooke has published numerous articles and book chapters, and she is the author of the book *Information Services to Diverse Populations: Developing Culturally Competent Library Professionals* (Libraries Unlimited, 2016) and a new ALA monograph titled *Fake News and Alternative Facts: Information Literacy in a Post-Truth Era* (ALA Editions, 2018). Nicole can be reached at nacooke@illinois.edu.

ALLISON HOSIER, MSIS, is Information Literacy Librarian at the University at Albany, SUNY. Her research has focused on the dual nature of research as both an activity and a subject of study and practical applications of the ACRL *Framework for Information Literacy* as part of information literacy instruction. Allison's e-mail address is ahosier@albany.edu.

KRISTIN KLUCEVSEK, PhD, holds a doctorate in Biological Sciences from the University of Pittsburgh. She is Assistant Teaching Professor in the English Department of Duquesne University in Pittsburgh, Pennsylvania, where she teaches scientific writing for science majors. Her research focuses on scientific literacy and information literacy as well as on how students transfer skills from one context to another. She is particularly interested in the practical and ethical challenges students encounter as they evaluate and use scientific resources. Kristin's recent publications include "The Intersection of Information and Science Literacy" in *Communications in Information Literacy* (2017) and "Information Literacy in Science Writing: How Students Find, Identify, and Use Scientific Literature" in the *International Journal of Science Teaching* (2016). Kristin can be reached by e-mail at klucevsekk@duq.edu.

MARC KOSCIEJEW, MLIS, PhD, from Western University in London, Ontario, Canada, is Lecturer and previous Head of Department of Library, Information, and Archive Sciences at the University of Malta. His research interests concentrate on documentation studies, information philosophy/theory, records and information management, library science, and the intersections of information, institutions, and individuals. His research has been published in peer-reviewed scholarly and professional journals—including the *Journal of Documentation, Information Management,* the *Minnesota Review, Library and Information History,* and *Tate Papers*—as well as in various magazines, newspapers, and blogs. He has conducted original research in North Korea on the isolated Communist state's library system, becoming one of the first English speakers to publish and present on this specific topic. He has lectured in Europe and North America and presented worldwide at diverse conferences, workshops, and events. He was appointed by Malta's Minister for Education and Employment as Chairperson of the Malta Libraries Council, a government-appointed national council stipulated in the Malta Libraries Act, 2011, to provide strategic advice on libraries, learning, and literacy to senior cultural and political figures, including the National Librarian of Malta and the Minister responsible for libraries. Marc's e-mail address is marc.kosciejew@um.edu.mt.

RACHEL M. MAGEE, PhD, MA, is Youth Advocate and Assistant Professor at the University of Illinois Urbana–Champaign, where her work in the School of Information Sciences is informed by her background as a public librarian. Her research and teaching are focused on youth, the ways they interact with technology, and what those practices mean for their engagement with information. In 2018, she was awarded an early career grant by the Institute of Museum and Library Services to support her work with teens as co-researchers, collaboratively investigating youth technology practices. Magee holds a PhD in Information Studies from Drexel University, a master's degree in Information Resources and Library Science from the University of Arizona, and a BS in Radio-Television-Film as well as a BA in English from the University of Texas at Austin. Rachel can be contacted by e-mail at rmmagee@illinois.edu.

THOMAS PALMER, MS, is Digital Media Lecturer for the Journalism Program at the University of Albany in New York. He teaches visual culture and multiplatform digital media courses. His research concentrates on the intersemiotic contextual misrepresentation in photojournalism and other modes in online news publishing. His *Albany Times Union* media criticism blog, *Picture Prosecutor*, immerses readers and students in this real-time research. His diverse experiences spanning three decades have included design directing, news editing, mobile platform UX (user experience) design, picture editing, copyediting, and photojournalism in news media. He works part-time at the *Albany Times Union* as Executive News Editor and Design Director. Thomas earned his master's degree at Syracuse University in the S. I. Newhouse School of Public Communications. He can be reached via e-mail at tpalmer@albany.edu.

JACLYN PARTYKA, PhD, is Instructor of English and First-Year Writing at Temple University, where she also received her PhD in English. Her research focuses on authorship, narrative theory, and contemporary multimodal literacies. Her work has appeared in *Contemporary Literature*, and she is currently at work on a monograph titled *Notorious Doppelgängers: Reading the Anxieties of Contemporary Authorship*. Jaclyn's e-mail address is jaclyn.partyka@temple.edu.

KIMMIKA L. H. WILLIAMS-WITHERSPOON, PhD (Cultural Anthropology), MA (Anthropology), MFA (Theater), Graduate Certificate (Women's Studies), BA (Journalism), is Associate Professor of Urban Theater and Community Engagement in the Theater Department at Temple University. She is the author of *Through Smiles and Tears: The History of African American Theater (From Kemet to the Americas)* (Lambert Academic Publishing, 2011) and the *Secret Messages in African American Theater: Hidden Meaning Embedded in Public Discourse* (Edwin Mellen Publishing, 2006). She is a recipient of the 2013 Miriam Maat Ka Re Award for scholarship; 2013 Associate Provosts' Arts Grant; 2008 Seed Grant; 2003 Provosts' Arts Grant; 2001 Independence Foundation Grant; 2000 Pew Fellowship; 1999 DaimlerChrysler National Poetry Competition; 1996 Lila Wallace Creative Arts Fellowship with the American Antiquarian Society; and a two-time returning playwright with the Minneapolis Playwrights' Center and Pew Charitable Trusts Playwrights Exchange. Williams-Witherspoon has had more than twenty-nine plays produced. Her stage credits include more than twenty productions and eight one-woman shows, and she has performed poetry in more than ninety-three national and international venues. Williams-Witherspoon is a contributing poet to thirty-one anthologies, the author of eleven books of poetry, and the recipient of a host of awards and citations. Kimmika's e-mail address is kwilli01@temple.edu.

Index